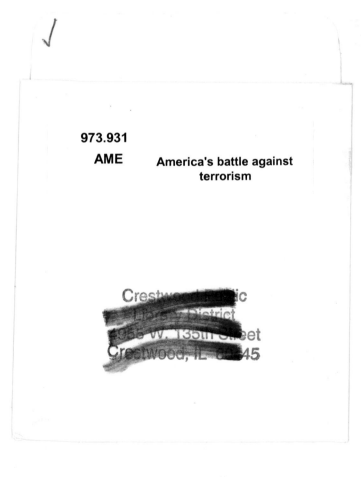

America's Battle Against Terrorism

Other books in the Current Controversies series:

America's Battle Against Terrorism

Andrea C. Nakaya, *Book Editor*

Bruce Glassman, *Vice President*
Bonnie Szumski, *Publisher*
Helen Cothran, *Managing Editor*

CURRENT CONTROVERSIES

GREENHAVEN PRESS
An imprint of Thomson Gale, a part of The Thomson Corporation

Detroit • New York • San Francisco • San Diego • New Haven, Conn.
Waterville, Maine • London • Munich

THOMSON
★
™
GALE

LIBRARY OF CONGRESS CATALOGING-IN-PUBLICATION DATA

America's battle against terrorism / Andrea C. Nakaya, book editor.
   p. cm. — (Current controversies)
  Includes bibliographical references and index.
  ISBN 0-7377-2783-7 (lib. : alk. paper) — ISBN 0-7377-2784-5 (pbk. : alk. paper)
   1. Terrorism—United States—Prevention. 2. Terrorism—Government policy—United States. 3. War on Terrorism, 2001– . 4. Civil Rights—United States. 5. United States—Foreign relations—2001– . I. Nakaya, Andrea C., 1976– . II. Series.
  HV6432.A5254 2005
  973.931—dc22
                                   2004054122

Contents

Chapter 1: Is America's Battle Against Terrorism Justified?

Yes: America's Battle Against Terrorism Is Justified

No: America's Battle Against Terrorism Is Not Justified

capabilities and erroneously claimed that Iraq had ties to the al Qaeda terrorist network.

Chapter 2: How Should America Fight Terrorism Worldwide?

Chapter 3: Are Civil Liberties Being Compromised in the Domestic Battle Against Terrorism?

Yes: Civil Liberties Are Being Compromised

Chapter 4: Has the Battle Against Terrorism Been Successful?

Foreword

By definition, controversies are "discussions of questions in which opposing opinions clash" (Webster's Twentieth Century Dictionary Unabridged). Few would deny that controversies are a pervasive part of the human condition and exist on virtually every level of human enterprise. Controversies transpire between individuals and among groups, within nations and between nations. Controversies supply the grist necessary for progress by providing challenges and challengers to the status quo. They also create atmospheres where strife and warfare can flourish. A world without controversies would be a peaceful world; but it also would be, by and large, static and prosaic.

The Series' Purpose

The purpose of the Current Controversies series is to explore many of the social, political, and economic controversies dominating the national and international scenes today. Titles selected for inclusion in the series are highly focused and specific. For example, from the larger category of criminal justice, Current Controversies deals with specific topics such as police brutality, gun control, white collar crime, and others. The debates in Current Controversies also are presented in a useful, timeless fashion. Articles and book excerpts included in each title are selected if they contribute valuable, long-range ideas to the overall debate. And wherever possible, current information is enhanced with historical documents and other relevant materials. Thus, while individual titles are current in focus, every effort is made to ensure that they will not become quickly outdated. Books in the Current Controversies series will remain important resources for librarians, teachers, and students for many years.

In addition to keeping the titles focused and specific, great care is taken in the editorial format of each book in the series. Book introductions and chapter prefaces are offered to provide background material for readers. Chapters are organized around several key questions that are answered with diverse opinions representing all points on the political spectrum. Materials in each chapter include opinions in which authors clearly disagree as well as alternative opinions in which authors may agree on a broader issue but disagree on the possible solutions. In this way, the content of each volume in Current Controversies mirrors the mosaic of opinions encountered in society. Readers will quickly realize that there are many viable answers to these complex issues. By questioning each author's conclusions, students and casual readers can begin to develop the critical thinking skills so important to evaluating opinionated material.

Current Controversies is also ideal for controlled research. Each anthology in the series is composed of primary sources taken from a wide gamut of informational categories including periodicals, newspapers, books, United States and foreign government documents, and the publications of private and public organizations. Readers will find factual support for reports, debates, and research papers covering all areas of important issues. In addition, an annotated table of contents, an index, a book and periodical bibliography, and a list of organizations to contact are included in each book to expedite further research.

Perhaps more than ever before in history, people are confronted with diverse and contradictory information. During the Persian Gulf War, for example, the public was not only treated to minute-to-minute coverage of the war, it was also inundated with critiques of the coverage and countless analyses of the factors motivating U.S. involvement. Being able to sort through the plethora of opinions accompanying today's major issues, and to draw one's own conclusions, can be a complicated and frustrating struggle. It is the editors' hope that Current Controversies will help readers with this struggle.

> *"America's foreign policy has changed dramatically as a result of the terrorist attacks and the ensuing battle against terrorism."*

Introduction

Prior to the September 11, 2001, terrorist attacks, U.S. foreign policy was largely based on nonintervention and nonaggression toward other nations, with multilateral action the preferred strategy for dealing with international threats. One section of the 1991 National Security Strategy of the United States summarizes the principles intended to guide U.S. foreign policy at that time. The document maintains that:

> The United States seeks, whenever possible in concert with its allies, to:
>
> • deter any aggression that could threaten the security of the United States and its allies . . .
>
> • effectively counter threats to the security of the United States and its citizens and interests short of armed conflict, including the threat of international terrorism; . . .
>
> • foster restraint in global military spending and discourage military adventurism.

Ten years later, however, on September 11, 2001, terrorists attacked America and caused the deaths of more than three thousand people. In response, the United States announced that it was embarking on a war on terrorism, which eventually included the invasions of two sovereign countries that were suspected of supporting terrorism—Afghanistan in 2001 and Iraq in 2003. The Iraq invasion was launched in opposition to the United Nations and many of America's allies around the world. As these actions illustrate, America's foreign policy has changed dramatically as a result of the terrorist attacks and the ensuing battle against terrorism, moving away from the restraint and deterrence delineated in the 1991 strategy and focusing on preventing threats to its security through intervention and unilateral action.

Professor Philip Zelikow describes the way U.S. foreign policy has operated historically. "In the past," says Zelikow, "threats tended to emerge slowly, often visibly, as weapons were forged, armies were conscripted, units were trained and deployed, and enemy forces were massed in position to move. The greatest threats, too, came from large states. . . . Because of their size . . . these large states had much to lose in war." For example, during the 1945 to 1990 Cold War between the United States and the former Soviet Union, each side amassed nuclear weapons, yet neither side launched an attack. Direct conflict was avoided because of self-interest; each country knew that the resulting retaliation would escalate into a conflict that might result in the destruction of both countries. Thus, the United States relied on maintaining a great military power so that it would not actually have to use it.

As America has become engaged in the worldwide battle against terrorism, however, its foreign policies have changed. Often referred to as the Bush Doctrine, after President George W. Bush, America's foreign policy is now based on preventing another terrorist attack. It aims to do this through preemptive war against imminent threats and unilateral action. In addition, the Bush Doctrine includes the policy of actively promoting democracy and freedom in all regions of the world in order to reduce poverty and other problems that may lead to terrorism. The new policy is described in the 2002 National Security Strategy of the United States:

> The United States possesses unprecedented—and unequaled—strength and influence in the world. . . . The great strength of this nation must be used to promote a balance of power that favors freedom. . . . We will disrupt and destroy terrorist organizations by:
>
> • direct and continuous action using all elements of national and international power . . .
>
> • defending the United States, the American people, and our interests at home and abroad by identifying and destroying the threat before it reaches our borders. While the United States will constantly strive to enlist the support of the international community, we will not hesitate to act alone, if necessary, to exercise our right of self-defense by acting preemptively against such terrorists, to prevent them from doing harm against our people and our country.

This new policy is based on the idea that terrorists are a new type of enemy that cannot be deterred. The British news magazine *Economist* sees the September 11 attacks as a catalyst for America's new foreign policy because they showed how vulnerable the nation was to terrorism. "Stung by the events of September 11th," states the *Economist*, "America is no longer shy about spilling blood, even its own." Author and international relations expert Jack Snyder explains why this more aggressive defense strategy is necessary to fight terrorism:

> No strictly defensive strategy against terrorism can be foolproof. Similarly, deterring terrorist attack by the threat of retaliation seems impossible when the potential attackers welcome suicide. Bizarre or diabolical leaders of potentially nuclear-armed rogue states may likewise seem undeterrable. If so, attacking the sources of potential threats before they can mount their own attacks may seem the only safe option.

Many people support the Bush Doctrine, arguing that by taking preventative action against terrorists and spreading freedom and democracy, the United States will reduce terrorism and improve life for Americans and many others around the world. According to President Bush, "We will extend the peace by encouraging free and open societies on every continent." Zelikow defends the right of the United States to use its power to effect change in other countries. He argues:

> The terrorists have no vision of a future that can assure Muslim parents that their children will lead a better life; the United States does. There are only a few states that could start a new wave of dangerous WMD [weapons of mass destruction] proliferation, and deflecting them now may nudge history in the right direction. Failure to do so, however, may condemn millions to needless suffering and the American people to years of living in fear.

However, there are also many critics of the Bush Doctrine. These analysts believe that the United States is not justified in taking aggressive, preemptive action against other nations, even if it believes the goal is a good one, such as fighting terrorism or spreading democracy. Writer Gene Healy criticizes the U.S. invasion of Iraq. He asks, "How can it be legitimate for the United States government to 'collaterally damage' hundreds or thousands of Iraqi civilians into oblivion because of the benefits our action may confer on the survivors?" In addition, he argues, it is not America's place to spread liberty around the world: "We Americans are pledged to assist each other in the defense of our liberties from enemies foreign and domestic. . . . We've set up a government to provide for 'the common defense' of the United States, not the defense or liberation of oppressed people throughout the world."

In 2004, three years after it began its battle against terrorism, the United States continues to pursue a new foreign policy, eliciting both praise and criticism. This controversial policy is only one of many facets of the battle against terrorism that have provoked fierce debate. Other issues that have arisen in America's war against terrorism include whether it is justified, how it should be fought, whether civil liberties are being compromised, and whether the battle has been successful.

Chapter 1

Is America's Battle Against Terrorism Justified?

Chapter Preface

In 1973 the Organization of Petroleum Exporting Countries (OPEC), which includes many of the world's largest oil-exporting nations, imposed an oil embargo on the United States. Severe shortages resulted, and oil prices in America doubled and tripled. Rationing of oil began, and gas station lines snaked around city blocks. The U.S. economy, which had become highly dependent on cheap and plentiful oil, went into a major recession. The embargo was lifted in 1974, but it had long-lasting effects on the economy, highlighting the importance of oil to the stability of the United States and the nation's vulnerability to the policies of oil-producing countries.

In the twenty-first century America remains highly dependent on oil. While the United States accounts for about 10 percent of world oil production, it consumes more than double that, resulting in the need to import much of its oil. It was this fact that led to skepticism when in 2003 the United States led an invasion of Iraq, which possesses the second largest proven oil reserve in the world. The invasion was justified as necessary to depose Iraqi leader Saddam Hussein, who was accused of aiding terrorists, but many people were quick to point out the connection between Iraq's plentiful oil supplies and the U.S. need for oil. There were accusations that the real motivation behind the invasion was not to fight terrorism but to take control of Iraq's oil fields and ensure a steady supply of energy for the United States.

The U.S. government has continued to state that these accusations are not true. In March 2004 President George W. Bush made one of many speeches justifying the invasion and occupation of Iraq. He argued that the primary reason for the war was the liberation of America and the rest of the world from terrorism. According to Bush,

> We have set out to encourage reform and democracy in the greater Middle East as the alternatives to fanaticism, resentment, and terror. We've set out to break the cycle of bitterness and radicalism that has brought stagnation to a vital region, and destruction to cities in America and Europe and around the world. This task is historic, and difficult; this task is necessary and worthy of our efforts.

As the occupation of Iraq continues, with the United States in control of Iraqi oil fields, there have been repeated assurances from the Bush administration that any profits from that oil will go exclusively to the Iraqi people.

However, many people are critical of these assertions, believing that the 2003 war was motivated by America's need for oil. Writer Pamela Ann Smith believes that the war on terrorism was merely used as an excuse to gain control of Iraqi oil. She writes in the *Middle East*,

Those two indefatigable allies in the invasion and conquest of Iraq, US President George Bush and British Prime Minister Tony Blair, may have succeeded in linking the conflict [in Iraq] with "the war on terrorism"—at least in the eyes of many Americans. But while both denied that it was also linked with "oil," the evidence is mounting that the reverse is true.

One example of that evidence is believed to be the way that, immediately following the war, it seems that there was little effort by the United States to stop the looting and destruction of many public buildings, including hospitals and universities, while in contrast U.S. troops carefully guarded the Iraqi Ministry of Oil. "Why?" asks journalist Robert Fisk. "The archives and files of Iraq's most valuable asset—its oilfields and, even more important, its massive reserves—are safe and sound, sealed off from the mobs and looters, and safe to be shared, as Washington almost certainly intends, with American oil companies."

The possible connection between oil and the U.S. occupation of Iraq is only one controversial aspect of America's battle against terrorism. As the battle continues, the heated debate over whether or not it is justified continues as well. The authors in the following chapter offer various viewpoints on this contentious issue.

The Battle Against Terrorism Is Necessary to Protect the World from al Qaeda

by J. Cofer Black

About the author: *On December 3, 2002, J. Cofer Black became the state department coordinator for counterterrorism. Prior to that he was the director of the Central Intelligence Agency Counterterrorist Center.*

Editor's Note: The following viewpoint was originally given as testimony before the U.S. House of Representatives on April 1, 2004.

Just over two and a half years ago, our nation suffered a devastating attack on its own soil, a day that none of us will forget. Since that terrible day of September 11, 2001, we have undergone a transformation as a nation, and have been fully engaged in a war with terrorism. The President's vision and message for the world has been crystal clear: Any person, organization, or government that supports, protects, or harbors terrorists is complicit in the murder of the innocent, and will be held to account.

We are carrying out the President's clear directive, and are taking the battle to terrorists worldwide using all the elements of national power. We are also enlisting the support of friends and allies in the international community, to great effect. We have made great progress in marshalling the collective strength of the international community into the counterterrorism fight, but we must continue to press forward to face and defeat terrorism.

Although there are numerous terrorist organizations of concern in the world today, the top priority of our efforts has been on the al-Qaida organization, its affiliates, and those who support them. Al-Qaida remains a potent force, despite

J. Cofer Black, testimony before the Subcommittee on International Terrorism, House Internal Relations Committee, Washington, DC, April 1, 2004.

the continuing efforts of the community of civilized nations to remove this evil from the world. Al-Qaida is determined to strike the United States, our allies and interests wherever it can, using the most destructive means at its disposal. I have no doubt that al-Qaida would use unconventional weapons if it possessed the capability to do so.

Since the Coalition's successful ouster of the Taliban regime from Afghanistan, the al-Qaida organization has been deeply wounded.[1] It has been forced to evolve in ways not entirely by its own choosing. However, it remains bent on murdering Americans, whether overseas or in our own country. Al-Qaida has amply demonstrated its willingness to kill and maim large numbers of innocent civilians around the world, regardless of faith, nationality, race, class, and creed.

> *"Al-Qaida is determined to strike the United States, our allies and interests wherever it can, using the most destructive means at its disposal."*

The Madrid Attack

The tragic events of 11 March [2004] in Madrid[2] demonstrate the potent global terrorist threat. We continue to see mounting evidence of al-Qaida's links to the attacks, although we are still awaiting the conclusions of the ongoing investigation by the Spanish government.

The Spanish government is uncovering evidence of linkages between suspects in custody and the perpetrators of the 16 May 2003 Casablanca [suicide] bombings [that killed twenty-six people]. Time and Spain's progress in its investigation will tell us about the extent of al-Qaida's involvement, particularly its senior leadership.

One lesson from the Madrid bombings is clear. We have learned this lesson before on the streets of Istanbul, Riyadh, Casablanca, Bali, Moscow, and Mombasa: No country is safe from the scourge of terrorism. No country is immune from attack, and neither demographics nor policies of deterrence or accommodation will ward off attack. Al-Qaida seeks only death and chaos, which is why we will continue to pursue the only viable course of action before us: to destroy this enemy utterly, both with the cooperation of our allies and by unilateral action when necessary.

Sanctuary Lost

The removal of the Taliban regime from Afghanistan stripped al-Qaida of its primary sanctuary and support, and shut down long-standing terrorist training camps. Although our work continues in Afghanistan to root-out the remnants of

---

1. In October 2001 a U.S.-led coalition invaded Afghanistan, ousting the Taliban, an Islamist group that had ruled most of Afghanistan since 1996 and was believed to be supporting al-Qaida. 2. a series of coordinated terrorist bombings against commuter trains in Madrid that killed 191 people and wounded more than 1,800

al-Qaida's former strength, al-Qaida has lost a vital safe haven. With the loss of Afghanistan and its terrorism infrastructure there, al-Qaida has also been separated from facilities central to its chem-bio and poisons development programs.

We and our coalition partners have also removed the regime of [former Iraqi president] Saddam Hussein in Iraq, a long-time state sponsor of terror. The al-Qaida-affiliated Zarqawi network continues to spread terror and death as the Iraqi people move toward a brighter future free from the tyranny of Saddam Hussein.

Iraq is currently serving as a focal point for foreign jihadist fighters, who are united in a common goal with former regime elements, criminals and more established foreign terrorist organization members to conduct attacks against Coalition and Iraqi civilian targets. These jihadists view Iraq as a new training ground to build their extremist credentials and hone the skills of the terrorist. We are aggressively rooting out the foreign fighters in Iraq, and we will continue to devote the resources necessary to ensure that al-Qaida and other terrorist groups will be unable to use Iraq as a training ground or sanctuary.

We have relied on the support of our partners in the global coalition against terrorism to ensure that al-Qaida is unable to establish a new secure base of operations like that which existed under the Taliban in Afghanistan. The partnership of Saudi Arabia, Pakistan, Yemen, and others has been, and will continue to be, essential to ensuring that al-Qaida is never able to reestablish comfortable sanctuary anywhere in the world.

The State of al-Qaida Leadership

Historically, al-Qaida has been a top-down organization with strong central leadership control over almost all aspects of its operations. However, our ongoing operations against al-Qaida have served to isolate its leadership, and sever or complicate communications links with its operatives scattered around the globe. Unable to find easy sanctuary in Afghanistan and elsewhere, the al-Qaida leadership must now devote much more time to evading capture or worse.

This has further complicated al-Qaida's communication and coordination efforts, which are much harder and time-consuming in the current operating environment. We have also seen examples of terrorist activities delayed for extended periods as al-Qaida affiliates await instructions from an increasingly isolated central leadership.

"No country is immune from attack, and neither demographics nor policies of deterrence or accommodation will ward off attack."

Also, as al-Qaida's known senior leadership, planners, facilitators, and operators are brought to justice, a new cadre of leaders is being forced to step up. These individuals are increasingly no longer drawn from the old guard, no longer the seasoned veteran al-Qaida trainers from Afghanistan's camps or close associates of al-Qaida's founding members.

Critical gaps have been cut out of the al-Qaida leadership structure, and these relatively untested terrorists are assuming far greater responsibilities. We are relentlessly going after these new leaders as they are identified.

This confluence of factors may be resulting in a lack of clear strategic direction and operational mistakes by al-Qaida. An example is the November 8, 2003 bombing of the Muhaya housing compound in Riyadh which killed 18 persons, predominantly Muslims during the month of Ramadan. This target selection, made either by mistake or due to poor judgment, was a public relations disaster for al-Qaida, which in turn has assisted aggressive Saudi efforts to roll-up the al-Qaida presence in the Kingdom [of Saudi Arabia]. Whether this operation was plagued by operational or strategic error is still a matter of debate, but I believe that it is indicative of the complications faced by al-Qaida in its truncated and besieged state.

> *"Unable to find easy sanctuary in Afghanistan and elsewhere, the al-Qaida leadership must now devote much more time to evading capture or worse."*

Allies in Sowing Terror

A few words now on how al-Qaida's influence has spread to other terrorist organizations. There are growing indications that a number of largely Sunni Islamic extremist groups are moving to pick up al-Qaida's standard and attempting to pursue global jihad against the United States and our allies.

There are also growing indications that al-Qaida's ideology is spreading well beyond the Middle East, particularly its virulent anti-American rhetoric. This has been picked up by a number of Islamic extremist movements which exist around the globe. This greatly complicates our task in stamping out al-Qaida, and poses a threat in its own right for the foreseeable future.

Literally scores of such groups are present around the world today. Some groups have gravitated to al-Qaida in recent years, where before such linkages did not exist. This has been, at times, merely an effort to gain greater public renown for their group or cause, but more troubling have been the groups seeking to push forward al-Qaida's agenda of worldwide terror.

In particular, groups like Ansar al-Islam and the Zarqawi network pose a real threat to U.S. interests. This has been demonstrated very clearly by their deadly activities in Iraq. Other groups of great concern include the Salafist Group for Call and Combat (GSPC), which operates mainly in the countries of North Africa, and Salifiya Jihadia, which claimed responsibility for the May 2003 Casablanca bombings. Jemaah Islamiya (JI) and the Islamic Movement of Uzbekistan (IMU) should also be on this short list.

While it would be a mistake to believe that we are now confronted by a monolithic threat posed by legions of like-minded terrorist groups working in concert against our interests, it would be fair to say that we are seeing greater cooperation between al-Qaida and smaller Islamic extremist groups, as well as even more localized organizations.

Identifying and acting against the leadership, capabilities, and operational plans of these groups poses a serious challenge now and for years to come.

In addition to these groups, there are literally thousands of jihadists around the world who have fought in conflicts in Kosovo, Kashmir, Chechnya, and elsewhere. As I said earlier, we see these "foreign fighters" operating in Iraq, where we are fighting them on a daily basis with the Coalition and Iraqi partners. These jihadists will continue to serve as a ready source of recruits for al-Qaida and other affiliated terrorist groups.

A Strategy to Defeat Terrorism

Let me go back for a moment to frame the overall strategy we have been employing to defeat terrorism.

Following the September 11 attacks, we have forcefully applied the Bush doctrine: any person or government that supports, protects, or harbors terrorists is complicit in the murder of the innocent, and will be held to account. We have done so through our National Strategy to Combat Terrorism, which creates the policy framework for coordinated actions to prevent terrorist attacks against the United States, its citizens, its interests, and its friends around the world and, ultimately, to create an international environment inhospitable to terrorists and all those who support them. We have implemented this strategy to act simultaneously on four fronts:

- Defeat terrorist organizations of global reach by attacking their sanctuaries, leadership, finances, and command, control and communications;
- Deny further sponsorship, support, and sanctuary to terrorists by cooperating with other states to take action against these international threats;
- Diminish the underlying conditions that terrorists seek to exploit by enlisting the international community to focus its efforts and resources on the areas most at risk; and
- Defend the United States, its citizens and interests at home and abroad. The National Strategy highlights that success will only come through the sustained, steadfast, and systematic application of all elements of national power—diplomatic, financial, law enforcement, intelligence, and military.

While the United States is committed to combating terrorism the world over, in whatever form it takes to threaten the American people and American interests, the focus of our efforts since September has been on the al-Qaida organization. Let me tell you about the progress we have made, and how the al-Qaida organization looks far different than it did in September 2001.

U.S. Accomplishments, al-Qaida Losses

A global dragnet has tightened around al-Qaida, made possible by a broad coalition of 84 nations, all focused on the common goal of eradicating the terrorist threat that endangers all civilized nations. Since September 11, 2001, 70% of al-Qaida senior leadership and more than 3,400 lower-level al-Qaida operatives or associates have been detained or killed in over 100 countries, largely as a result of cooperation among law enforcement and intelligence agencies. Terrorist cells have been wrapped up in nations in all corners of the globe, from Singapore to Italy and Saudi Arabia, as well as here at home in Buffalo, Portland, and North Carolina.

> *"There are literally thousands of jihadists around the world. . . . These jihadists will continue to serve as a ready source of recruits for al-Qaida."*

A growing list of senior al-Qaida leaders and associates will no longer threaten the United States and our allies:

- al-Qaida operations chief Khalid Sheikh Mohammad,
- Senior planner for Southeast Asia Hambali,
- Persian Gulf operations chief Nashiri and his suspected successor Khaled Ali al-Haj,
- Yemen's most senior al-Qaida figures Abu Ali al-Harithi and Abu Assem al-Makki.

The al-Qaida figures we take out of circulation performed roles in all operational areas, including financing, logistics, training and procurement, among others. This has sapped al-Qaida's strength by disrupting its ability to coordinate complex operational plans and gather the operatives, materials and funding required to carry them out.

We have made extensive efforts to attack al-Qaida's financing, which is the lifeblood of its murderous activities, providing for the movement of operatives, the cooption of officials and local populations, and the acquisition of arms and explosives. More than 172 countries have issued orders freezing or seizing approximately $200 million in terrorism-related financial assets and accounts.

In addition to attacking known accounts, more than 100 countries worldwide have introduced new terrorist-related legislation or regulations, including new laws to block money-laundering and the misuse of charities in the support of terrorists.

An important tool in countering terrorism financing is the authority the Secretary of State uses to formally designate Foreign Terrorist Organizations. This authority, under the Anti-Terrorism and Effective Death Penalty Act of 1996 freezes a designated group's assets in the United States, makes it a criminal offense for Americans to provide funding and other forms of material support and denies visas to members of the designated group. Thirty-six groups are currently designated. . . .

Meanwhile, we have strengthened our defenses here at home, including a comprehensive reorganization of our government to better protect the homeland. We have also implemented more stringent screening measures, and engaged with our international community to raise global standards. For example, in Africa, we and our colleagues in the Departments of Transportation and Homeland Security are implementing a program to secure airports in countries where the danger to aviation is particularly striking (Safe Skies for Africa).

We must also continue to provide frontline countries the training and assistance needed to support their counterterrorisrn efforts. The Department of State's Anti-Terrorism Training Assistance (ATA) Program, Terrorist Interdiction Program (TIP), and other counterterrorism training are vital parts of this effort.

The support of the Congress for this and other capacity-building programs will be essential to eradicating al-Qaida and other terrorist groups. Many of our most important successes have come through joint or unilateral actions by foreign governments. Improving the counterterrorisrn capacity of key states is clearly in our interest. While the dividends of such investment may not be immediately apparent, we must think of our global war on terrorism as a long-term fight that will take years or, indeed, decades, as was the case with the Cold War.

Eradication of al-Qaida

In conclusion, I should stress that while we have made substantial progress toward eradicating the threat posed by al-Qaida, we are on a long, tough road, and we cannot afford to falter.

The al-Qaida organization has been gravely wounded, and forced to evolve in new ways to survive. However, al-Qaida is a patient, resourceful and flexible organization and is able to draw from a global support base of jihadists and international mujahedin movement. It must be denied safe haven and kept on the run, while we starve it of its resources, dismantle its cells, and apprehend its foot soldiers at our borders. We must more than match its flexibility and resolve, and commit to combat al-Qaida over the long haul, for there can be no accommodation with this evil.

As President [George W.] Bush recently said, "The war on terror is not a figure of speech. It is an inescapable calling of our generation. . . . There can be no separate peace with the terrorist enemy. Any sign of weakness or retreat simply validates terrorist violence, and invites more violence for all nations. The only certain way to protect our people is by early, united, and decisive action."

> *"While we have made substantial progress toward eradicating the threat posed by al-Qaida, we are on a long, tough road, and we cannot afford to falter."*

Our continued dedication to the eradication of al-Qaida with the support of our international partners is the only way to ensure the elimination of the threat posed by al-Qaida. The fates of the civilized nations of the world are inextricably linked—we must face this fight together and eradicate the al-Qaida scourge from the face of the Earth.

The Invasion of Afghanistan Is Justified

by George W. Bush

About the author: *George W. Bush, former governor of Texas, is the forty-third president of the United States.*

Editor's Note: In October 2001 a U.S-led coalition invaded Afghanistan and overthrew the Islamist Taliban government that had ruled the country since 1996. In justification for the attack, the United States claimed that the Taliban was harboring al Qaeda, the terrorist group responsible for the September 11, 2001, attacks on America. The following speech was given in Warsaw, Poland, by George W. Bush on November 6, 2001, as coalition and Taliban forces fought one another in Afghanistan.

For more than 50 years, the peoples of [Central and Eastern Europe] suffered under repressive ideologies that tried to trample human dignity. Today, our freedom is threatened once again. Like the fascists and totalitarians before them, these terrorists—al Qaeda, the Taliban regime that supports them, and other terror groups across our world—try to impose their radical views through threats and violence. We see the same intolerance of dissent; the same mad, global ambitions; the same brutal determination to control every life and all of life.

We have seen the true nature of these terrorists in the nature of their attacks—they kill thousands of innocent people and then rejoice about it. They kill fellow Muslims, many of whom died in the World Trade Center [terrorist attack on September 11, 2001] that terrible morning—and then they gloat. They condone murder and claim to be doing so in the name of a peaceful religion.

We have also seen the true nature of these terrorists in the nature of the regime they support in Afghanistan—and it's terrifying. Women are imprisoned in their homes, and are denied access to basic health care and education. Food sent to help starving people is stolen by their leaders. The religious monuments of other faiths are destroyed. Children are forbidden to fly kites, or sing songs, or build snowmen. A girl of seven is beaten for wearing white shoes. Our ene-

George W. Bush, address to the Warsaw Conference on Combating Terrorism, Warsaw, Poland, November 6, 2001.

mies have brought only misery and terror to the people of Afghanistan—and now they are trying to export that terror throughout the world.

Fighting al Qaeda

Al Qaeda operates in more than 60 nations, including some in Central and Eastern Europe. These terrorist groups seek to destabilize entire nations and regions. They are seeking chemical, biological and nuclear weapons. Given the means, our enemies would be a threat to every nation and, eventually, to civilization itself.

So we're determined to fight this evil, and fight until we're rid of it. We will not wait for the authors of mass murder to gain the weapons of mass destruction. We act now, because we must lift this dark threat from our age and save generations to come.

The people of my nation are now fighting this war at home. We face a second wave of terrorist attacks in the form of deadly anthrax that has been sent through the U.S. mail.[1] Our people are responding to this new threat with alertness and calm. Our government is responding to treat the sick, provide antibiotics to those who have been exposed and track down the guilty, whether abroad or at home.

> *"We will not rest until terrorist groups of global reach have been found, have been stopped, and have been defeated."*

And we fight abroad with our military, with the help of many nations, because the Taliban regime of Afghanistan refused to turn over the terrorists. And we're making good progress in a just cause. Our efforts are directed at terrorist and military targets because—unlike our enemies—we value human life. We do not target innocent people, and we grieve for the difficult times the Taliban have brought to the people of their own country.

Our military is systematically pursuing its mission. We've destroyed many terrorist training camps. We have severed communication links. We're taking out air defenses, and now [in November 2001] we're attacking the Taliban's front lines.

I've seen some news reports that many Afghanistan citizens wish the Taliban had never allowed the al Qaeda terrorists into their country. I don't blame them. And I hope those citizens will help us locate the terrorists—because the sooner we find them, the better the people's lives will be. It may take a long time, but no matter how long it takes, those who killed thousands of Americans and citizens from over 80 other nations will be brought to justice, and the misuse of Afghanistan as a training ground for terror will end.

As I've said from the start, this is a difficult struggle, of uncertain duration.

---

1. This 2001 bioterrorism incident resulted in several anthrax infections and five deaths. No one was charged in the attacks.

We hunt an enemy that hides in shadows and caves. We are at the beginning of our efforts in Afghanistan. And Afghanistan is the beginning of our efforts in the world. No group or nation should mistake America's intentions: We will not rest until terrorist groups of global reach have been found, have been stopped, and have been defeated. And this goal will not be achieved until all the world's nations stop harboring and supporting such terrorists within their borders.

International Cooperation

The defeat of terror requires an international coalition of unprecedented scope and cooperation. It demands the sincere, sustained actions of many nations against the network of terrorist cells and bases and funding. . . . No nation can be neutral in this conflict, because no civilized nation can be secure in a world threatened by terror.

I thank the many nations of Europe, including our NATO [North Atlantic Treaty Organization] allies, who have offered military help. I also thank the nations who are sharing intelligence and working to cut off terrorist financing. . . . The war against terrorism will be won only when we combine our strengths.

We have a vast coalition that is uniting the world and increasingly isolating the terrorists—a coalition that includes many Arab and Muslim countries. I am encouraged by what their leaders are saying. The head of the 22 nation Arab League rejected the claims of the terrorist leader and said he—Osama bin Laden—"doesn't speak in the name of Arabs and Muslims." Increasingly, it is clear that this is not just a matter between the United States and the terror network. As the Egyptian Foreign Minister said, "There is a war between bin Laden and the whole world."

All of us here today understand this: We do not fight Islam, we fight against evil.

I thank all of our coalition partners, and all of you, for your steadfast support. [In June 2001], I talked of our shared vision of a Europe that is whole and free and at peace. I said we are building a House of Freedom, whose doors are open to all of Europe's people, and whose windows look out to global opportunities beyond. Now that vision has been challenged, but it will not change. With your help, our vision of peace and freedom will be realized. And with your help, we will defend the values we hold in common.

War Against Iraq Is Necessary to Protect America from Weapons of Mass Destruction

by Donald Rumsfeld

About the author: *Donald Rumsfeld was appointed U.S. secretary of defense in 2001. He also served as secretary of defense from 1975 to 1977 under President Gerald Ford.*

Editor's Note: The following speech was given in September 2002—prior to the U.S.-led war on Iraq that took place the following year. In that war, beginning on March 20, 2003, a U.S.-led coalition invaded Iraq, toppling the regime there, and beginning an occupation that continues as of this writing.

[On September 11, 2002,] we commemorated the one-year anniversary of the most devastating attack our nation has ever experienced—more than 3,000 innocent people killed in a single day [in the September 11, 2001, terrorist attacks].

Today, I want to discuss the task of preventing even more devastating attacks—attacks that could kill not thousands, but potentially tens of thousands of our fellow citizens.

As we meet, state sponsors of terror across the world are working to develop and acquire weapons of mass destruction. As we speak, chemists, biologists, and nuclear scientists are toiling in weapons labs and underground bunkers, working to give the world's most dangerous dictators weapons of unprecedented power and lethality.

The threat posed by those regimes is real. It is dangerous. And it is growing with each passing day. We cannot wish it away.

We have entered a new security environment, one that is dramatically differ-

Donald Rumsfeld, testimony before the House and Senate Armed Services Committees, Washington, DC, September 18–19, 2002.

ent than the one we grew accustomed to over the past half-century. We have entered a world in which terrorist movements and terrorist states are developing the capacity to cause unprecedented destruction.

A New Threat

Today, our margin of error is notably different. In the 20th century, we were dealing, for the most part, with conventional weapons—weapons that could kill hundreds or thousands of people, generally combatants. In the 21st century, we are dealing with weapons of mass destruction [WMD] that can kill potentially tens of thousands of people—innocent men, women and children.

Further, because of the nature of these new threats, we are in an age of little or no warning, when threats can emerge suddenly—at any place or time—to surprise us. Terrorist states have enormous appetite for these powerful weapons—and active programs to develop them. They are finding ways to gain access to these capabilities. This is not a possibility—it is a certainty. In word and deed, they have demonstrated a willingness to use those capabilities.

Moreover, after September 11th, they have discovered a new means of delivering these weapons—terrorist networks. To the extent that they might transfer WMD to terrorist groups, they could conceal their responsibility for attacks. And if they believe they can conceal their responsibility for an attack, then they would likely not be deterred.

We are on notice. Let there be no doubt: an attack will be attempted. The only question is when and by what technique. It could be months, a year, or several years. But it will happen. It is in our future. Each of us needs to pause, and think about that for a moment—about what it would mean for our country, for our families—and indeed for the world.

If the worst were to happen, not one of us here today will be able to honestly say it was a surprise. Because it will not be a surprise. We have connected the dots as much as it is humanly possible—before the fact. Only by waiting until after the event could we have proof positive. The dots are there for all to see. The dots are there for all to connect. If they aren't good enough, rest assured they will only be good enough after another disaster—a disaster of still greater proportions. And by then it will be too late.

The question facing us is this: what is the responsible course of action for our country? Do you believe it is our responsibility to wait for a nuclear, chemical or biological 9/11? Or is it the responsibility of free people to do something now—to take steps to deal with the threat before we are attacked?

> *"We have entered a world in which terrorist movements and terrorist states are developing the capacity to cause unprecedented destruction."*

The President has made his position clear: the one thing that is not an option is doing nothing.

There are a number of terrorist states pursuing weapons of mass destruction—Iran, Libya, North Korea, Syria, to name but a few. But no terrorist state poses a greater and more immediate threat to the security of our people, and the stability of the world, than the regime of [Iraqi president] Saddam Hussein in Iraq.

No living dictator has shown the murderous combination of intent and capability—of aggression against his neighbors; oppression of his own people; genocide; support of terrorism; pursuit of weapons of mass destruction; the use of weapons of mass destruction; and the most threatening hostility to its neighbors and to the United States, than Saddam Hussein and his regime. . . .

A Murderous Regime

These facts about Saddam Hussein's regime should be part of this [congressional] record and of our country's considerations:

• Saddam Hussein has openly praised the attacks of September 11th. . . .

• On the anniversary of 9/11, his state-run press called the attacks "God's punishment."

• He has repeatedly threatened the U.S. and its allies with terror—once declaring that "every Iraqi [can] become a missile."

• He has ordered the use of chemical weapons—Sarin, Tabun, VX, and mustard agents—against his own people, in one case killing 5,000 innocent civilians in a single day.

• His regime has invaded two of its neighbors, and threatened others.

• In 1980, they invaded Iran, and used chemical weapons against Iranian forces.

> *"There are ways Iraq could easily conceal responsibility for a WMD attack."*

• In 1990, they invaded Kuwait and are responsible for thousands of documented cases of torture, rape and murder of Kuwaiti civilians during their occupation.

• In 1991, they were poised to march on and occupy other nations—and would have done so, had they not been stopped by the U.S. led coalition forces.

• His regime has launched ballistic missiles at four of their neighbors—Israel, Iran, Saudi Arabia and Bahrain.

• His regime plays host to terrorist networks, and has directly ordered acts of terror on foreign soil.

• His regime assassinates its opponents, both in Iraq and abroad, and has attempted to assassinate the former Israeli Ambassador to Great Britain, and a former U.S. President. . . .

• His regime has amassed large, clandestine stockpiles of biological weapons—including anthrax and botulism toxin, and possibly smallpox.

• His regime has amassed large, clandestine stockpiles of chemical weapons—including VX, sarin, cyclosarin and mustard gas.

• His regime has an active program to acquire and develop nuclear weapons.

• They have the knowledge of how to produce nuclear weapons, and designs for at least two different nuclear devices.

• They have a team of scientists, technicians and engineers in place, as well as the infrastructure needed to build a weapon.

• Very likely all they need to complete a weapon is fissile material—and they are, at this moment [in 2002] seeking that material—both from foreign sources and the capability to produce it indigenously.

> *"[Saddam Hussein] has incentives to make common cause with terrorists. He shares many common objectives with groups like al-Qaeda."*

• His regime has dozens of ballistic missiles, and is working to extend their range in violation of UN restrictions.

• His regime is pursuing pilotless aircraft as a means of delivering chemical and biological weapons.

• His regime agreed after the Gulf War to give up weapons of mass destruction and submit to international inspections—then lied, cheated and hid their WMD programs for more than a decade. . . .

As the President warned the United Nations [in September 2002] "Saddam Hussein's regime is a grave and gathering danger." It is a danger to its neighbors, to the United States, to the Middle East, and to international peace and stability. It is a danger we do not have the option to ignore. . . .

Some have asked whether an attack on Iraq would disrupt and distract the U.S. from the Global War on Terror.

The answer to that is: Iraq is a part of the Global War on Terror—stopping terrorist regimes from acquiring weapons of mass destruction is a key objective of that war. We can fight all elements of this war simultaneously.

Our principal goal in the war on terror is to stop another 9/11—or a WMD attack that could make 9/11 seem modest by comparison—before it happens. Whether that threat comes from a terrorist regime or a terrorist network is beside the point. Our objective is to stop them, regardless of the source.

In his State of the Union address last January [2001], President [George W.] Bush made our objectives clear. He said: "by seeking weapons of mass destruction, these regimes pose a grave and growing danger. They could provide these arms to terrorists, giving them the means to match their hatred. They could attack our allies or attempt to blackmail the United States. In any of these cases the price of indifference would be catastrophic." Ultimately, history will judge us all by what we do now to deal with this danger. . . .

How Much Evidence Is Necessary?

In our country, it has been customary to seek evidence that would prove guilt "beyond a reasonable doubt" in a court of law. That approach is appropriate when the objective is to protect the rights of the accused. But in the age of

WMD, the objective is not to protect the "rights" of dictators like Saddam Hussein—it is to protect the lives of our citizens. And when there is that risk, and we are trying to defend against the closed societies and shadowy networks that threaten us in the 21st century, expecting to find that standard of evidence, from thousands of miles away, and to do so before such a weapon has been used, is not realistic. And, after such weapons have been used it is too late.

I suggest that any who insist on perfect evidence are back in the 20th century and still thinking in pre-9/11 terms. On September 11th, we were awakened to the fact that America is now vulnerable to unprecedented destruction. That awareness ought to be sufficient to change the way we think about our security, how we defend our country—and the type of certainty and evidence we consider appropriate.

In the 20th century, when we were dealing largely with conventional weapons, we could wait for perfect evidence. If we miscalculated, we could absorb an attack, recover, take a breath, mobilize, and go out and defeat our attackers. In the 21st century, that is no longer the case, unless we are willing and comfortable accepting the loss not of thousands of lives, but potentially tens of thousands of lives—a high price indeed. . . .

"The issue for the U.S. is not vengeance, retribution or retaliation—it is whether the Iraqi regime poses a growing danger to the safety and security of our people."

We do know that the Iraqi regime has chemical and biological weapons of mass destruction and is pursuing nuclear weapons; that they have a proven willingness to use the weapons at their disposal; that they have proven aspirations to seize the territory of, and threaten, their neighbors; proven support for and cooperation with terrorist networks; and proven record of declared hostility and venomous rhetoric against the United States. Those threats should be clear to all. . . .

Iraq's Links to Terrorist Networks

Some have argued Iraq is unlikely to use WMD against us because, unlike terrorist networks, Saddam has a "return address.". . .

There is no reason for confidence that if Iraq launched a WMD attack on the U.S. it would necessarily have an obvious "return address." There are ways Iraq could easily conceal responsibility for a WMD attack. They could deploy "sleeper cells" armed with biological weapons to attack us from within—and then deny any knowledge or connection to the attacks. Or they could put a WMD-tipped missile on a "commercial" shipping vessel, sail it within range of our coast, fire it, and then melt back into the commercial shipping traffic before we knew what hit us. Finding that ship would be like searching for a needle in a haystack—a bit like locating a single terrorist. Or they could recruit and utilize a terrorist network with similar views and objectives, and pass on weapons of mass destruction to them. It is this nexus between a terrorist state like Iraq with WMD and terrorist networks that has so significantly changed the U.S. security environment. . . .

Some have opined there is scant evidence of Iraq's ties to terrorists, and he has little incentive to make common cause with them.

> *"Taking military action in Iraq does not mean that it would be necessary or appropriate to take military action against other states that possess or are pursuing WMD."*

That is not correct. Iraq's ties to terrorist networks are long-standing. . . . We know that [the terrorist group] al-Qaeda is operating in Iraq today [2002] and that little happens in Iraq without the knowledge of the Saddam Hussein regime. We also know that there have been a number of contacts between Iraq and al-Qaeda over the years. We know Saddam has ordered acts of terror himself, including the attempted assassination of a former U.S. President.

He has incentives to make common cause with terrorists. He shares many common objectives with groups like al-Qaeda, including an antipathy for the Saudi royal family and a desire to drive the U.S. out of the Persian region. Moreover, if he decided it was in his interest to conceal his responsibility for an attack on the U.S., providing WMD to terrorists would be an effective way of doing so.

Some have said that they would support action to remove Saddam if the U.S. could prove a connection to the attacks of September 11th—but there is no such proof.

The question implies that the U.S. should have to prove that Iraq has already attacked us in order to deal with that threat. The objective is to stop him before he attacks us and kills thousands of our citizens.

The case against Iraq does not depend on an Iraqi link to 9/11. The issue for the U.S. is not vengeance, retribution or retaliation—it is whether the Iraqi regime poses a growing danger to the safety and security of our people, and of the world. There is no question but that it does.

Why Iraq?

Some argue that North Korea and Iran are more immediate threats than Iraq. North Korea almost certainly has nuclear weapons, and is developing missiles that will be able to reach most of the continental United States. Iran has stockpiles of chemical weapons, is developing ballistic missiles of increasing range, and is aggressively pursuing nuclear weapons. The question is asked: why not deal with them first?

Iran and North Korea are indeed threats—problems we take seriously. That is why President Bush named them specifically, when he spoke about an "Axis of Evil." And we have policies to address both.

But Iraq is unique. No other living dictator matches Saddam Hussein's record of waging aggressive war against his neighbors; pursuing weapons of mass destruction; using WMD against his own people and other nations; launching ballistic missiles at his neighbors; brutalizing and torturing his own citizens; harboring terrorist networks; engaging in terrorist acts, including the attempted assassination of foreign officials; violating his international commitments; lying, cheating and hiding his WMD programs; deceiving and defying the express will of the United Nations over and over again.

As the President told the UN, "in one place—in one regime—we find all these dangers in their most lethal and aggressive forms.". . .

Some have asked whether military intervention in Iraq means the U.S. would have to go to war with every terrorist state that is pursuing WMD?

The answer is: no. Taking military action in Iraq does not mean that it would be necessary or appropriate to take military action against other states that possess or are pursuing WMD. For one thing, preventive action in one situation may very well produce a deterrent effect on other states. After driving the Taliban from power in Afghanistan [in 2001] we have already seen a change in behavior in certain regimes.

Moreover, dealing with some states may not require military action. In some cases, such as Iran, change could conceivably come from within. The young people and the women in Iran are increasingly fed up with the tight clique of Mullahs—they want change, and may well rise up to change their leadership at some point.

Some say that there is no international consensus behind ousting Saddam—and most of our key allies are opposed.

First, the fact is that there are a number of countries that want Saddam Hussein gone. Some are reluctant to say publicly just yet. But, if the U.S. waited for a consensus before acting, we would never do anything. Obviously, one's first choice in life is to have everyone agree with you at the outset. In reality, that is seldom the case. It takes time, leadership and persuasion. Leadership is about deciding what is right, and then going out and persuading others. . . .

A Critical Choice

As the President has made clear, this is a critical moment—for our country and for the world. Our resolve is being put to the test. It is a test that, unfortunately, the world's free nations have failed before in recent history—with terrible consequences.

Long before the Second World War, Hitler wrote in *Mein Kampf* indicating what he intended to do.[1] But the hope was that maybe he would not do what he said. Between 35 and 60 million people died because of a series of fatal miscal-

---

1. *Mein Kampf*, or *My Struggle*, published in 1926, outlines the main ideas that culminated in the Holocaust of World War II.

culations. He might have been stopped early—at a minimal cost of lives—had the vast majority of the world's leaders not decided at the time that the risks of acting were greater than the risks of not acting.

Today, we must decide whether the risks of acting are greater than the risks of not acting. Saddam Hussein has made his intentions clear. He has used weapons of mass destruction against his own people and his neighbors. He has demonstrated an intention to take the territory of his neighbors. He has launched ballistic missiles against U.S. allies and others in the region. He plays host to terrorist networks. He pays rewards to the families of suicide bombers in Israel—like those who killed five Americans at the Hebrew University earlier this year [2002]. He is hostile to the United States, because we have denied him the ability he has sought to impose his will on his neighbors. He has said, in no uncertain terms that he would use weapons of mass destruction against the United States. He has, at this moment [in 2002] stockpiles of chemical and biological weapons, and is pursuing nuclear weapons. If he demonstrates the capability to deliver them to our shores, the world would be changed. Our people would be at great risk. Our willingness to be engaged in the world, our willingness to project power to stop aggression, our ability to forge coalitions for multilateral action, could all be under question. And many lives could be lost.

We need to decide as a people how we feel about that. Do the risks of taking action to stop that threat outweigh these risks of living in the world we see? Or is the risk of doing nothing greater than the risk of acting? That is the question President Bush has posed to the Congress, to the American people and to the world community.

The question comes down to this: how will the history of this era be recorded? When we look back on previous periods of our history, we see there have been many books written about threats and attacks that were not anticipated. . . .

The list of such books is endless. And, unfortunately, in the past year, historians have added to that body of literature—there are already books out on the September 11th attacks and why they were not prevented. . . .

Each is an attempt by the authors to "connect the dots"—to determine what happened, and why it was not possible to figure out that it was going to happen.

Our job today—the President's, the Congress' and the UN's is to connect the dots before the fact—to anticipate vastly more lethal attacks before they happen—and to make the right decision as to whether we should take preventive action—before it is too late.

We are on notice—each of us. Each has a solemn responsibility to do everything in our power to ensure that, when the history of this period is written, the books won't ask why we slept—to ensure that history will instead record that on September 11th the American people were awakened to the impending dangers—and that those entrusted with the safety of the American people made the right decisions and saved our nation, and the world, from 21st century threats.

The Threat of al Qaeda Has Been Exaggerated

by John L. Scherer

About the author: *John L. Scherer, a freelance writer, edited the yearbook* Terrorism: An Annual Survey *in 1982 and 1983, and the quarterly* Terrorism *from 1986 to 2001.*

The threat of terrorism in the U.S. is not over, but [the September 11, 2001, terrorist attacks] may have been an anomaly. Intelligence agencies are unlikely to uncover an impending attack, no matter what they spend on human intelligence, because it is virtually impossible to infiltrate terrorist cells whose members are friends and relatives. At least five of the 19 Al Qaeda hijackers came from Asir province in Saudi Arabia, and possibly eight were related.

The U.S. was not defended on 9/11. As soon as the aircraft were hijacked, helicopters armed with missiles should have risen to protect coastal cities. Two F-16s dispatched from Langley and Otis Air Force bases in Virginia and New Jersey, respectively, were too distant to reach New York and Washington, D.C., in time. On a cautionary note, the penetration of White House air space by a Cessna aircraft in June, 2002, and by several other flights since the World Trade Center and Pentagon attacks, indicates nothing much has been done.

Major Al Qaeda Operations Are Over

Although there will be small-scale terrorist attacks in the U.S. in the next 10 years, major Al Qaeda operations are over. Of the more than 1,200 people arrested after 9/11, none has been charged in the conspiracy. This suggests the hijackers did not and do not have an extensive operational American network. Some intelligence officials have estimated that up to 5,000 "sleepers"—persons with connections to Al Qaeda—are living in this country, including hundreds of hard-core members, yet nothing significant has happened in more than a year.

The arrests in the Buffalo, N.Y., area back up the possibility of such sleeper cells.[1]

Al Qaeda attacks are more likely to occur abroad, but the danger of this group is being exaggerated overseas as well. Members of Al Qaeda cells have been arrested in Spain, Italy, England, Germany, Malaysia, and elsewhere, but scarcely more than a score anywhere except Pakistan.

The threat of terrorism in the U.S. has greatly diminished, but Al Qaeda and Taliban[2] prisoners realize they can terrorize citizens merely by "confessing" to plans to blow up bridges in California, attack schools in Texas, bomb apartments in Florida, rob banks in the Northeast, set off a series of "dirty bombs," [radioactive devices] and have scuba divers operate in coastal areas.

A recent book on Al Qaeda states that the organization plans 100 attacks at any one time. This is nonsense. There have been a handful of small-scale attacks with fatalities linked to Al Qaeda since Sept. 11, nothing near 100. These include a church bombing in Islamabad (five deaths); the explosion of a gasoline truck and bus outside a synagogue on Djerba Island, Tunisia (19 dead); a bus bombing outside the Sheraton Hotel in Karachi (14 killed); and a bombing at the U.S. consulate in Karachi (12 fatalities). Three of these incidents occurred in Pakistan. In addition, Al Qaeda links are suspected in late-2002 bombings in Bali and Kenya.[3] The claim by Sept. 11 terrorist suspect Zacarias Moussaoui of an ongoing Al Qaeda plot in this country is a subterfuge to save himself.

Al Qaeda had planned attacks in London, Paris, Marseilles, Strasbourg, Singapore, and Rome, but most of the conspirators were arrested a short time after the Sept 11 attacks. Meanwhile, no one had hijacked an aircraft in the U.S. using a "real" weapon in almost 15 years, although crashing planes into structures is not new. The Israelis shot down a Libyan jetliner they said was headed for a building in Tel Aviv in the 1980s. A Cessna 150 fell 50 yards short of the White House in September, 1994. French commandos prevented a jumbo jet, hijacked in Algeria by the Armed Islamic Group, from crashing into the Eiffel Tower the following December. In the mid 1990s, terrorist Ramzi Yousef plotted to have his friend Abdul Hakim Murad fly a light plane

> *"Although there will be small-scale terrorist attacks in the U.S. in the next 10 years, major Al Qaeda operations are over."*

loaded with chemical weapons into CIA headquarters at Langley, Va., or to have him spray the area with poison gas. A Turkish hijacker attempted to crash an aircraft into the tomb of former Pres. Kemal Ataturk in Ankara in 1998. With enhanced security on at airports and passengers on commercial airliners who will react to any danger, this threat has diminished.

---

1. In late 2002 six suspected Al Qaeda terrorists were arrested in Buffalo, New York.   2. The Taliban is an Islamist group that ruled most of Afghanistan from 1996 until 2001, when it was deposed by U.S. forces. The United States accused the Taliban of supporting Al Qaeda.   3. Al Qaeda was also suspected in the March 2004 terrorist bombings in Madrid that killed 191 people and wounded more than 1,800.

Terrorists have attacked on holidays, but authorities are now especially alert on those occasions, and the number and violence of anniversary attacks have lessened. Al Qaeda has never staged an incident on a holiday.

CBN Attacks Unlikely

Chemical, biological, and nuclear (CBN) attacks are possible, but difficult and unlikely. Only one has succeeded over the last two decades—the 1995 Sarin incident on the Tokyo subway [when members of the Aum Shinrikyo cult released sarin gas]. Thousands were injured, but just six people died. There have been no CBN attacks with mass fatalities anywhere. Terrorist "experts" simply have thought up everything terrible that can happen, and then assumed it will. Terrorists would encounter problems dispersing biological toxins. Most quickly dilute in any open space, and others need perfect weather conditions to cause mass casualties. Some biological agents, although not anthrax, are killed by exposure to ultraviolet light. The Washington, D.C., subway system has devices that can detect biological toxins. New York has the highest-density population of any American city, and for this reason might have the greatest probability of such an attack, but it also has the best-prepared public health system.

"Americans must remain vigilant, of course, but there is no need to raid the Treasury or turn the country upside down pursuing phantoms."

In one instance, Essid Sami Ben Khemais, a Moroccan who ran Al Qaeda's European logistics center in Milan, Italy, received a five-year prison sentence in February, 2002. His cell planned to poison Rome's water supply near the U.S. embassy on the Via Veneto. This group had 10 pounds of potassium ferro-cyanide, a chemical used to make wine and ink dye, but extracting a deadly amount of cyanide from this compound would have proved extremely difficult.

Americans are rightly concerned about a strike against a nuclear power facility, but terrorists would have to get through a series of gates and fences, bypass motion sensors, and outfight a heavily armed security force to enter a containment building. Once inside the structure, they would need to know the exact sequence to shut down a reactor. An aircraft diving at a nuclear station would have to hit a small target, nothing like the World Trade Center buildings, which rose 1,400 feet into the air. Containment vessels are 160 feet high by 130 feet wide, and storage casks are even smaller.

Politicians have proposed creating a bureau to protect food from terrorists, but no one in the U.S. has ever died from a terrorist food poisoning. In fact, the nation has experienced just one instance of tampering with agricultural produce, when members of a cult contaminated several salad bars at restaurants in Oregon. The biggest danger to the food supply would be from salmonella, E. coli 0157, clostridium botulinum, and cholera, but careless handling and improper preparation of food are far-greater menaces than terrorism.

There are 168,000 public water systems in the U.S. Some serve as many as 8,000,000 people, while others as few as 25. None has ever been poisoned, although there have been attempts.

Recognizing U.S. Defenses

The FBI may need reorganization, especially since its failures preceding Sept. 11 resulted from officials making bad decisions. It is well-known that in mid August, 2001, officials at a flight school in Eagan, Minn., told the FBI that a French citizen of Algerian descent, Moussaoui, had offered $30,000 cash for lessons on a flight-simulator to learn how to fly a Boeing 747. He had no interest in learning how to land the plane. Moussaoui was arrested three weeks before the attacks. One week before the hijackings, French intelligence informed the FBI that he was an Islamic militant who had visited Afghanistan and had links to Al Qaeda. FBI agents could have entered Moussaoui's computer and obtained his phone records using the Federal statutes already in place, but which were ignored or forgotten by officials.

Reorganizations refuse to acknowledge that some individuals are smarter and more knowledgeable than others, and new personnel will eventually resolve these problems. The new Department of Homeland Security will disrupt normal channels of communication and create even more bureaucratic confusion. It will compete for resources with the National Security Council and it will be costly trying to coordinate 46 agencies and, judging from actual terrorist events in the U.S., wholly unnecessary. Americans must remain vigilant, of course, but there is no need to raid the Treasury or turn the country upside down pursuing phantoms.

The Invasion of Afghanistan Was Not Justified

by W. Pal S. Sidhu

About the author: *W. Pal S. Sidhu is an associate at the New York–based International Peace Academy, an institution dedicated to promoting the prevention and settlement of armed conflicts between and within states.*

The taking of innocent lives—be they American, Indian, Pakistani, Palestinian or Israeli—cannot be justified on any grounds whatsoever and should be condemned. Therefore the events of September 11, 2001 on the United States, the largest-ever terrorist attack in terms of both mass destruction and mass disruption, must be condemned in the strongest and most unequivocal of terms. Perhaps this is why organisations as diverse and disparate as the Organisation of the Islamic Conference and the Asia Pacific Economic Cooperation forum had no hesitation in unanimously condemning the acts of Terrible Tuesday [September 11, 2001].

As a logical corollary, therefore, there can be no doubt that any country which is a victim of such heinous attacks has every right to retaliate against the perpetrators of such acts as laid out in Article 51 (in Chapter VII) of the United Nations [UN] Charter, which recognises the "inherent right of individual or collective self-defence if an armed attack occurs against a member of the United Nations." This right was reiterated in United Nations Security Council (UNSC) Resolution 1373 passed on September 28, 2001—the same day that the Nobel Peace Committee awarded the prize jointly to the UN and Secretary General Kofi Annan. The resolution reaffirmed not only the "inherent right of individual or collective self-defence" but also the "need to combat by all means, in accordance with the Charter of the United Nations, threats to international peace and security caused by terrorist act. . . ." Therefore, at the very least it could be ar-

W. Pal S. Sidhu, "Can the US War on Terrorism Be Justified?" *Nautilus Institute Special Forum*, vol. 41, November 21, 2001. Copyright © 2001 by the Nautilus Institute. Reproduced by permission.

gued that the US has fundamental grounds to go to war to punish those responsible for the horrible acts of 11 September.

Conditions for Justification

There are, however, several other important conditions that should be met before the war can be justified. First, only the guilty party or parties should be punished. As per the principles of just war the retaliation should be aimed to redress only the wrong suffered and should not be seen as an excuse to launch a crusade against people or states that one does not like (even though there are, clearly, many states that Washington loves to hate).

Second, the operation should also take into consideration whether there is a reasonable chance of success. Apart from the objective of punishing those responsible, the military action should also ensure as far as possible that the perpetrators are not free to strike again, and that the crime cannot be repeated. Consequently, it is crucial that those responsible for the dastardly acts have been correctly identified, and equally important that the guilt of the terrorists can be publicly proven.

Third, in carrying out the punishment it should be ensured that innocent victims are spared, otherwise the distinction between those who have committed the crime and those who are doling out the punishment becomes blurred. This is in line with the just war principle that war must discriminate between combatants and non-combatants.

Finally, the ultimate goal of the military operation should be to re-establish peace. The peace established after the war must be preferable to the peace that would have prevailed if the war had not been fought. This implies not only achieving the short-term military objectives, but also taking long-term measures to ensure that the conditions—political, economic, ideological—that led to the initiation of these terrorist acts in the first place are resolved. Failing to do so risks a recurrence of similar terrorist acts in the future.

No Support for War in Afghanistan

How do these conditions hold up when applied to the present war on terrorism, which is now [in 2001] erroneously being equated with the war in Afghanistan? First, even today there is no evidence that will stand up to legal scrutiny . . . and conclusively prove that these terrorists were linked to [the terrorist group] Al-Qaeda or [Al-Qaeda leader] Osama bin Laden. Even assuming for a moment that these terrorists were connected to Al-Qaeda and bin Laden, how does that link them to the Taliban and Afghanistan?[1] There is no evidence to suggest that the corporate headquarters of Terrorism Inc. is located in Afghanistan. None of the hijackers were from Afghanistan nor were they trained in

---

1. The Taliban is an Islamist group that ruled Afghanistan from 1996 until its overthrow by a U.S.-led coalition in 2001. A justification for the U.S.-led invasion in 2001 was that the Taliban was supporting the Al-Qaeda terrorist group.

camps run by the Taliban. It is not even clear whether any of them ever went to Afghanistan. By most accounts they were reasonably well off men from Egypt, Saudi Arabia and the United Arab Emirates who used Germany as a base for their operations. Does this make all these countries legitimate targets of retaliation as well? How then is the Taliban regime (a truly contemptible regime in its own right) culpable in the September 11 attacks?

The only crime Afghanistan is accountable for is having the misfortune of being the last Cold War battleground of the US and the Soviet Union. As a result of this struggle between two superpowers, Afghanistan has been reduced to a non-state leaving it vulnerable to exploitation by the likes of bin Laden and Al-Qaeda.

> *"The ultimate goal of the military operation [in Afghanistan] should be to re-establish peace. . . . Failing to do so risks a recurrence of similar terrorist attacks."*

On the issue of innocent victims, there is already evidence that civilians have become what the military euphemistically calls "collateral damage." However, a greater humanitarian disaster is looming on the horizon. According to UN estimates [as of November 2001] as many as 7.5 million people—a quarter of the total population of Afghanistan—is on the verge of starvation. Even worse, the original token food drops carried out by the US have backfired, literally, because many of the yellow food packets looked very similar to the yellow coloured cluster bombs that are particularly civilian unfriendly. Thus the situation has been further exacerbated by the US-led war. According to one estimate, between [November] and December 2001 the number of innocent Afghanis who will die will be more than the number of innocent victims of the twin tower tragedy. Sadly neither group had anything to do with the horrific events of September 11 and yet both have become hapless victims.

Finally, despite the realisation that Washington's disastrous decision to walk away at the end of the Cold War has compelled its desperate return now to Afghanistan, it seems Washington is likely to repeat this same mistake, as soon as its short-term military objective of eliminating bin Laden, dismantling the Al-Qaeda network and defeating the Taliban is achieved. Senior members of the present Bush administration have admitted that they may fail to achieve their originally prescribed goals. Defense Secretary Donald Rumsfeld publicly confessed that bin Laden may never be caught and that Al-Qaeda might never be destroyed. This failure is likely to haunt them not only abroad but also at home. The American intelligence agencies, while candidly acknowledging the presence of Al-Qaeda cells within the US, have been spectacularly unsuccessful in exposing them, let alone destroying them.

However, whatever the outcome of the war, the administration's stalwarts have already publicly expressed their aversion to getting their hands dirty with the messy business of nation-building. This shortsighted policy will essentially guarantee that Afghanistan will remain ripe for the picking by yet another group of extremists who would no doubt exploit the vulnerability of the Afghani people and perpetuate the cycle of terrorist violence. The only difference is that this time around the repercussions are not going to be confined strictly to Afghanistan, but will also have serious ramifications for the six countries that surround it.

Alternatives

Given the moot justification and serious limitations in the present US approach to combating terrorism, what are the alternatives? Strategically, there are three parallel paths: first, there is a need to create a truly global and multilateral anti-terrorist coalition—not just fragile alliances of convenience that exist at the moment. This coalition must be based on universally accepted norms, ideally located in the various UN conventions, declarations and resolutions. Here the record of the 12 anti-terrorist conventions adopted by the UN since 1963 is telling. While most of these are already in force, compliance to them remains patchy at best. Moreover, one critical convention—the International Convention for the Suppression of the Financing of Terrorism adopted in 1999—which obligates state parties either to prosecute or to extradite persons accused of funding terrorist activities and requires banks to enact measures to identify suspicious transactions has yet to enter into force. It requires 22 countries to ratify the treaty to enter into force, but until the end of October 2001 only five countries (Azerbaijan, Botswana, Sri Lanka, the United Kingdom and Uzbekistan) have ratified it.

Second, this counter-terrorism norm should be enforced universally. In this context the difficult experience of bringing those responsible for Pan Am 103 to justice could serve as a model for future approaches to dealing with the scourge of terrorism.[2] Here the establishment of UNSC Counter-Terrorism Committee, headed by the United Kingdom, to "deny space, money [and] haven to terrorism" is a step in the right direction.

Finally, a long-term engagement policy, which could stretch into decades, will have to be sustained with states of concerns or non-states to ensure that they do not play willing or unwilling hosts to terrorists. In this context the tendency to follow a blunt "sanction only" approach should be avoided. Instead a sanctions-cum-incentive approach should be adopted. Simultaneously, the UN, particularly the Secretary General, should agree to get involved only when they have received an extended mandate and the necessary resources to support the mandate. Here the role of [UN] Ambassador Lakhdar Brahimi, who has been adept in traversing the minefield in the UN (when he chaired the Panel on

2. In 1988, 270 people died when a bomb exploded on board this flight travelling from London to New York. Subsequent investigation concluded that two Libyans were responsible; however, Libya initially refused to hand over the suspects. Finally, in a 1999 trial in the neutral country of the Netherlands, one of the men was convicted and imprisoned. However, there is continuing disagreement over his conviction.

United Nations Peace Operations) as well as in Afghanistan (where he has had vast experience negotiating with the various warring parties) will be critical.

Clearly, the US could play a lead role in strengthening both the UN's normative and operational capability in combating terrorism. However, in order to be taken seriously Washington must abandon its multilateralism a la carte policy in favour of a policy of genuine multilateralism, which implies not walking away from treaties or conventions that are perceived to be unpalatable. The question is: will it?

The War Against Iraq Was Unjustified

by Edward M. Kennedy

About the author: *Edward M. Kennedy was elected to the U.S. Senate in 1962, representing Massachusetts, and has been reelected to the seat ever since.*

[In 2004] the nation is engaged in a major ongoing debate about why America went to war in Iraq, when Iraq was not an imminent threat, had no nuclear weapons, no persuasive links to [the terrorist group] Al Qaeda, no connection to the terrorist attacks of September 11th, and no stockpiles of weapons of mass destruction.

Over two centuries ago, [former U.S. president] John Adams spoke eloquently about the need to let facts and evidence guide actions and policies. He said, "Facts are stubborn things; and whatever may be our wishes, our inclinations, or the dictates of our passions, they cannot alter the state of facts and evidence." Listen to those words again, and you can hear John Adams speaking to us now about Iraq. "Facts are stubborn things; and whatever may be our wishes, our inclinations, or the dictates of our passions, they cannot alter the state of facts and evidence."

Tragically, in making the decision to go to war in Iraq, the Bush Administration allowed its wishes, its inclinations and its passions to alter the state of facts and the evidence of the threat we faced from Iraq. . . .

It is not sufficient for [CIA director George] Tenet to say only, as he did [in March 2004] to the Senate Intelligence Committee, that we must be patient. When he was appointed Director of Central Intelligence in 1997, Tenet said to [former] President [Bill] Clinton. ". . . I have believed that you . . . and the Vice President must be provided with . . . complete and objective intelligence. . . . We must always be straight and tell you the facts as we know them." The American people and our men and women serving in Iraq deserve the facts and they deserve answers now.

Edward M. Kennedy, address to the Council on Foreign Relations, Washington, DC, March 5, 2004.

44

The rushed decision to invade Iraq cannot all be blamed on flawed intelligence. If we view these events simply as an intelligence failure—rather than a larger failure of decision-making and leadership—we will learn the wrong lessons.

Intelligence Manipulation

The more we find out, the clearer it becomes that any failure in the intelligence itself is dwarfed by the Administration's manipulation of the intelligence in making the case for war. Specific warnings from the intelligence community were consistently ignored as the Administration rushed toward war.

We now know that from the moment President [George W.] Bush took office, Iraq was given high priority as unfinished business from the first Bush Administration [1989–1993].

According to former Treasury Secretary Paul O'Neill's account in [journalist] Ron Suskind's book, *The Price of Loyalty*, Iraq was on the agenda at the very first meeting of the National Security Council, just ten days after President Bush's inauguration in 2001. At that meeting, the President quickly—and wrongly—concluded that the U.S. could not do much about the Israeli-Palestinian conflict. He said we should "pull out of that situation," and then turned to a discussion of "how Iraq is destabilizing the region."

Secretary O'Neill remembers: "Getting [former Iraqi president Saddam] Hussein was now the Administration's focus. From the start, we were building the case against Hussein and looking at how we could take him out and change Iraq into a new country. And, if we did that, it would solve everything. It was all about finding a way to do it. That was the tone of it. The President saying, 'Fine. Go find me a way to do this.'"

By the end of February 2001, the talk on Iraq was mostly about how—and how quickly—to get rid of Saddam Hussein. President Bush was clearly frustrated with what the intelligence community was providing. According to Secretary O'Neill, on May 16, 2001, he and the other principals of the National Security Council met with the President to discuss the Middle East. Tenet presented his intelligence report, and told the President that it was still only speculation whether Saddam had weapons of mass destruction, or was even starting a program to build such weapons.

Secretary O'Neill says: "Everything Tenet sent up to Bush and [Vice President Richard] Cheney about Iraq

> *"The Bush Administration allowed its wishes, its inclinations and its passions to alter the state of facts and the evidence of the threat we faced from Iraq."*

was very judicious and precisely qualified. The President was clearly very interested in weapons or weapons programs—and frustrated about our weak intelligence capability—but Tenet was clearly being careful to say, here's the little that we know and the great deal that we don't. That wouldn't change, and I read those CIA reports for two years," said O'Neill.

Effect of 9/11

Then came [the September 11, 2001, terrorist attacks]. In the months that followed, the war in Afghanistan and the hunt for [terrorist leader] Osama bin Laden had obvious priority. Al Qaeda was clearly the most imminent threat to our national security. In fact, in his testimony to Congress in February 2001, one month after President Bush's inauguration and seven months before 9/11, Tenet had said: "Osama bin Laden and his global network of lieutenants and associates remain the most immediate and serious threat." That testimony emphasized the clear danger of bin Laden in light of the specific attacks in previous years on American citizens and American institutions.

In February 2002, five months after 9/11, Tenet testified: "Last year, I told you that Osama bin Laden and the Al Qaeda network were the most immediate and serious threat this country faced. This remains true despite the progress we have made in Afghanistan and in disrupting the network elsewhere."

Even during the buildup to the war in Iraq, in February 2003, Tenet again testified, "the threat from Al Qaeda remains . . . We place no limitations on our expectations of what Al Qaeda might do to survive . . . Al Qaeda is living in the expectation of resuming the offensive."

> *"Any failure in the intelligence itself is dwarfed by the Administration's manipulation of the intelligence in making the case for war."*

In his testimony [in March 2004] to the Senate Intelligence Committee, Tenet repeated his earlier warnings. He said again that Al Qaeda is not defeated and that "We are still at war . . . This is a learning organization that remains committed to attacking the United States, its friends and allies."

Tenet never used that kind of strong language to describe the threat from Iraq. Yet despite all the clear and consistent warnings about Al Qaeda, by the summer of 2002, President Bush was ready for war with Iraq. The war in Afghanistan was no longer in the headlines or at the center of attention. Bin Laden was hard to find, the economy was in trouble, and so was the President's approval rating in the polls.

[Political strategist for George W. Bush] Karl Rove had tipped his hand earlier by stating that the war on terrorism could bring political benefits as well. The President's undeniable goal was to convince the American people that war was necessary—and necessary soon, because soon-to-be-acquired nuclear weapons in the hands of Saddam Hussein could easily be handed off to terrorists.

This conclusion was not supported by the facts, but the intelligence could be retrofitted to support it. Greg Thielmann, former Director of the State Department's Bureau of Intelligence and Research, put it bluntly last July [2003]. He said, "Some of the fault lies with the performance of the intelligence community, but most of it lies with the way senior officials misused the information they were provided." He said, "They surveyed the data, and picked out what they liked. The whole thing was bizarre. The Secretary of Defense had this huge Defense Intelligence Agency, and he went around it." Thielmann also said, "This administration has had a faith-based intelligence attitude, its top-down use of intelligence: we know the answers;

> *"The President's undeniable goal was to convince the American people that war was necessary—and necessary soon."*

give us the intelligence to support those answers. . . . Going down the list of administration deficiencies, or distortions, one has to talk about, first and foremost, the nuclear threat being hyped," he said.

David Albright, the former weapons inspector with the International Atomic Energy Agency, put it this way: "Leaders will use worst case assessments that point to nuclear weapons to generate political support because they know people fear nuclear weapons so much."

An Imminent Threat

Even though they make semantic denials, there is no doubt that senior Administration officials were suggesting the threat from Iraq was imminent.

At a roundtable discussion with European journalists [in February 2004], Secretary [of Defense Donald] Rumsfeld insisted: "I never said imminent threat."

In fact, Secretary Rumsfeld had told the House Armed Services Committee on September 18, 2002, ". . . Some have argued that the nuclear threat from Iraq is not imminent—that Saddam is at least 5–7 years away from having nuclear weapons. I would not be so certain."

In February 2003, with war only weeks away, then Deputy Press Secretary Scott McClellan was asked why NATO [North Atlantic Treaty Organization] allies should support Turkey's request for military assistance against Iraq. His clear response was, "This is about an imminent threat." In May 2003, White House spokesman Ari Fleischer was asked whether we went to war "because we said WMD [weapons of mass destruction] were a direct and imminent threat to the United States." Fleischer responded, "Absolutely."

What else could National Security Adviser Condoleezza Rice have been suggesting, other than an imminent threat—an extremely imminent threat—when she said on September 8, 2002, "We don't want the smoking gun to be a mushroom cloud."

President Bush himself may not have used the word "imminent," but he carefully chose strong and loaded words about the nature of the threat—words that the intelligence community never used—to persuade and prepare the nation to go to war against Iraq.

In the [White House] Rose Garden on October 2, 2002, as Congress was preparing to vote on authorizing the war, the President said the Iraqi regime "is a threat of unique urgency."

In a speech in Cincinnati on October 7, President Bush echoed Condoleezza Rice's image of nuclear devastation: "Facing clear evidence of peril, we cannot wait for the final proof—the smoking gun—that could come in the form of a mushroom cloud."

At a political appearance in New Mexico on October 28, 2002, after Congress had voted to authorize war, and a week before the election, President Bush said Iraq is a "real and dangerous threat."

At a NATO summit on November 20, 2002, President Bush said Iraq posed a "unique and urgent threat."

In Fort Hood, Texas on January 3, 2003, President Bush called the Iraqi regime a "grave threat."

Nuclear weapons. Mushroom cloud. Unique and urgent threat. Real and dangerous threat. Grave threat. This was the Administration's rallying cry for war. But those were not the words of the intelligence community. The community recognized that Saddam was a threat, but it never suggested the threat was imminent, or immediate, or urgent.

In his speech [in February 2004] at Georgetown, CIA Director Tenet stated that, despite attempts to acquire a nuclear capability, Saddam was many years away from acquiring a nuclear weapon. Tenet's precise words were: "We said Saddam did not have a nuclear weapon, and probably would have been unable to make one until 2007 to 2009."

The acquisition of enough nuclear material is an extremely difficult task for a country seeking nuclear weapons. Tenet bluntly stated that the intelligence community had "detected no such acquisition" by Saddam. The October 2002 National Intelligence Estimate also outlined the disagreement in the intelligence community over whether the notorious aluminum tubes were intended for nuclear weapons or not. Tenet clearly distanced himself from the Administration's statements about the urgency of the threat from Iraq in his speech at Georgetown. But he stopped short of saying the Administration distorted the intelligence or relied on other sources to make the case for war. He said he only gave the President the CIA's daily assessment of the intelligence, and the rest he did not know.

> *"There is no doubt that senior Administration officials were suggesting the threat from Iraq was imminent."*

Truth Comes Too Late

Tenet needs to explain to Congress and the country why he waited until [February 2004]—nearly a year after the war started—to set the record straight. Intelligence analysts had long been frustrated about the way intelligence was being misused to justify war. In February 2003, an official described the feelings of some analysts in the intelligence agencies to the *New York Times*, saying "I think there is also a sense of disappointment with the community's leadership that they are not standing up for them at a time when the intelligence is obviously being politicized."

Why wasn't CIA Director Tenet correcting the President and the Vice President and the Secretary of Defense a year ago, when it could have made a difference, when it could have prevented a needless war, when it could have saved so many lives?

It was Vice President Cheney who first laid out the trumped up argument for war with Iraq to an unsuspecting public. In a speech on August 26, 2002, to the Veterans of Foreign Wars, he asserted: ". . . We now know that Saddam has resumed his efforts to acquire nuclear weapons . . . Many of us are convinced that Saddam will acquire nuclear weapons fairly soon." As we now know, the intelligence community was far from certain. Yet the Vice President had been convinced.

On September 8, 2002, Cheney was even more emphatic about Saddam. He said, "[We] do know, with absolute certainty, that he is using his procurement system to acquire the equipment he needs in order to enrich uranium to build a nuclear weapon." The intelligence community was deeply divided about the aluminum tubes, but Cheney was absolutely certain.

Where was the CIA Director when the Vice President was going nuclear about Saddam going nuclear? Did Tenet fail to convince the policy makers to cool their overheated rhetoric? Did he even try to convince them?

One month later, on the eve of the watershed vote by Congress to authorize the war, President Bush said it even more vividly. He said, "Iraq has attempted to purchase high-strength aluminum tubes . . . which are used to enrich uranium for nuclear weapons. If the Iraqi regime is able to produce, buy, or steal an amount of highly enriched uranium a little larger than a single softball, it could have a nuclear weapon in less than a year. And if we allow that to happen, a terrible line would be crossed . . . Saddam Hussein would be in a position to pass nuclear technology to terrorists."

In fact, as we now know, the intelligence community was far from unified on Iraq's nuclear threat. The Administration attempted to conceal that fact by classifying the information and the dissents within the intelligence community until after the war, even while making dramatic and excessive public statements about the immediacy of the danger.

Distorting the Facts

In a February 2004 article in the *Atlantic Monthly*, Ken Pollack, a former CIA analyst who supported the war, said, ". . . Time after time senior Administration officials discussed only the worst case and least likely scenario, and failed to mention the intelligence community's most likely scenario." In a January

[2004] interview, Pollack added, "Only the Administration has access to all the information available to various agencies of the U.S. government—and withholding or downplaying some of that information for its own purposes is a betrayal of that responsibility."

In October 2002, the intelligence agencies jointly issued a National Intelligence Estimate stating that "most agencies" believed that Iraq had restarted its nuclear program after inspectors left in 1998, and that, if left unchecked, Iraq "probably will have a nuclear weapon during this decade."

The State Department's intelligence bureau, however, said the "available evidence" was inadequate to support that judgment. It refused to predict when "Iraq could acquire a nuclear device or weapon."

The National Intelligence Estimate cited a foreign government report that, as of early 2001, Niger planned to send several tons of nuclear material to Iraq. The Estimate also said, "reports indicate that Iraq has sought uranium ore from Somalia and possibly the Democratic Republic of the Congo." The State Department's intelligence bureau, however, responded that claims of Iraq seeking to purchase nuclear material from Africa were "highly dubious." The CIA sent two memos to the White House stressing strong doubts about those claims.

> *"The intelligence community was far from unified on Iraq's nuclear threat. The Administration attempted to conceal that fact."*

But the following January, the President included the claims about Africa in his State of the Union Address, and conspicuously cited the British government as the source of that intelligence.

Information about nuclear weapons was not the only intelligence distorted by the Administration. On the question of whether Iraq was pursuing a chemical weapons program, the Defense Intelligence Agency concluded in September 2002 that "there is no reliable information on whether Iraq is producing and stockpiling chemical weapons, or where Iraq has—or will—establish its chemical warfare agent production facilities."

That same month, however, Secretary Rumsfeld told the Senate Armed Services Committee that Saddam has chemical-weapons stockpiles.

He said that "we do know that the Iraqi regime has chemical and biological weapons of mass destruction," that Saddam "has amassed large clandestine stocks of chemical weapons," that "he has stockpiles of chemical and biological weapons," and that Iraq has "active chemical, biological and nuclear programs." He was wrong on all counts.

Yet the October 2002 National Intelligence Estimate actually quantified the size of the stockpiles, finding that "although we have little specific information on Iraq's CW [chemical weapons] stockpile, Saddam probably has stocked at least 100 metric tons and possibly as much as 500 metric tons of CW agents—

much of it added in the last year." In his speech at the United Nations on February 5, 2003, Secretary of State Powell went further, calling the 100–500 metric ton stockpile a "conservative estimate."

Secretary Rumsfeld made an even more explicit assertion in his March 30, 2003, interview on [the television show] "This Week with [political analyst] George Stephanopoulos." When asked about Iraqi weapons of mass destruction, he said, "We know where they are. They're in the area around Tikrit and Baghdad and east, west, south and north somewhat."

No Link with Al Qaeda

The second major claim in the Administration's case for war was the linkage between Saddam Hussein and Al Qaeda.

Significantly here as well, the Intelligence Estimate did not find a cooperative relationship between Saddam and Al Qaeda. On the contrary, it stated only that such a relationship might happen if Saddam were "sufficiently desperate"—in other words, if America went to war. But the estimate placed "low confidence" that, even in desperation, Saddam would give weapons of mass destruction to Al Qaeda.

A year before the war began, senior Al Qaeda leaders themselves had rejected a link with Saddam. The *New York Times* reported last June [2003] that a top Al Qaeda planner and recruiter captured in March 2002 told his questioners last year that "the idea of working with Mr. Hussein's government had been discussed among Al Qaeda leaders, but Osama bin Laden had rejected such proposals." According to the *Times*, an Al Qaeda chief of operations had also told interrogators that the group did not work with Saddam.

Mel Goodman, a CIA analyst for 20 years, put it bluntly: "Saddam Hussein and bin Laden were enemies. Bin Laden considered and said that Saddam was the socialist infidel. These were very different kinds of individuals competing for power in their own way and Saddam Hussein made very sure that Al Qaeda couldn't function in Iraq."

In February 2003, investigators at the FBI told the *New York Times* they were baffled by the Administration's insistence on a solid link between Al Qaeda and Iraq. One investigator said: "We've been looking at this hard for more than a year and you know what, we just don't think it's there."

But President Bush was not deterred. He was relentless in using America's fears after the devastating 9/11 tragedy. He drew a clear link—and drew it repeatedly—between Al Qaeda and Saddam.

In a September 25, 2002, statement at the White House, President Bush flatly declared: "You can't distinguish between Al Qaeda and Saddam when you talk about the war on terror."

In his State of the Union Address in January 2003, President Bush said, "Evidence from intelligence sources, secret communications, and statements by people now in custody reveal that Saddam Hussein aids and protects terrorists, including members of Al Qaeda," and that he could provide "lethal viruses" to a "shadowy terrorist network."

Two weeks later, in his radio address to the nation, a month before the war began, President Bush described the ties in detail, saying, "Saddam Hussein has longstanding, direct and continuing ties to terrorist networks . . . "

He said: "Senior members of Iraqi intelligence and Al Qaeda have met at least eight times since the early 1990s. Iraq has sent bomb-making and document-forgery experts to work with Al Qaeda. Iraq has also provided Al Qaeda with chemical and biological weapons training. An Al Qaeda operative was sent to Iraq several times in the late 1990s for help in acquiring poisons and gases. We also know that Iraq is harboring a terrorist network headed by a senior Al Qaeda terrorist planner. This network runs a poison and explosive training camp in northeast Iraq, and many of its leaders are known to be in Baghdad."

> *"There was no operational link and no clear and persuasive pattern of ties between the Iraqi government and Al Qaeda."*

In fact, there was no operational link and no clear and persuasive pattern of ties between the Iraqi government and Al Qaeda. That fact should have been abundantly clear to the President. Iraq and Al Qaeda had diametrically opposing views of the world.

Fear-Mongering

In the march to war, the President exaggerated the threat anyway. It was not subtle. It was not nuanced. It was pure, unadulterated fear-mongering, based on a devious strategy to convince the American people that Saddam's ability to provide nuclear weapons to Al Qaeda justified immediate war. . . .

The evidence so far leads to only one conclusion. What happened was not merely a failure of intelligence, but the result of manipulation and distortion of the intelligence and selective use of unreliable intelligence to justify a decision to go to war. The Administration had made up its mind, and would not let stubborn facts stand in the way. . . .

America went to war in Iraq because President Bush insisted that nuclear weapons in the hands of Saddam Hussein and his ties to Al Qaeda were too dangerous to ignore. Congress never would have voted to authorize the war if we had known the facts.

Chapter 2

How Should America Fight Terrorism Worldwide?

Chapter Preface

On May 1, 2003, less than two months after U.S. forces invaded Iraq as part of America's battle against terrorism, U.S. president George W. Bush gave a speech announcing the end of major combat operations in that country. In his speech, he described America's victory in Iraq as an important step toward victory in the war against terrorism. He said:

> The liberation of Iraq is a crucial advance in the campaign against terror. We've removed an ally of [terrorist group] al Qaeda, and cut off a source of terrorist funding. . . . The advance of freedom is the surest strategy to undermine the appeal of terror in the world. Where freedom takes hold, hatred gives way to hope. When freedom takes hold, men and women turn to the peaceful pursuit of a better life. American values and American interests lead in the same direction: We stand for human liberty.

A year after Bush's speech, however, many people argue that the invasion of Iraq was not a good way to fight terrorism because it has caused worldwide hatred against America, which has actually increased the terrorist threat to the United States.

In 2004, as the United States continues to occupy Iraq, anti-Americanism is expressed loudly around the world. According to *International Economy* magazine, "At the beginning of the 21st century, the United States has become the world's chief bogeyman, the object of global spite." A 2004 survey by the Pew Research Center found that anti-Americanism is widespread, particularly in the Muslim world:

> Discontent with America and its policies has intensified rather than diminished. . . . In the predominantly Muslim countries surveyed, anger toward the United States remains pervasive. . . . [Al Qaeda leader] Osama bin Laden, however, is viewed favorably by large percentages in Pakistan (65%), Jordan (55%) and Morocco (45%). Even in Turkey, where bin Laden is highly unpopular, as many as 31% say that suicide attacks against Americans and other Westerners in Iraq are justifiable.

Many people believe that this anger is the result of the way America invaded and occupied Iraq. Writing in *New Statesman* in October 2003, author Lutz Kleveman gives an illustration of how the invasion of Iraq and America's treatment of Iraqis has generated anti-Americanism, which may be contributing to increasing support for terrorism against the United States. He recounts a conversation with Kudair Abbass, the brother of twenty-eight-year-old truck driver Yaass Abbass, who was accidentally shot in Iraq by U.S. soldiers: "'The Americans treat us like animals,' said Kudair Abbass. . . . When asked if he wanted revenge, he kept silent but his eyes, filled with tears and hate, gave a clear answer. And it had nothing to do with any loyalty to [former Iraqi president] Saddam Hussein." Kleveman concludes, "The irony is that, by invading Iraq without clear ideas of what to do after a ceasefire, the Bush administration has created what it set out to destroy: a terrorist haven." Jonathan Freedland echoes this in the *Guardian:* "Before the war President Bush told us Iraq was a throbbing hub of terror. It wasn't, of course. But it is now."

As the United States continues to battle terrorism in Iraq and around the world, there is debate over how this battle should be fought. The authors of the following viewpoints offer various opinions on this controversial topic.

America Should Use Preemptive Strikes to Fight Terrorism

by Jack Spencer

About the author: *Jack Spencer is policy analyst for defense and national security at the Kathryn and Shelby Cullom Davis Institute for International Studies at the Heritage Foundation, a public policy research institute.*

The president of the United States has no greater responsibility than protecting the American people from threats both foreign and domestic. He is vested by the Constitution with the authority and responsibility to accomplish this essential task. In taking the oath of office, the president swears to "preserve, protect and defend the Constitution of the United States," the preamble of which makes providing for the "common defense" a top priority.

As the nature of threats to the United States changes, so must the nation's approach to its defense. To fulfill his constitutional responsibility, the president must have the flexibility to address these threats as they emerge. Given the proliferation of weapons of mass destruction [WMD] by nations hostile to America, in an increasing number of cases, this may require applying military power before the United States or its interests are struck. In situations where the evidence demonstrates overwhelmingly that behavioral trends, capability and motives all point to imminent threat, it may be necessary for the president to attack preemptively.

While few arguments have been made against the use of armed force in Afghanistan to retaliate against acts of aggression,[1] the idea of preemptively striking adversaries has garnered far more criticism. However, the president is

---

1. In October 2001, the United States invaded Afghanistan, which it suspected of supporting the September 11, 2001, terrorist attacks against America.

legally obliged—both domestically and internationally—to preemptively strike in self-defense adversaries that present imminent threat.

Right to Self-Defense

The right to self-defense is codified in customary international law and in the charter of the United Nations. The most basic expression of a nation's sovereignty is action taken in self-defense. Traditional international law recognizes that right, and the U.N. Charter is wholly consistent with it. Article 51 states: "Nothing in the present Charter shall impair the inherent right of individual or collective self-defense if an armed attack occurs against a Member of the United Nations."

One of the challenges of achieving national security in the 21st century is that nations or organizations wishing to challenge America or Western powers increasingly are seeking weapons of mass destruction to reach their political objectives. The only effective response is to destroy those capabilities before they are used. The tenet of customary international law that allows for this preventive or preemptive action is "anticipatory self-defense."

An oft-cited incident that validates the practice of anticipatory self-defense as part of international law occurred in 1837. That year, British forces crossed into American territory to destroy a Canadian ship, anticipating that the ship would be used to support an anti-British insurrection. The British government claimed its actions were necessary for self-defense, and the United States accepted that explanation.

> *"The president is legally obliged—both domestically and internationally—to preemptively strike in self-defense adversaries that present imminent threat."*

While debate continues as to whether or not this principle of international law survived the adoption of the U.N. Charter, neither the charter, nor the actions of member states since the charter came into force, outlaw the principle. Israel has invoked the right of anticipatory self-defense numerous times throughout its history, including incidents in 1956 when it preemptively struck Egypt and in 1967 when it struck Syria, Jordan and Egypt as those nations were preparing an attack.

The United States also has asserted its right to anticipatory self-defense. A classic example occurred in 1962 when President John Kennedy ordered a blockade of Cuba—a clear act of aggression—during the Cuban missile crisis. Although no shots were fired, President Kennedy's preemptive action was imperative for the protection of American security. During the 1980s, President Ronald Reagan invoked this right at least twice: first, in 1983, when he ordered an invasion of Grenada to protect U.S. nationals from potential harm, and again in 1986, when he ordered the bombing of terrorist sites in Libya.

When any nation that is overtly hostile to America or its allies is developing weapons of mass destruction, has ties to international terrorist and intelligence data, and gives reason to believe that it intends to attack, the threshold of the U.S. right to invoke a response based on anticipatory self-defense has clearly been passed.

Authority to Use Force

The U.S. government alone has the authority to determine what constitutes a threat to its citizens and what should be done about it. The Constitution of the United States gives this power only to the president, as commander in chief, and Congress, which has authority to raise and support armies and to declare war. So long as U.S. actions are in accord with the Constitution, no treaty or agreement can transfer this authority to an international body or give that body veto power over a U.S. decision to use military force in its own defense.

Furthermore, the president as commander in chief has the authority to use America's armed forces to "provide for the common defense." The Constitution gives Congress the authority to declare war but makes the president commander in chief. Since the birth of the nation, this division of power has given rise to tension between the executive and legislative branches of government regarding who can authorize the use of force.

Debate regarding this matter gave rise to the War Powers Resolution, which states that the president can use force to protect the nation without congressional authorization for 60 to 90 days. Many, including every president since this resolution came into force in 1973, have regarded the document as unconstitutional. Most, however, agree that the president has the authority to defend America from attack, even in the absence of congressional authorization. It should be noted that if Congress is truly opposed to any military action authorized by the president, it has the power to deny funds for that mission, making it impossible to carry out.

Lessons from September 11

The president is justified in applying preemptive military force to fight the war on terrorism. To fail to do so in spite of a threat of imminent attack would be to ignore the lessons learned from [the September 11, 2001, terrorist attacks] regarding the nature of threats that face America in the 21st century. Before those attacks, U.S. authorities were aware of Osama bin Laden, his resources and his hatred for America. They knew he was a terrorist and that he had attacked America in the past. They also were aware that he was running terrorist training camps in Afghanistan with the blessing of the Taliban[2] regime. Despite this information, neither the United States nor the international community took decisive action to address bin Laden's imminent aggression.

---

2. Islamic group that ruled most of Afghanistan from 1996 until 2001

In the post–Sept. 11 world, such complacency is not acceptable. A series of lessons can be learned from the Sept. 11 attacks and the initial prosecution of the war on terrorism. These lessons must be taken into consideration when future action against terrorists and terrorist states is contemplated.

One of these lessons is that deterrence alone is not sufficient to suppress aggression. The Taliban and bin Laden could have predicted that the United States would respond to their attacks, yet they acted anyway. Although numerous reports and studies warned of the growing threat of catastrophic terrorism, the United States, for the most part, ignored those warnings. The activities of a worldwide organized terrorist network were treated instead as criminal behavior.

> *"The U.S. government alone has the authority to determine what constitutes a threat to its citizens and what should be done about it."*

The conclusion of recent studies has been that the risk of America being struck with a weapon of mass destruction has increased. In other words, the effectiveness of deterrence has decreased. Such massive acts of terrorism could be perpetrated by an organization acting alone, an organization working with a nation or a nation acting alone. It would be nearly impossible to deter all of these hostile entities, given that each state and each organization has a different motivation.

The Sept. 11 attacks also demonstrated that large-scale strikes can occur with little or no warning. The emergence of global communications, advances in technology and the globalization of terrorism have significantly decreased the time it takes for a potential threat to be identified and for that threat to emerge as an act of aggression. In many instances, a specific threat may not be identified until the act of aggression has taken place, rendering preventive measures irrelevant.

In this world of drastically shortened time lines, the president's authority to act decisively to quickly defeat aggressors is essential when a preponderance of information points to a threat of imminent attack. For example, although the president did not have information that al-Qaida[3] operatives were going to commandeer four passenger jets and use them as guided cruise missiles, ample evidence existed to show that threats to the United States would likely emerge from Afghanistan, where al-Qaida—an organization responsible for past attacks on America—was present and supported by the Taliban.

Also, the use of a weapon of mass destruction is reasonably likely. On Sept. 11, Americans were killed on a massive scale. Hostile entities increasingly view weapons of mass destruction as political assets. North Korea has admitted to a covert nuclear program and may already have two nuclear weapons; Iran has active chemical-, biological- and nuclear-weapons programs; and Iraq has ac-

---

3. the terrorist group believed to be responsible for the September 11, 2001, terrorist attacks

tive WMD programs and a history of using such weapons. All three countries have ballistic- and cruise-missile programs.

Even terrorist organizations, such as al-Qaida, are involved in developing and using WMD, as was evidenced by videos in which al-Qaida was experimenting with chemical weapons on dogs. Other reports link bin Laden to the pursuit of a nuclear or radiological device. In 1995, terrorists in Japan used sarin gas to kill civilians in a Tokyo subway.

The world must understand that a deadly synergy is created when hostile state and non-state agents conspire. While hostile states continue to threaten America and its interests, the threat of non-state actors, such as al-Qaida, is growing. The danger increases when states and non-state actors work together. States have resources—including territory, finances, an international diplomatic presence and trade—that non-state actors do not have. On the other hand, non-state actors are able to operate globally and can act largely undetected.

The reality of the 21st century is that a state like Iraq can harness its resources to develop a weapon of mass destruction and collude with non-state actors to deliver that weapon. This symbiotic relationship can operate undercover, possibly without the knowledge of the American government. Thus, a state hostile to the United States may appear to be acting within the bounds of normal diplomatic behavior while at the same time covertly supporting aggressive endeavors of its non-state allies.

Failure of "Soft Diplomacy"

The future envisioned by America's enemies is incompatible with U.S. security. Prior to Sept. 11, "soft diplomacy"—including multilateral arms control, aid incentives and appeals to reason—was the preferred approach in dealing with hostile regimes. Although the ideals of those regimes and those of the West are in direct contrast, there was hope that, eventually, these despots would transform, fall or simply discontinue their threatening activities. This policy continued as the approach of choice even though it has been demonstrably ineffective: North Korea continues to sell ballistic missiles, Iran continues to support terrorism and Iraq continues to develop nuclear bombs.

> *"In many instances, a specific threat may not be identified until the act of aggression has taken place, rendering preventive measures irrelevant."*

On Sept. 11, however, the idea that such hostile regimes and the United States could simultaneously pursue their respective interests lost all credibility. It was clear that America's enemies were willing to use unprovoked violence to achieve their objectives. The United States could no longer postpone acting against terrorists and nations that support them.

More than a year after the terrorist attacks of Sept. 11, the United States remains at war. Indeed, Vice President Dick Cheney says, "We are still closer to the beginning of this war than to its end." Although the Taliban has fallen, and al-Qaida is on the run, the reality is that the United States and its interests abroad remain directly threatened by global terrorism and weapons of mass destruction in the hands of terrorist states.

On Sept. 11, 2001, America came to a new awareness of its own vulnerability and the nature of the threats that now face the nation. No longer can the United States wait passively while hostile regimes foment terrorism, build weapons of mass destruction and propagate hatred for America. The war on terrorism will be long and difficult, but the president has the authority to prosecute this just war and the responsibility to do so, using whatever means are at his disposal.

America Should Not Use Preemptive Strikes to Fight Terrorism

by Paul Craig Roberts

About the author: *Paul Craig Roberts, a former columnist for the* Wall Street Journal *and* Business Week, *is a senior research fellow at the Hoover Institution, a public policy research center.*

The United States is more at risk as a result of President George W. Bush's new policy of pre-emptive attack. Consider just a few reasons for the decline in America's safety.

A policy of pre-emptive attack creates instability by encouraging other countries to adopt the same strategy. The policy easily can be a guise for other agendas: control over oil, enhancing the safely of an ally, reconstruction contracts for a political donor base or a messianic militarism determined to impose "American exceptionalism" on the rest of the world. Once other countries believe or suspect that such motives are the reasons for U.S. pre-emptive attacks, those countries will form alliances that will isolate the United States from former allies.

Undersecretary of State John Bolton, [writer and commentator] Norman Podhoretz and other neoconservatives have indicated that the U.S. invasion of Iraq is but the opening step of a plan for cleansing the Muslim Middle East. On April 2 [2003], former CIA director James Woolsey said the U.S. invasion of Iraq was the beginning of World War IV, a war that will last many years while "we move toward a new Middle East."

Such a war is likely to create unity and alliances among Muslim states. An alliance could form between Iran and nuclear-armed Pakistan. Both countries are believed to harbor far more terrorists and al-Qaeda [terrorist group] operatives than Iraq. A pre-emptive attack on a nuclear-armed adversary could require the United States to use nuclear weapons. Such action would isolate the United

States, alarm other powers and possibly subject the United States itself to pre-emptive attack from Russia, China and "old Europe"[1]—all of which could be said to be harboring terrorists in their large Muslim populations. We should not forget that Russia possesses nuclear missiles capable of destroying the United States and that China, thanks to former president Bill Clinton and U.S. defense firms, possesses the technology for nuclear-weapon capability equal to our own.

A case for pre-emptive attack rests on propaganda, assumptions and intelligence information that may be false. Iraq may not possess weapons of mass destruction.[2] . . .

Pre-Emptive Attack Will Cause a Loss of Good Will

Misinformation abounds within the American public. Polls indicate that 50 percent of Americans believe that Iraqis hijacked the airliners that were crashed into the World Trade Center twin towers and the Pentagon [on September 11, 2001]. If Americans, with their free press, can be so misinformed, imagine the misconceptions possible in the Middle East, Russia and China. Once the United States adopts a policy of attacking countries based on unproven suspicions, every country becomes a potential target, thus provoking pre-emptive attack against this country.

International law is a nebulous concept. Regardless, the United States has spent the last half-century building support for world order and enlisting world opinion behind its foreign policy. Having poured authority into the United Nations, the United States now has defied its own creation and acted unilaterally in the face of world opinion. This gives America's enemies propaganda with which to brand the United States an outlaw nation. It is difficult for a country perceived as an outlaw to convince the world that it has a moral case for pre-emptive war. If Muslims respond to the invasion of Iraq with more terror, much of world opinion will believe that the United States shares the blame. The sympathy and cooperation enjoyed by the United States since [the September 11, 2001, terrorist attacks] have been squandered.

> *"A policy of pre-emptive attack creates instability by encouraging other countries to adopt the same strategy."*

The loss of good will makes our country less safe. On March 27 [2003], Samir Ragab, chairman of the *Egyptian Gazette*, editorialized: "The U.S. has just shown its true colors. And the world can rest assured that both the U.S. and Israel are one and the same thing. Their common objective is to enfeeble Arabs and tear their nations to pieces." The *Gazette*, established in 1880, is not a radi-

1. This term was used in January 2003 by U.S. secretary of defense Donald Rumsfeld to refer to those European countries who were not in favor of the 2003 invasion of Iraq.   2. One of the justifications for the 2003 war against Iraq was that it possessed weapons of mass destruction and thus threatened U.S. security. Following the war, however, these weapons were not found.

cal Islamic newspaper, and Ragab is not a known anti-American. His editorial indicates that the U.S. invasion of Iraq has hurt America's standing with moderate Muslims. Reporting from Jakarta on March 26 [2003], Reuters [news agency] said that the U.S. invasion of Iraq has disillusioned American-educated Muslim elites throughout Asia. Moderate Muslims in the Middle East and pro-American ones in Asia are washing their hands of us. By attacking Iraq, the United States has achieved the "Palestinization" of the Muslim world. The consequence

> *"[President George W.] Bush has initiated a war in a manner that expands the powers of his office to give the president attributes of a Caesar."*

will be more terror. On March 31 [2003], Egyptian President Hosni Mubarak said: "This war will have horrible consequences. Instead of having one [terrorist leader Osama] bin Laden, we will have 100 bin Ladens."

Pre-Emptive War Threatens the Constitution

Another aspect of U.S. safety is threatened by pre-emptive war. The Founding Fathers realized that not all enemies are foreign. What keeps U.S. citizens safe is adherence to the U.S. Constitution. Losing any part of the Constitution is precedent for losing other parts. Congress—the American people's representative—now has lost the constitutional right to declare war.

In the past the U.S. has fought war without declaring it, as in Vietnam. But Vietnam was a "proxy war" fought to contain communist expansion without directly confronting communist states, which could have provoked nuclear holocaust. There was no such danger in attacking Iraq. Moreover, the U.S. invasion of Iraq was not a surprise attack, but a war that the U.S. publicly initiated. There is no excuse in this instance for circumventing a congressional declaration of war. The U.S. invasion of Iraq is the result of a presidential decision and personal ultimatum. Bush has initiated a war in a manner that expands the powers of his office to give the president attributes of a Caesar.

Pre-emptive war is the foreign-policy version of [legal and social reformer] Jeremy Bentham's proposal pre-emptively to arrest citizens who might commit crimes in the future. Bentham "proved" that it served "the greatest interest of the greatest number" to round up people who fit profiles predisposed to commit criminal acts. How would such citizens be identified? The same way that we "know" which countries are going to attack us in the future: by assumption, probability, speculation and bad information, such as the forged nuclear documents offered as proof that Iraq has a nuclear-weapons program. Fairfax County, Va., police recently used pre-emptive reasoning when they arrested bar patrons on the grounds that some might later be guilty of driving under the influence.

Arresting people before they commit crimes is a violation of mens rea—the principle that there can be no crime without intent—and a violation of actus rea—the principle that a criminal act must occur before an arrest can take place. These principles are foundations of Anglo-American law. Once people can be arrested for suspected future misdeeds, liberty is dead. Similarly, pre-emptive war is based in surmise.

A Recipe for Armageddon

Pre-emptive war commits the United States to empire. It was Rome's policy to subdue potential enemies in advance by constructing an empire. Empire cost the Roman citizens their republic, destroyed the power of the Roman senate and brought crashing taxation, inflation, division and resentments. Finding themselves overextended, Romans withdrew from their far-flung posts. Their enemies followed them back to Rome and, ultimately, the ancient city was sacked and plundered.

Pre-emptive war is a recipe for Armageddon. Each time the U.S. pre-emptively attacks a future enemy, new enemies will be created. This is especially the case in the Middle East. Such an aggressive policy likely will lead to the reinstatement of conscription in the United States and the militarization of the entire country. To understand why, consider the miscalculations and difficulties evident by the fifth day of the U.S. invasion of Iraq.

It is difficult to imagine a more inviting target for attack than Iraq, a divided country containing three mutually hostile groups—Kurds, and Sunni and Shiite Muslims. Iraq's army has outmoded weapons and has been weakened by defeat in the 1991 Persian Gulf War and 12 years of embargoes and bombings. . . .

> *"When Americans realize the recklessness behind the pre-emptive attack on Iraq they will feel very unsafe indeed."*

Yet, by the fifth day of the invasion, it was obvious that the war was not going to be a cakewalk for the United States. U.S. generals began complaining that their warnings were ignored and that sufficient forces were not committed to the invasion, and reinforcements were sent. If a quarter-million-man, high-tech army supported by a powerful navy and unquestionable air superiority is insufficient force, what happens when we attack a unified, more populous Muslim state? What happens if U.S. aggression unites the Muslims and they come to one another's aid? What would have been the fate of our army in Iraq if Syria, Iran and Turkey had joined the fray?

Prior to the next pre-emptive attack, even the tamed political U.S. generals will put their foot down and demand "sufficient" forces so that there is no question about the outcome. Whose sons, grandsons, brothers and fathers will provide these forces? Whose taxes will pay the enormous cost? Will critics of U.S. pre-emptive wars be silenced by knocks on the door from "Homeland Security"?

Meanwhile, on U.S. soil other wars are being lost. The Bush tax cut, which was to restore the economy, has been sacrificed to the war. The Supreme Court has just refused to hear a case that would have questioned the right of government to spy on citizens. And the silent invasion of America by 1 million illegal immigrants per annum continues unabated. How is a country that is not capable of defending its own borders made safe by sending its army halfway around the world to confront ancient and unresolvable animosities?

When Americans realize the recklessness behind the pre-emptive attack on Iraq, they will feel very unsafe indeed.

The United States Should Fight Terrorism by Building Democracy in the Middle East

by Chuck Hagel

About the author: *Chuck Hagel is a U.S. senator from Nebraska, first elected to the Senate in 1996 and reelected in 2002.*

On March 5, 1946, at Westminster College in Fulton, Mo., British Prime Minister Winston Churchill, with Pres. Harry Truman at his side, gave one of the greatest speeches of our time. Its power and majesty are not limited to time and place, although Churchill's warning of a Soviet "Iron Curtain"[1] in Europe vividly captured the communist threat of that era. That day, he also conveyed something unique and special about America's international role: ". . . The United States stands at this time at the pinnacle of world power. It is a solemn moment for the American democracy. For with this primacy in power is also joined an awe-inspiring accountability to the future. As you look around you, you must feel not only the sense of duty done, but also you must feel anxiety lest you fall below the level of achievement. Opportunity is here now, clear and shining, for both our countries. To reject it or ignore it or fritter it away will bring upon us all the long reproaches of the aftertime."

With new eras come new challenges, and today [2003] the U.S. again stands at a pinnacle of power and again bears a heavy burden for securing a better tomorrow, for our citizens and for all the peoples of the world. At this critical juncture, the success of our actions will be determined not by the extent of our power, but by an appreciation of its limits. America must approach the world

---

1. This term refers to the boundary line that divided Europe into two separate areas of interest at the end of World War II: Soviet control in the East, and political freedom in the West.

Chuck Hagel, "Defining America's Role on the Global Stage," *USA Today Magazine*, vol. 131, May 2003. Copyright © 2003 by the Society for the Advancement of Education. Reproduced by permission.

with a sense of purpose in global affairs that is anchored by our ideals, a principled realism that seeks not to remake the world in our image, but to help make a better world.

We must avoid the traps of hubris and imperial temptation that come with great power. Our foreign policy should reflect the hope and promise of America tempered with a mature wisdom that is the mark of our national character. In this new era of possibilities and responsibilities, America will require a wider-lens view of how the world sees us, so that we can better understand the world, and our role in it.

International Challenges

Just as Churchill pointed out in 1946, when historic opportunities for leadership are before us, they cannot be rejected, ignored, or frittered away. There would have been grave consequences if the U.S. had shrunk from its responsibilities in 1946, as there will be grave consequences if America shrinks from today's challenges. The war in Iraq and a long-term engagement with the Middle East offer as much peril as promise. We also face an urgent threat from North Korea and the potential for nuclear war between India and Pakistan. The AIDS epidemic in Africa, Russia, and Asia poses one of the most-deadly threats to all humanity. Moreover, we cannot overlook our own hemisphere, where Colombia and Venezuela are involved with continued violence and instability.

The complexities of an interconnected world give us little margin for error in dealing with these great international challenges. The first priority for the U.S. and all sovereign nations is to protect its citizens. To do so we must build and sustain global institutions and alliances that share our interests and values. Harold Ickes, Secretary of the Interior under Pres. Franklin Roosevelt, put it powerfully in a speech on May 18, 1941, when he said, in response to those who urged the U.S. to stay out of World War II, that American support for Britain was "the sort of enlightened selfishness that makes the wheels of history go around. It is the sort of enlightened selfishness that wins victories. Do you know why? Because we cannot live in a world alone, without friends and without allies."

The serious obligations of global leadership come with a price. Beating the burdens and costs in defeating global terrorism, countering nuclear proliferation by nations and terrorist networks, and ending poverty and hunger on this planet are investments in our own security, as well as in the stability and security of the world. Security at home cannot be separated from dangers abroad.

Need for Cooperation

The war against international terrorism and its sponsors is unlike any one we have ever known. There is no battlefield, no clash of armies. It is a war fought in the shadows and recesses of the world. Terrorism breeds among the hopeless and the alienated, in societies where democracy and economic opportunity are out of reach for most people. Military power alone will not end this scourge of mankind. Victory will require extensive international cooperation in the intelligence, economic, diplomatic, law enforcement, and humanitarian fields. It will require a seamless network of cooperation between the U.S. and its allies.

Terrorism and the proliferation of weapons of mass destruction are the enemies of all peoples—not just Americans. We must build relationships upon this common denominator of common interests. The U.S. cannot defeat terrorism alone.

America's ability to build lasting and flexible coalitions will be the measure of our success, the only assured means of long-term security for future generations. We cannot lose sight of the wider view of what is before us, that it is about much more than Iraq. We are setting the tone for America's role in the world for the next decade and beyond. At this critical time, our policies and our rhetoric should not create distance between the U.S. and its allies. If that is the price of waging war in Iraq, then victory, in the long run, in the war on terrorism, in the Middle East, on the Korean peninsula, and against weapons of mass destruction will not be ours. As Churchill reminded us, the "aftertime"—the long run—is what measures victory.

> *"We must avoid the hubris and imperial temptation that come with great power."*

America must remain on a steady course to empower alliances and institutions committed to disarmament in Iraq, North Korea, Iran, and elsewhere. In Europe and in many corners of the globe, the U.S. is perceived as determined to use force to the exclusion of world opinion or the interests of our allies, even those who share our concerns about [Iraqi president] Saddam Hussein's weapons programs. America must balance its determination with patience and not be seen as in a rush to war. As *Washington Post* columnist David Ignatius has written, "A nation heading into war needs prudence and good judgment. America's best generals, people such as [Ulysses S.] Grant and [George] Marshall and [Dwight] Eisenhower, were at once cautious and decisive. Their greatness lay in the fact that they never lost sight of the long-term interests of the United States."

America must steer away from actions that could produce the unintended results of fracturing those very institutions that have helped avoid global conflagration since World War II. Allowing war in Iraq to create divisions in those institutions and alliances that will help sustain American security and world stability is a shortsighted and dangerous course of action.

In order for America to address the differences between ourselves and our allies, we must understand those differences. We don't enhance our relationships and bridge differences by impugning the motives of our friends. Let us not forget that they, too, are democracies. They, too, are accountable to their people and respond to the judgment of their citizens. Isn't that the essence of our noble purpose as democratic governments? We must listen and learn, then forge a coalition based upon our common interests.

A Post-Saddam Future

American purpose requires more than the application of military might to rid Iraq of its weapons of mass destruction. War should be a means, not an end, to achieve a plan of action to encourage conflict resolution and change in Iraq and throughout the Middle East.

Iraq cannot be considered in a vacuum, detached from the politics and culture of its region and the Muslim world. The American use of military force to dislodge Saddam will bring change to Iraq and to the region, but we cannot foresee the nature of that change. What comes after him? The uncertainties of a post-Saddam, postconflict Middle East should give us pause, encourage prudence, and force us to recognize the necessity of a coalition in seeing it through.

America will need to remain in Iraq and the Middle East to help lead this post-Saddam transition. This will require adroit diplomacy, long-term commitment, and dynamic coalition building. There is no other way. Regime change in Iraq will not alone be the endgame for a region devoid of democratic institutions, economic development, and effective regional organizations. It must be seen as just the beginning of a long transitional period towards stability, development, and individual freedom for millions who have never known the hope and promise of an open and free society.

Priorities for U.S. Policy

How do we meet the opportunities and challenges now before us? Allow me to suggest five priorities for U.S. policy towards Iraq that will be critical to helping support and sustain stability and prosperity in the Middle East in the years ahead.

First, a post-Saddam transition in Iraq must focus on security, economic stability, and creating the conditions for democratic change. We should put aside the mistaken delusion that democracy is just around the corner, or that by force of arms we can place Iraq on the path to democracy by overlaying a blueprint for democracy on the region—a so-called "Democratic Domino effect." The spade work of building a free Iraq will take time. Anthony Zinni, Special Advisor to the Secretary of State and former Commanding General, U.S. Central Command, reminded the Senate Foreign Relations Committee in February [2003] that, with regard to Iraq, "there will not be a spontaneous democracy, so the re-

> *"America's ability to build lasting and flexible coalitions will be the measure of our success, the only assured means of long-term security for future generations."*

construction of the country will be a long, hard course regardless of whether a modest vision of the end state is sought or a more-ambitious one is chosen." Building nations and democracy in the Middle East or anywhere is complicated and difficult, and success is never assured. We can try to help create the conditions for democratic change, but we must assume that it will not come quickly or easily.

Second, the U.S. should place its operations in a post-Saddam Iraq under a United Nations [UN] umbrella as soon as possible. A conspicuous American occupation force in Iraq or in any Arab or Muslim country would only fuel anti-Americanism, nationalism, and resentment. By working through the UN, the U.S. will neutralize the accusations that a war in Iraq is anti-Muslim or driven by oil or American Imperialism.

> *"Regime change in Iraq will not alone be the endgame for a region devoid of democratic institutions, economic development, and effective regional organizations."*

Third, America should encourage the convening of a regional conference to deal with outstanding Iraqi and regional security issues. The Middle East has a lack of regional political institutions to deal with conflict prevention and resolution. Ending Saddam's regime would not necessarily mean the end of long-standing border disputes between Iraq and its neighbors—Turkey, Iran, and Kuwait—disputes that predate Saddam Hussein. Stability in northern Iraq is not assured, given the potential for conflict between Turkey and Iraq's Kurdish parties. A regional conference, arranged under UN auspices, would play an important role in building confidence among the states of the region so that future conflicts can be prevented.

Fourth, America must act immediately to restart the Israeli-Palestinian peace process. There will be no lasting peace between Israel and its Arab neighbors without the U.S. taking the lead to broker a settlement. The road to peace in the Middle East does not end in Baghdad. Long-term stability in the region depends on progress toward Israeli-Palestinian peace. There is no other way. We must work with Russia, the European Union, and the United Nations as well as Israel, the Palestinians, and our Arab allies to put the peace effort back on track. Every day that passes without active American mediation contributes to the radicalization of Palestinian and Arab politics, and the likelihood of greater terrorism visited on Israel.

Fifth, America should create partnership with the governments and peoples of the Arab world to take the necessary steps to help them open up their political systems and economies, such as the Middle East Partnership Initiative proposed by the President to encourage democratic, educational, and economic reforms. It is vital to promote private-sector development and educational reform there. For too long, the governments of this region have deferred or opposed governmental and societal reform.

Peaceful Change

Former Secretary of State Henry Kissinger once said that "modern politics too often produces an orgy of self-righteousness amidst a cacophony of sounds." If we do not complement our disarmament efforts in Iraq with a program of peaceful change in the Middle East, our policies may encourage the perception of a hard-edged American security doctrine that offers little more than self-righteous ideology. That would result in many in the Arab and Muslim worlds seeing their interests as being compromised to U.S. power. Instead of contributing to stabilization and democratization in the Middle East, just the opposite could occur, intensifying the radicalization of the region's politics.

The U.S.'s purpose in the world requires a commitment to a kind of principled realism that promotes America's values, strengthens international institutions, builds coalitions, and recognizes what is possible. The opportunities for helping create a better world are as real today as any time in our history, just as they were when Churchill spoke at Westminster College 57 years ago.

Opportunities for moments of reflection during times of great decisions are fleeting, but they are crucial, in order to place current events in an important perspective. Churchill, [former U.S. president Harry] Truman, [American military leader George] Marshall, and other leaders understood the magnitude of challenges the world would face in the second half of the 20th century. We face comparable challenges today, and we can learn from history.

It was America's investment in international organizations such as the United Nations, World Bank, International Monetary Fund, NATO [North Atlantic Treaty Organization], and other institutions that helped maintain international stability and prevent world wars. These and other multinational institutions have given structure and force to global consensus and commitment to face the challenges of our time. America has helped build and reinforce these institutions with a judicious use of its power. All nations and institutions are imperfect, but the world today is more hopeful and more just because the U.S. and its friends took this responsible and far-sighted course of coalitions of common interest and multilateral institutions.

What distinguishes America is not its power, for the world has known great power. It is the U.S.'s purpose and commitment to making a better life for all people. That is the America the world needs to see—a wise, thoughtful, and steady nation, worthy of its power, generous of spirit, and humble in its purpose.

Building Democracy Worldwide Is an Ineffective Way to Fight Terrorism

by Charles V. Peña

About the author: *Charles V. Peña is director of defense policy studies at the Cato Institute, a nonprofit public policy research foundation.*

In making the case to go to war against Iraq, President [George W.] Bush said: "America must not ignore the threat gathering against us. Facing clear evidence of peril, we cannot wait for the final proof—the smoking gun—that could come in the form of a mushroom cloud." That statement was made not long after the release of the *National Security Strategy of the United States of America*, which outlined a doctrine of preemption: "[A]s a matter of common sense and self-defense, America will act against such emerging threats before they are fully formed." The [2003] Iraq war thus became the first test of the administration's national security strategy. But persistent questions about the threat posed by Iraq, the quality of the intelligence about the threat, and how that information was used by the administration to make its case for war are cause to be skeptical about the wisdom of the new national security strategy.

Aboard the aircraft carrier USS *Abraham Lincoln* on May 1, 2003, President Bush declared an end to major combat operations in Iraq and told U.S. military personnel, "Because of you, our nation is more secure." The assertion that the war in Iraq has made the United States more secure is the subject of important debate. But perhaps more important than the Iraq war itself is the larger issue of whether the *National Security Strategy*, which served as the blueprint for going to war, will indeed make the United States more secure.

The Constitution makes clear that one of the paramount responsibilities of the federal government is to "provide for the common defense." Therefore, the security of the American homeland and public should be the primary objective of any national security strategy. [The September 11, 2001, terrorist attacks] only further reinforced the need for U.S. national security strategy to focus on protecting America against the threat of terrorism. Yet, the *National Security Strategy* speaks little about directly protecting the U.S. homeland. Indeed, homeland security seems more of a passing reference rather than a central theme:

> *"U.S. national security is not predicated on spreading freedom and democracy, however desirable they may be."*

• "While we recognize that our best defense is a good offense, we are also strengthening America's homeland security to protect against and deter attack."

• "This broad portfolio of military capabilities must also include the ability to defend the homeland."

• "We must strengthen intelligence warning and analysis to provide integrated threat assessments for national and homeland security."

• "At home, our most important priority is to protect the homeland for the American people."

To be sure, protecting America against terrorist attack is implied in these goals:

• "strengthen alliances to defeat global terrorism and work to prevent attacks against us and our friends"; and

• "prevent our enemies from threatening us, our allies, and our friends, with weapons of mass destruction."

But the other goals, however noble and worthwhile, are clearly not directed at protecting the nation against terrorism:

• "champion aspirations for human dignity,"

• "work with others to defuse regional conflicts,"

• "ignite a new era of global economic growth through free markets and free trade,"

• "expand the circle of development by opening societies and building the infrastructure of democracy,"

• "develop agendas for cooperative action with other main centers of global power," and

• "transform America's national security institutions to meet the challenges and opportunities of the twenty-first century."

Indeed, the new *National Security Strategy* describes itself as "based on distinctly American internationalism," which is "the union of our values and our national interests." The outcome is a strategy whose "aim . . . is to help make the world not just safer but better."

That is a surprising posture for a president who previously talked about a more humble foreign policy and criticized nation building. It draws on [former U.S. president] Woodrow Wilson's belief that it is America's mission to spread democracy. It also reproduces a rather Clintonesque foreign policy vision of promoting democracy. After all, President [Bill] Clinton declared in a speech at the United Nations in 1993: "Our overriding purpose must be to expand and strengthen the world's community of market-based democracies. During the Cold War, we fought to contain a threat to the survival of free institutions. Now we seek to enlarge the circle of nations that live under those free institutions." To be sure, the neoconservatives would challenge the liberal interventionists' preference for working with the United Nations and having the support of the international community. But both arrive at the same end point. The result is an alliance of strange bedfellows brought together by the belief that American security is best served by using military power to spread democracy throughout the world. . . .

The reality is that "national" security strategy is a misnomer. It is a global security strategy to "defend liberty and justice because these principles are right and true for all people everywhere" based on the false belief that the best and only way to achieve U.S. security is by forcibly creating a better and safer world in America's image. Although the administration's original argument for military action against Iraq was the purported threat of Iraqi weapons of mass destruction (WMD),

> *"U.S. national security strategy . . . should be focused more narrowly on protecting the United States itself."*

at the eleventh hour the larger and more noble goal of spreading democracy was added as a rationale: "The world has a clear interest in the spread of democratic values, because stable and free nations do not breed the ideologies of murder. They encourage the peaceful pursuit of a better life."

No one would dispute that promoting democracy is a worthy goal. And certainly the United States should encourage the formation of liberal democracies throughout the world. But U.S. national security is not predicated on spreading freedom and democracy, however desirable they may be. National security is based on being able to counter (by either deterrence or defeat) direct threats. Thus, the litmus test is not whether a country meets U.S.-imposed criteria of democratic government but whether it has hostile intentions and real military capability to directly threaten the United States.

Defining the Threats to U.S. National Security

In the past, the primary threats to the United States and U.S. interests were nation-states. But since the end of the Cold War, the United States is in a unique geostrategic position. The military threat posed by the former Soviet Union is gone. Two great oceans act as vast moats to protect America's western and eastern flanks. And America is blessed with two friendly and stable neighbors to the north and south. Thus, the American homeland is safe from a traditional conventional military invasion, and the U.S. strategic nuclear arsenal acts as an effective and credible deterrent against possible nuclear attack—even by rogue states that might eventually acquire nuclear weapons.

Not only is the United States relatively insulated from possible attack; it is defended by the most dominant military force on the planet. Indeed, in 2001 the U.S. defense budget (nearly $348 billion) exceeded those of the next 13 nations combined (most of whom are allies or friendly to the United States). The country closest in defense spending to the United States was Russia ($65 billion). But it is clear that under President Vladimir Putin Russia has charted a course to move closer to the United States and the West, both politically and economically. China—which many observers see as the next great threat—had estimated defense expenditures of $47 billion. Moreover, it is not a given that China will become an aggressive great power that challenges the United States. According to a Council on Foreign Relations task force chaired by former secretary of defense Harold Brown:

> The People's Republic of China is pursuing a deliberate and focused course of military modernization but . . . it is at least two decades behind the United States in terms of military technology and capability. Moreover, if the United States continues to dedicate significant resources to improving its military forces, as expected, the balance between the United States and China, both globally and in Asia, is likely to remain decisively in America's favor beyond the next twenty years.

And the combined defense spending of the so-called axis of evil nations (North Korea, Iran, and Iraq) was only $5.3 billion, or 1.5 percent of the U.S. defense budget.

Not only does the United States outspend most of the rest of the world, but its military is technologically superior to that of any other country. The swift and decisive U.S. military victory in Iraq is a testament to that superiority. Thus, it should be abundantly clear that, with the fall of the Soviet Union, the United States no longer faces a serious military challenger or a global hegemonic threat. The only potential traditional nation-state threat would be the rise of a hostile global hegemonic power, but none is on the horizon. The resulting bottom line is that a conventional military threat to the U.S. homeland is, for all intents and purposes, nonexistent.

This is a welcome situation for America. It does not call for isolationism but demands a judicious, realistic, and prudent deployment of the strengths bestowed by such good fortune.

The Real Threat Is Terrorism

That is not to say that no threats exist. As September 11 so devastatingly demonstrated, the real threat to the U.S. homeland is not a foreign military power but terrorist groups. Yet the United States remains preoccupied with nation-state threats and an extended forward defense perimeter. The result is fear of overextending the U.S. military to meet the requirements of forward defense.

The real problem, however, is not overextension but overcommitment of military forces that dilutes the United States' ability to focus on the al Qaeda terrorist threat. Despite the demise of the Soviet Union as a military threat to Europe, the United States has nearly 100,000 troops deployed [in 2003] to defend the Continent. In another obsolete, Cold War–era obligation, the United States still has about 37,000 troops stationed in South Korea. Yet the South has more than twice the population of the North (48 million vs. 22 million) and an economy 20 times larger than the North's (on a par with the lesser economies of the European Union). Those characteristics should enable it to defend itself against the North. The U.S. military also maintains in Japan a military presence similar to that in South Korea. But a country with the world's second largest economy certainly possesses the resources to defend itself rather than be a security ward of the United States.

> *"The United States needs to stop meddling in the internal affairs of other countries and regions."*

As Ted Galen Carpenter at the Cato Institute points out: "The terrorist attacks on America have given added urgency to the need to adjust Washington's security policy. . . . [W]e cannot afford the distraction of maintaining increasingly obsolete and irrelevant security commitments around the globe." Therefore, the United States should "clear the decks" and focus its national security strategy more pointedly on the terrorist threat posed by those responsible for the September 11, 2001, attacks: the al Qaeda terrorist network. More specifically, the core element and primary objective of a national security strategy should be to protect the homeland against future terrorist attacks. U.S. national security strategy should not aim to make the world a better place; instead, it should be focused more narrowly on protecting the United States itself—the country, the population, and the liberties that underlie the American way of life. . . .

National Security Strategy Stuck in a Cold War Paradigm

In the post–Cold War environment, the United States no longer needs to check the advances of a superpower enemy. Instead, it is faced with an unconventional foe in a war that has no distinct battle lines. Indeed, the many layers of the extended U.S. defense perimeter designed to defend against the Soviet threat during the Cold War were not able to prevent al Qaeda from carrying out the attacks on September 11. Nonetheless, U.S. national security thinking remains largely on Cold War autopilot, guided by the belief that a global U.S. military presence is fundamental to making the United States more secure. Most striking is that such thinking permeates the administration's approach to homeland security. According to the *National Strategy for Homeland Security* issued by the White House in July 2002:

For more than six decades, America has sought to protect its own sovereignty and independence through a strategy of global presence and engagement. In so doing, America has helped many other countries and peoples advance along the path of democracy, open markets, individual liberty, and peace with their neighbors. Yet there are those who oppose America's role in the world, and who are willing to use violence against us and our friends. Our great power leaves these enemies with few conventional options for doing us harm. One such option is to take advantage of our freedom and openness by secretly inserting terrorists into our country to attack our homeland. Homeland security seeks to deny this avenue of attack to our enemies and thus to provide a secure foundation for America's ongoing global engagement.

Thus, even the administration admits that our aggressive forward presence abroad spurs terrorism. Yet maintaining a global presence appears to have become an end in itself for U.S. national security strategy. The national security strategy is less about national security and more about exercising American power (military, economic, and political) to make a better and safer world. However grand and noble the cause of spreading freedom and democracy throughout the world may be, the reality is that it has little to do with protecting America against more terrorist attacks from al Qaeda—the one real threat we face.

"What We Do" vs. "Who We Are"

Conventional wisdom holds that other countries and people hate the United States for "who we are." In his address to a joint session of Congress and the American people after the September 11 terrorist attacks, President Bush said: "Why do they hate us? They hate what we see right here in this chamber—a democratically elected government. They hate our freedoms—our freedom of religion, our freedom of speech, our freedom to vote and assemble and disagree with each other."

To be sure, suicide terrorists who fly airplanes into buildings probably do hate the United States. But it would be misleading to assume that such hatred is the primary reason and motivation for terrorism against the United States. Throughout the world there is a deep and widespread admiration for America and what it has accomplished domestically, including

> *"A better approach to national security policy would be for the United States to adopt a less interventionist policy abroad."*

its energy, productivity, much of its culture, and its values. But there is also a "love/hate" relationship with America: many people love what we are, but they often hate what we do. That is, anti-Americanism is fueled more by our actions than by our existence.

Evidence for that can be found in various polls taken around the world. For example, the Pew Global Attitudes Project, which has surveyed more than 66,000 people around the world, states:

• "Despite soaring anti-Americanism and substantial support for [al Qaeda leader] Osama bin Laden, there is considerable appetite in the Muslim world for democratic freedoms. The broader, 44-nation survey shows that people in Muslim countries place a high value on freedom of expression, freedom of the press, multi-party systems, and equal treatment under the law."

> *"Clearly, the United States was a lightning rod for terrorism even before [the September 11, 2001, terrorist attacks]."*

• "The broad desire for democracy in Muslim countries and elsewhere is but one indication of the global acceptance of ideas and principles espoused by the United States. The major survey also shows that the free market model has been embraced by people almost everywhere."

• "This is not to say that they accept democracy and capitalism without qualification, or that they are not concerned about many of the problems of modern life. By and large, however, the people of the world accept the concepts and values that underlie the American approach to governance and business."

But according to the Pew project, in the aftermath of the Iraq war:

> [T]he bottom has fallen out of support for America in most of the Muslim world. Negative views of the U.S. among Muslims, which had been largely limited to countries in the Middle East, have spread to Muslim populations in Indonesia and Nigeria. Since last summer, favorable ratings for the U.S. have fallen from 61% to 15% in Indonesia and from 71% to 38% among Muslims in Nigeria.

> In the wake of the war, a growing percentage of Muslims see serious threats to Islam. Specifically, majorities in seven of eight Muslim populations surveyed express worries that the U.S. might become a military threat to their countries. Even in Kuwait, where people have a generally favorable view of the United States, 53% voice at least some concern that the U.S. could someday pose a threat.

The Zogby International "Impressions of America" poll of ten nations (five Arab, Muslim nations; three non-Arab, Muslim nations: and two non-Arab, non-Muslim countries) reveals that while "majorities do favor American movies, television and products, all ten nations were in great opposition to a potential U.S. attack on Iraq" and gave the United States "extremely negative ratings for its policy toward Iraq." Another Zogby poll found that Arabs look favorably on American freedoms and political values but have a strongly negative overall view of the United States based largely on their disapproval of U.S. policy toward the Middle East.

Those views are not confined to countries that might somehow be inherently predisposed to dislike the United States. A poll conducted for the Chicago

Council on Foreign Relations and the German Marshall Fund of the United States showed that "a majority of people surveyed in six European countries believe American foreign policy is partly to blame for the Sept. 11 attacks." And the results of a Gallup International poll of 36 countries showed that in 23 countries (9 of which were Western European countries and included Great Britain) "more people think U.S. foreign policy is negative rather than positive in its effects on their country."

The obvious conclusion to be drawn by American policymakers is that the United States needs to stop meddling in the internal affairs of other countries and regions, except when they directly threaten U.S. national security interests, that is, when the territorial integrity, national sovereignty, or liberty of the United States is at risk.

September 11 further highlights the need for the United States to distance itself from problems that are not truly vital to U.S. national security. Much of the anti-American resentment around the world—particularly in the Islamic world—is the result of interventionist U.S. foreign policy. Such resentment breeds hatred, which becomes a steppingstone to violence, including terrorism.

> *"If the United States does not change its policies to stem the growing tide of anti-American sentiment overseas . . . [it] will continue to be a target [for terrorists]."*

Indeed, the linkage between an interventionist foreign policy and terrorism against the United States was recognized by upper levels of the U.S. government long before September 11. According to a 1997 study by the Defense Science Board, a panel of experts that advises the secretary of defense:

> As part of its global power position, the United States is called upon frequently to respond to international causes and deploy forces around the world. America's position in the world invites attacks simply because of its presence. Historical data shows a strong correlation between U.S. involvement in international situations and an increase in terrorist attacks against the United States. . . .

Less Intervention Equals More Security: Reducing the "Lightning Rod" Problem

A better approach to national security policy would be for the United States to adopt a less interventionist policy abroad and to pull back from the Cold War–era extended security perimeter (with its attendant military commitments overseas). Such an approach recognizes that conflict and instability per se do not automatically jeopardize U.S. national security. It also recognizes that many of the problems plaguing the world, such as civil wars and ethnic strife, are largely impervious to external solutions (even from a country as powerful as the United States).

Instead of being the balancer of power around the world, the United States should allow countries to establish their own balance of power arrangements in their own regions (as the dominant military power in the world, the United States could always step in as a balancer of last resort if a serious imbalance that jeopardized vital U.S. national security interests were to develop). And instead of viewing all crises and conflicts as vitally important, the United States would be able to distinguish between those that demand its attention and those that can be left to run their natural course.

Recognizing the link between an interventionist American foreign policy, however noble or well intentioned, and terrorism against U.S. targets is even more important now. The United States must do everything in its power to dismantle the al Qaeda terrorist network worldwide, but the United States must avoid needlessly making new terrorist enemies or fueling the flames of virulent anti-American hatred.

According to statistics compiled by the State Department:

• In 1998, there were 274 total terrorist incidents worldwide, 111 (41 percent) of which were anti-U.S.,

• In 1999, there were 395 total terrorist incidents worldwide, 169 (43 percent) of which were anti-U.S.,

• In 2000, there were 426 total terrorist incidents worldwide, 200 (47 percent) of which were anti-U.S., and

• In 2001, there were 355 total terrorist incidents worldwide, 219 (62 percent) of which were anti-U.S.

Clearly, the United States was a lightning rod for terrorism even before September 11. Given that fact and given that even bin Laden's hatred of the United States is largely driven by U.S. policies, a vital component of U.S. national security policy must be to stem the tide of vehement anti-American sentiment. That is especially true in the Middle East, which is an incubator and recruiting pool for radical Islamist terrorists. . . .

If the United States does not change its policies to stem the growing tide of anti-American sentiment overseas—particularly within the Islamic world—all the time, effort, and money spent on other aspects of homeland security will be wasted because the pool of terrorist recruits will grow and the United States will continue to be a target.

The United States Should Cooperate with Europe in the Battle Against Terrorism

by Robin Niblett

About the author: *Robin Niblett is executive vice president of the Center for Strategic and International Studies, a center dedicated to providing world leaders with strategic insights and policy solutions for current and emerging global issues.*

Editor's Note: The following viewpoint was originally given as testimony to the U.S. Senate on March 31, 2004.

The terrorist attacks of March 11, 2004, in Madrid have had a profound effect on the political landscape in Europe. Their secondary, inevitable effect will be on transatlantic relations. However, the ways that the attacks will affect transatlantic relations and also transatlantic cooperation in the fight against international terrorism are not predetermined. While a deepening of the transatlantic rift that broke open a year ago [in 2003] in the lead-up to the war in Iraq is a possible outcome, it is not a necessary one. . . .

Spanish Reactions and European Conclusions

It is hard to dispute the fact that the terrorist attacks on March 11, 2004, swung the Spanish general election in favor of the Socialist Party, led by Jose Luis Rodriguez Zapatero. Collectively, some three and a half million voters either abandoned the ruling party or added their vote to the Socialists compared to the previous election, contradicting the poll numbers that stood at the start of that fateful week.

Robin Niblett, testimony before the U.S. Senate Subcommittee on European Affairs, Committee on Foreign Relations, Washington, DC, March 31, 2004.

Numerous American commentators and some senior legislators immediately accused Spanish voters of appeasing the terrorists by throwing out a leader—Prime Minister Jose Maria Aznar—who had stood shoulder to shoulder with the Bush administration in its strategy to fight global terrorism. Others—and I include myself in this group—argued that this was a simplistic interpretation of the events in Spain between March 11–13. While some voters may indeed have wanted to punish Prime Minister Aznar for putting Spaniards directly in the terrorists' cross-hairs, many more chose to punish him for the government's apparent determination to pin the blame for the attacks on the Basque separatist group ETA,[1] even when the evidence of the group's guilt was, at best, inconclusive and, at worst, lacking. . . .

> *"The overwhelming conclusion for most Europeans . . . is that the terrorist threat to them has widened and deepened as a result of the invasion of Iraq."*

But there was a second reason why the electorate turned so swiftly against Prime Minister Aznar's party after March 11, and this reason carries wider implications for the transatlantic relationship and the war against terror in the months ahead. The impression that the ruling government misled the public by blaming ETA also reminded Spaniards that the decision to go to war against Iraq was based on the apparently false premise that [former Iraqi president] Saddam Hussein represented an immediate danger because of his possession of weapons of mass destruction (WMD). Throughout Europe, the failure to find WMD in Iraq has severely undermined public confidence in the motives that drove the United States to go to war. And it has weakened the position of European leaders who chose to back the U.S. administration against the wishes of their public opinion.

Furthermore, the fact that the terrorist attacks in Madrid took place after the overthrow of Saddam Hussein has made not only Spaniards, but also other Europeans feel that they have now been placed on the terrorists' target list as a direct consequence of participating in a war that should not have been fought. The overwhelming conclusion for most Europeans, therefore, is that the terrorist threat to them has widened and deepened as a result of the invasion of Iraq. They now feel less rather than more safe and they hold the United States and governments that supported the war responsible. . . .

Impact on Transatlantic Relations

The impact of these events on transatlantic relations and cooperation in the war on terrorism are still hard to discern. One clear consequence is the disap-

---

1. Euskadi Ta Askatasuna, meaning "Basque Country and Liberty" is a terrorist group seeking an independent Socialist Basque state. The Basques are an ethnic group that inhabits parts of Spain and France.

pearance for the time being of the "New Europe" as a distinct collection of countries sharing an unquestioning commitment to support the United States in the pursuit of its foreign policy and security priorities. . . .

Despite the rapid military victory in Iraq, European public support for the decision to go to war and for U.S. leadership in general has now dropped off again precipitously, influenced not just by the failure to find WMD, but also to demonstrate rapid progress in Iraq's political and economic reconstruction. [The terrorist group] al Qaeda's apparent ability to operate successfully in Western Europe,[2] despite the huge investment of resources in Iraq, will harden this view.

The March 16, 2004 report from the Pew Global Attitudes Project paints this picture clearly, comparing polling figures prior to the war, immediately after the war, and [April 2004]. Perhaps most striking in terms of this [Senate] committee's interests are two trends. First, a fall in European public confidence in the sincerity of U.S. motives for pursuing the war on international terrorism. In France and Germany, two thirds of respondents now believe the motives are not sincere, and even in Britain 41% do not trust U.S. motives. Second, is the growing number of Europeans who believe they should chart a more independent foreign policy from the United States. As expected, French respondents favored a more independent European role by a margin of 75% to 21%. More surprisingly, German and British respondents also favored a more independent European role by margins of 63% to 36% and by 56% to 40% respectively.

> *"European public support for the decision to go to war [in Iraq] and for U.S. leadership in general has now dropped off . . . precipitously."*

So, in the aftermath of what appears to be the first major Al Qaeda terrorist attack in the European Union, a swing toward a more united Europe, and a deepening skepticism in Europe of U.S. motives and leadership in the war on global terrorism, what are the prospects for transatlantic relations in the coming year? Are relations destined to get worse, with unpredictable consequences for cooperation on the war on terror, or will the tentative efforts to overcome these differences, which had been visible earlier this year, take root?

Common Threat, but Different Responses

Before trying to answer these questions, there are two further issues to consider. The first is the apparent coming together of U.S. and European perceptions of the nature of the threat that they face. And the second is the continuing dichotomy between U.S. and European strategic approaches to deal with this threat.

---

2. A group affiliated with Al Qaeda claimed responsibility for the March 11, 2004, attacks.

On the first of these points, it is remarkable to note how closely the new European Security Strategy (ESS), that EU leaders developed last year and approved in December 2003, resembles the administration's 2002 National Security Strategy in terms of conceptualizing the changed nature of the threat to national security. The European paper specifically highlights international terrorism, WMD proliferation, "state failure," and organized crime as the central security concerns for Europe in the future. It also highlights, as has the U.S. administration, that "the most frightening scenario is the one in which terrorist groups acquire weapons of mass destruction." The paper concludes that the threats to Europe of the 21st century are "dynamic" and bear little resemblance to the 20th century European preoccupation with invasion.

It would be easy to surmise that the language contained in the ESS represents an effort to mimic the United States linguistically, but without true political conviction. The attacks of 3/11 in Madrid will surely lay this view to rest. Europeans are well aware that their geographic proximity to the Middle East, large Muslim populations, porous borders, and uncoordinated national law enforcement agencies make it possible for Islamic extremist groups to operate in their midst with relative ease. Although intelligence agencies have penetrated national terrorist groups such as ETA and the IRA [Irish Republican Army] the activities of loosely knit Islamic extremist groups pose new and unfamiliar challenges. Spain is a case in point.

Nor is this threat perceived as being limited to the countries that have supported the United States in Iraq. Most EU members have been active and willing participants in the U.S.-led war against the Taliban and Al Qaeda in Afghanistan.[3] Furthermore, European nations offer other sources of ire to Islamic extremist groups—the French government's decision to ban wearing of the veil in public schools being just the latest example.

Following the attacks of 3/11, European nations find themselves explicitly, not just theoretically, in the new security environment that U.S. leaders entered two and half years earlier. But agreeing on the threat does not mean that there is transatlantic agreement on the best way to

> *"As closely as Europeans might agree with U.S. perceptions of the nature of the threat, they tend to differ in their prescriptions."*

confront it. As closely as Europeans might agree with U.S. perceptions of the nature of the threat, they tend to differ in their prescriptions.

At heart, Europeans start from the premise that, in a war against terrorism, the effectiveness of military power is always limited and often counterproductive.

---

3. The Taliban is an Islamist movement that ruled most of Afghanistan from 1996 until 2001. In 2001 a U.S.-led attack was launched against Afghanistan—where Al Qaeda members were believed to be hiding—and the Taliban, which was believed to be supporting Al Qaeda.

Terrorism reflects a failure of sovereign governments and is a manifestation of societal, cultural, and religious fault lines. It is rarely, if ever, a battle of good versus evil or freedom versus tyranny. Whatever the merits of soft power (diplomacy, financial and other assistance) versus hard power (military suasion) in dealing with inter-state rivalries, all European governments perceive instinctively as well as from hard-earned experience that military actions alone cannot defeat terrorism. From the European perspective, the satisfaction and achievements of military action against terrorists are always short-lived unless governments simultaneously work to starve the roots of the terrorist cause. This explains the majority of European leaders' deep frustration with the U.S. decision to follow up the war against Afghanistan immediately with a war to overthrow Saddam Hussein.

> *"The need for parallel transatlantic coordination could serve as a catalyst for European efforts [against terrorism]."*

Central also to European thinking is the belief that a war against terrorism is a battle for legitimacy and not just for victory. Americans start from the view that their actions flow from a sense of what is right and wrong and that they are, therefore, intrinsically legitimate. Europeans are more cynical. Government action requires the legitimacy of international law and multilateral rules. In the international arena, such legitimacy can flow only from the United Nations, as imperfect an organization as it might be. Hence, also, Europe's general preference for an explicitly multilateral framework within which to pursue national actions to combat international terrorism.

Overcoming such fundamental differences in strategic outlook will be difficult, however much Europeans and Americans perceive a common threat to their security from international terrorism. Nevertheless, governments on both sides of the Atlantic must make a supreme effort not to allow the attacks of 3/11 to hand the terrorists a second victory by leading to a further fracturing of the transatlantic partnership. The stakes could not be greater. The United States, Europe, and key allies have built together a transatlantic community of democratic values, economic interests, prosperity, and individual freedoms that are spreading to the rest of the world. This growing community of modern, open, interconnected societies is especially vulnerable, however, to determined terrorist attack. . . .

One Step at a Time

Following the attacks in Madrid, U.S. and European officials face a series of difficult near-term decisions if they are to confront the threat of international terrorism together and not allow the war against terror to become a source of division rather than common action. Each decision must be tackled individually, one step at a time.

First, neither the United States nor Europe can afford to lose Iraq. The risks to European countries, which are on the door step of the Middle East, have growing domestic Muslim populations, and are heavily dependent on Gulf energy imports, are as great as they are for the United States. . . .

Second, U.S., European forces, and their coalition partners must continue to secure Afghanistan's transition away from lawlessness and economic despair. NATO [North Atlantic Treaty Organization] support for the gradual expansion of the role of Provincial Reconstruction Teams outside Kabul will be central to this process and to the credibility of the U.S. and European intention not only to defeat Al Qaeda and the Taliban militarily, but also to prevent their return.

Third, as many other commentators have noted, the United States and Europe must show a united front in their plans for long-term political and economic reform across North Africa and the Middle East. For such an initiative to be both credible and sustainable in the region, however, U.S. and European governments must be insistently and actively engaged in helping the Israeli and Palestinian peoples find a way out of their cycle of violence and toward a viable settlement.

Each of these steps will take time to bear fruit. In the interim, the United States and Europe can take more direct steps to confront the threat of international terrorism by closely integrating the domestic policies, procedures, technological standards, and organizations that they are putting in place to combat international terrorism in the wake of recent attacks and threats. In this context, the summit of EU heads of state on March 26 [2004] represented an important milestone in European commitment to coordinating their anti-terrorism initiatives. However, the summit declaration also highlighted how slowly EU governments are implementing the steps that they had identified two years earlier in the wake of the 9/11 attacks. The need for parallel transatlantic coordination could serve as a useful catalyst for European efforts, while making the transatlantic space a less attractive one for terrorist operatives.

> *"The [terrorist] threat is common and urgent, and we urgently need to build common responses."*

U.S. and European leaders were hugely successful in building an integrated military structure to confront the danger of Soviet military aggression during the cold war. At their upcoming EU and NATO summits this summer [2004], U.S. and European leaders should consider creating new standing institutional arrangements that would bring together officials covering the fields of home affairs, justice, law enforcement, intelligence, and emergency response. These groups are key components in the war on international terror. Only once they start working together effectively will it be possible to roll back the threat of international terrorism.

It is worth noting that the growing transatlantic gap in military capabilities and spending that has so often been cited as a structural impediment to future transatlantic security cooperation need not be a central obstacle to transatlantic cooperation in the war on terrorism. Organizational coordination, political will, and bureaucratic flexibility will be as important as financial resources in this war, where the deliberately low-tech approach of the terrorists often bypasses the sophisticated defense systems we have put in place.

A Common Threat

The attacks in Madrid heralded a new phase in the emerging post–cold war security environment. For their part, Europeans suddenly find themselves, once again, on the front-line of a non-traditional war. This is not a cold war of titanic, superpower proportions, as they experienced from 1948–1990. Nor is it a traditional war that threatens territorial conquest and identifiable enemies. In this new struggle the United States and Europe once again face a common enemy. But, as during the cold war, we see alternative and sometimes competing potential strategies to confront the threat.

Admittedly, Americans and Europeans entered the war against terrorism through different gateways—the United States through the exceptional events of September 11, 2001 and Europeans through decade-long struggles against domestic terrorist groups. After the events of March 11, 2004, however, we can no longer say that we confront different threats. The threat is common and urgent, and we urgently need to build common responses.

America Should Fight Terrorism by Encouraging Strong States in the Middle East

by Charles Hill

About the author: *Charles Hill is a research fellow at the Hoover Institution, a public policy research center at Stanford University in California.*

Terrorism thrives on myth. Many deceptive and dangerous delusions have been in the air since [the] September 11 [2001 terrorist attacks]. These include the myths that (1) terrorists are really freedom fighters struggling to establish their own state and peaceful relations with their neighbors; (2) Islam, a faith that fostered peace and a great civilization in the past, cannot be held responsible for providing a spawning ground for terror today; (3) terrorism is the last resort of the poor, the dispossessed, and the desperate peoples of the Middle East; (4) Arab states with stable governments and viable economies can control the rising tide of Islamic militancy within their borders; and (5) the nations of the West, especially the United States, are to blame for the authoritarian, corrupt, and backward status of the states of the Middle East.

We need to dispel the myths and look reality in the eye.

Terrorists Do Not Want Peace

The most frequent charge features the American role in negotiations between Palestinians and Israelis. Assertions that the United States has fallen short in the past and now must change its ways and that it must become more "evenhanded" are grossly misplaced.

Over the years, whenever Israelis and Palestinians have come close to a peace agreement, the terrorists have stepped up their attacks. They abhor the idea of such a peace.

Arab terrorism, with its commitment to the eradication of Israel, is the principal cause of the collapse of the peace process. Terrorism's primary targets are virtually all the Middle Eastern regimes—not just Israel's but those of the surrounding Arab countries as well. Fear of being overthrown by terrorists leads those regimes, in an effort to divert their people's attention toward external targets, to inundate them with anti-Israel propaganda. Israel's willingness in recent years to abandon its formerly non-negotiable position—and the withdrawal of Israel Defense Forces from southern Lebanon and the offer to give up the Golan Heights to Syria—has created a conviction among Arabs that terrorism is working and that no accommodation of Israel need be considered.

> *"Those who think that the United States can defuse Islamic fundamentalist rage . . . by imposing a peace agreement are out touch with the cruel reality of the Middle East."*

Thus the terrorists, the regimes that foster yet fear them, and most recently the Palestinian leadership all share one idea: None can tolerate a peace agreement between Israelis and Palestinians.

Those who think that the United States can defuse Islamic fundamentalist rage and end terrorism by imposing a peace agreement are out of touch with the cruel reality of the Middle East. To press for such a peace is to invite further terror. Anyone involved in the diplomacy of the Arab-Israeli conflict over the years, as I have been, understands that peace cannot be imposed from the outside. To attempt such a solution would shield one side or the other, or both, from the need to make the concessions necessary for a durable agreement. Under present circumstances, any indication that the United States is considering a dictated peace will be taken by the Arab side as a victory and a way station on the road to eliminating the state of Israel.

After Islamic terrorism is eradicated, and only then, can an Israeli-Palestinian peace agreement be achieved. Only after the American war on terrorism is won can peace in the Middle East become possible. The same holds true for many other supposedly intractable conflicts around the world; it is the terrorists who reject the very idea of peace. Suppress terrorism and diplomacy will get a new lease on life.

Frustration . . . Resentment . . . Terrorism?

In the aftermath of September 11, many Americans recommitted themselves to civil liberties and respect for the rights of individuals who share the appearance, ethnicity, or faith of the terrorist enemies of the United States.

The religious dimension of this terrorism, however, cannot be explained away. This version of Islam involves religious leaders instructing their followers that it is their religious duty to kill those who do not share their religious beliefs. Islam can be considered a faith that has fostered peace and civilization.

But, like some other religions, Islam has, during certain periods of history, been part of an environment in which evildoers can burrow and breed. The higher levels of Islam have not yet displayed adequate doctrinal defenses against this, nor have they condemned it. The Friday sermons in mosques across the Middle East and in Europe and North America as well, have ranged from a pro-Taliban[1] line to a transparent apologia for the terrorists (i.e., what they did was bad but understandable and no worse than the "terrorism" conducted by the United States and Israel).

Much public argumentation since September 11 has sidestepped this reality by stressing the anger and desperation of those peoples of the Middle East who lead lives of poverty, unemployment, and dispossession.

But the terrorists we pursue today are often not the poor and downtrodden. In case after case they come from strong families, are well-off and educated, and have optimistic prospects for their lives and careers. Most notably, Mohammed Atta, who flew American Airlines Flight 11 into the north tower of the World Trade Center [on September 11, 2001,] was the well-educated, well-traveled son of an affluent Cairo attorney.

Something else is at work here: frustration over the region's failure to succeed economically and resentment at the absence of political avenues toward progress.

Not many years ago, the states of the Arab Middle East seemed well placed to join Asian nations as entrants to the First World. In geographic extent, population size, and wealth, the region was an obvious candidate for world power and influence.

> *"The terrorists we pursue today are often not the poor and downtrodden. In case after case they come from strong families."*

Even without substantial oil resources, the Middle East and North Africa should command geopolitical importance by the shape and location of their lands on the globe. But the Arab-Islamic world has not attained full participation in the global economy. In fact, were it not for oil, the Middle East would rank lower than Africa in economic development.

Middle Eastern regimes base their power on a compact with their people that economic and social realities make virtually impossible to fulfill. As discontent grows, the tenets of Islamic fundamentalism provide grounds for an attack on any government in power, whatever its form or philosophy.

The Failure of Statehood

Neither history nor the authentic Islamic faith can account for the Middle East's lowly world ranking. So what can? The answer lies in the miserable state of politics and governance in that region.

---

1. Islamist movement that ruled most of Afghanistan from 1996 until 2001

States are the building blocks and fundamental actors of international relations, and diplomacy is the method by which states attempt to solve problems among them. The Islamic political tradition, however, stresses a seamless unity of faith and power, a concept incompatible with the very idea of statehood.

Traditional Islamic governance is based on the umma, the community of believers, which should know no boundaries other than the religion itself. Sharia—law based on a literal reading of the Koran—takes priority over the state; indeed, it does not require the existence of a state. The caliphate emerged from the need, following the Prophet's death, to establish a politico-religious center of power.[2] In the modern era the Ottoman Empire claimed the caliphate. In 1924, when the Turkish revolution overthrew the Ottomans, the caliphate was abolished.

Since then, Arab-Islamic political elites have failed to find a credible alternative to the traditional system of government. At present, the shadow of illegitimacy falls over all political power in Islam, and the very existence of states may be seen as evidence of non-Islamic practices. This grim reality makes all the more potent the fantastical suggestion that some charismatic figure such as [terrorist leader] Osama bin Laden could, through terrorist warfare, cleanse the Dar al Islam (the realm of Islam) of all unbelievers and reestablish the caliphate.

The Arab world today consists of 21 countries, all members of the League of Arab States. Few seem comfortable with their own statehood except as a means of casting a veil of international legitimacy over their own version of power politics. Some, such as Morocco, are hereditary paternalistic monarchies whose royal heads are uneasy indeed. Some are secular regimes on the national socialist model. . . . Still others, such as Egypt and Syria, borrowed Western constitutional forms but have never achieved legitimacy because they have not been accompanied by democratic freedoms. A look at the region as a whole reveals inauthentic "states" attempting to function within the concept of pan-Arabism (one Arab nation) within the wider body of states—members of the Organization of the Islamic Conference, where, if anywhere, the unfilled office of the caliphate resides—with a commitment to pan-Islam. All these concepts hamper the full participation of the region in the contemporary international system of states. The absence of credible political systems and the inability to participate in a world of state powers incite protests under the banner of Islam.

> *"Every regime of the Arab-Islamic world has proved a failure. . . . Religiously inflamed terrorists take root in such soil."*

Over the past decade, an immense contradiction has become evident between

---

2. The caliph claims rulership over all Muslims. This title was established following the death of Muhammad, whom Muslims consider the last prophet of God, in 632.

the ideals of pan-Arabism and pan-Islam on the one hand and efforts at state strengthening on the other. State security has been tightened, as has state control over the media. Legitimate opposition elements have been crushed, bought off, or co-opted.

What appear to be a variety of governmental forms in Middle Eastern states are variations of power being held by a strongman, surrounded by a praetorian guard: in Oman, a sultan; in Yemen, a military "president"; in Saudi Arabia, a king and family with special Islamic custodial responsibilities; in Jordan, a king of a simulated constitutional monarchy; in Egypt, a president and a parliament only nominally connected to the Western meaning of those institutions.

> *"An immense opportunity now exists to shape the war on terrorism to positive ends."*

A family or personal entourage clusters around the ruler. Those close to power gain; the weak are disregarded. The constant fear is that the repressed opposition will attempt a coup d'état. This pattern represents a fundamental and ancient political order.

Saudi Arabia most vividly embodies these contradictions. This fragile, conflict-ridden country is not just the homeland of Osama bin Laden but also the source of his fortune. The only nation-state with a family name and the only state whose legitimacy is based on its protection of Islam, Saudi Arabia is considered by its monarchy to be a complete embodiment of Islam. Indeed, with its vast oil wealth, huge expenditures on infrastructure and private enterprise, and enthusiasm for expanding science and higher education, Saudi Arabia can be viewed as a great experiment to determine whether modern economic and technological life can be compatibly achieved alongside a rigorous interpretation of Islam. Yet Saudi Arabia, for all its application of the Koran to every aspect of society, is denounced as virtually non-Islamic by the new wave of terrorists. In 1996 bin Laden issued a fatwa—a religious decree on a matter of Islamic law— setting as his primary goals the takeover of [holy Islamic cities] Mecca and Medina and the overthrow of the Saudi regime. Bin Laden's pronouncements make clear that, as long as the United States has any presence or influence in the Islamic world, he will be unable to achieve his goals.

Every regime of the Arab-Islamic world has proved a failure. Not one has been able to provide its people with realistic hopes for a free and prosperous future. The regimes have found no way to respond to their people's frustration other than by a combination of internal oppression and propaganda to generate rage against external enemies. Religiously inflamed terrorists take root in such soil. Their threats extort facilities and subsidies from the regimes that increase their strength and influence. The result is a downward spiral of failure, fear, and hatred.

Such feelings are deepened by a cultural infection that has spread across the

Middle East: the deeply rooted conviction that every societal shortcoming can be attributed to a foreign plot or conspiracy and that every local problem is beyond solution without some action—perniciously withheld—by the United States or some other foreign power.

Over the past few decades, even Americans have begun to fall prey to the idea that virtually every problem in the world can be attributed to some fault of ours.

What Next?

Nevertheless, the situation in the Middle East presents the United States with some opportunities to shape the region and the international scene in a positive way. Many governments in the Arab-Islamic region that have accommodated and provided support for terrorists have felt a shock of recognition at the September 11 attacks. These regimes have been playing a dangerous game, stirring up their people's hatred of external forces without focusing on the terrorists themselves. The attacks on New York City and Washington, D.C., made clear that the terrorism beast may have escaped the control of its keepers.

An immense opportunity now exists to shape the war on terrorism to positive ends in view of the nature and extent of the terrorist threat to virtually every state in the world.

State is the fundamental entity of international relations. The past decade has been marked by a widening belief that the sovereign state is on the way out, that the information revolution, international "civil society," globalization, and other inexorable forces of change are rendering the state obsolete; but the state remains the indispensable core entity of international life, with no replacement in sight.

The United States must help Arab regimes recognize that their commitment to their faith and to their people can best be strengthened through a commitment to the state. Although a more ideal form of government may be imaginable, none is realizable in this era of world history.

Terrorism is the ultimate assault weapon against the state. So the new war on terrorism provides a natural bonding agent for today's states and the international system of states that goes back to the seventeenth century. This system remains the foundation stone for all that is accomplished in the global arena.

A revitalized, state-centered, and clearly antiterrorist approach could help resolve some of the world's intractable conflicts, almost all of which involve two communities unwilling to be part of one state. If terrorism can truly be suppressed, the fear that stands in the way of accommodation will be sharply diminished in places such as Northern Ireland and Kashmir. These and other conflicts cannot be closed out quickly or easily, but victory in the war on terrorism could transform the international scene into one more accepting of peace and stability.

Chapter 3

Are Civil Liberties Being Compromised in the Domestic Battle Against Terrorism?

Chapter Preface

Following the September 11, 2001, terrorist attacks on America, the U.S. Department of Defense launched the Total Information Awareness (TIA) project. TIA, part of the U.S. government's attempts to guard against another terrorist attack, was designed to gather as much information as possible about everyone in the United States and to store the data in a centralized location for easy perusal by the U.S. government. This information could then be used to detect and prevent terrorist activity. Data for TIA would be collected, or mined, through sources such as Internet activity, credit card purchase histories, airline ticket purchases, car rental accounts, medical records, educational transcripts, driver's license applications, utility bills, and tax returns. When news of TIA was made public, an immediate outcry followed from critics who claimed the project disregarded the concept of individual privacy and was far too invasive and prone to abuse. In late 2003 this highly controversial program was suspended as a result of widespread protest.

After the September 11 attacks, the U.S. government has attempted to improve its intelligence systems in an effort to prevent another terrorist attack on America. While it has discontinued the TIA project, it continues to pursue other methods of gathering and analyzing information in order to find terrorists and prevent future attacks. In response, civil liberties advocates have argued that these new technologies are threatening the civil liberties of Americans. The result is an ongoing debate over the use of information mining and surveillance in the United States.

Advocates of these methods argue that they are invaluable tools against terrorism. Writer Michael Scardaville argues that data mining and analysis could be a vital tool in finding and preventing terrorism in the United States. He contends that the U.S. government is obligated to use whatever technology is available to protect its citizens. According to him, "Fear of abuse by corrupt individuals should not hinder the government's ability to complete its duty to protect Americans." Editor Eugenie Samuel argues that "spotting terrorists before they strike will save lives, so there is a need for surveillance technologies like TIA." According to Samuel, it is possible to implement adequate safeguards so that data mining can be used without intruding on the lives of innocent people.

However, civil liberties proponents argue that it will be impossible to mine information without compromising Americans' civil liberties. Writer Timothy Lynch argues that America must preserve its freedom above all else and that it is not worth winning the battle against terrorism if doing so means giving up our freedom. He contends:

It is . . . both wise and imperative to address the terrorist threat within the framework of a free society. . . . Here at home, it means resisting the implementation of a surveillance state. This course of action is, admittedly, fraught with danger. Innocent people at home and brave soldiers abroad will lose their lives to the barbaric forces of terrorism, but they will at least have died honorably as free people.

Journalist Clyde Wayne Crews Jr. claims that the information gathered on Americans could be easily misused. "The government has proven notoriously bad at safeguarding its information databases," says Crews. "Since 9/11, hackers have gained access to secret Department of Defense satellite photos and nuclear missile information."

As America continues to search for better ways to protect itself against terrorism, there is continuing disagreement over how to effectively protect Americans while ensuring that their civil liberties remain intact. The authors of the viewpoints in this chapter discuss whether or not civil liberties have been compromised in America's domestic battle against terrorism.

Civil Liberties Have Been Compromised by the Patriot Act

by Michael Stern

About the author: Michael Stern, a former journalist and English professor, is the head of the technology transactions group at Cooley Godward law firm.

In an America that remains as politically polarized into [liberal and conservative] states as it was in 2000—despite the [terrorist] attacks on September 11, 2001—the Bush administration's counterterrorism measures have created one striking, if unanticipated, consensus. Our three authors aren't people who would be expected to agree with each other about much. Nat Hentoff, the renowned jazz critic and longtime columnist for *The Village Voice*, has for decades championed free speech and opposed the national security state's efforts to squelch it. Philip Heymann, now [in 2004] a professor at Harvard Law School, ran the criminal division of [former U.S. president] Jimmy Carter's Justice Department and served as [former U.S. president] Bill Clinton's deputy attorney general. James Bovard is the libertarian policy adviser to the Future of Freedom Foundation, a winner of the National Rifle Association's Freedom Fund Award, a longtime contributor to *The American Spectator*, and a scourge of Bill Clinton's purported abuses of power. So what do these exemplary voices of left, center, and right agree about? That the USA Patriot Act (and the Bush administration's increasingly aggressive assertion of executive authority to curtail or eliminate judicial review of decisions about whom to surveil, interrogate, detain, and prosecute for what conduct) represents a dangerous, unprecedented—and above all, unjustifiable—threat to civil liberties.

Each author arrives at the ground he shares with the others from a different direction, of course, and that ground is a complex Venn diagram of intersecting indictments and policy prescriptions. Their sobering conclusions about the impact of the "war on terror" on American democracy have three core elements in common:

Undermining Constitutional Checks and Balances

As [former U.S. president] James Madison famously wrote in *The Federalist Papers* (No. 47): "The accumulation of all powers, legislative, executive and judiciary, in the same hands . . . may justly be pronounced the very definition of tyranny." The net effect of the Bush administration's post-9/11 antiterrorism campaign has been to massively concentrate power and authority in the executive branch, while seeking to conceal the results of this process.

The Patriot Act defines "domestic terrorism" as "activities that involve acts dangerous to human life that violate the laws of the United States or any state [and] appear to be intended to: (1) intimidate or coerce a civilian population; (2) influence the policy of a government by intimidation or coercion; or (3) affect the conduct of the government by mass destruction, assassination, or kidnapping. . . ." The sweeping vagueness of phrases such as "dangerous to human life," "appear to be intended," and "intimidate" could capture many forms of political protest—enabling the government, as Hentoff points out, to surveil, detain, interrogate, and ultimately charge as a terrorist anyone who provides any assistance to others engaged in purportedly terrorist activities, however innocuous such assistance might be. Examples (from Bovard): Eyad Alrababah, a Palestinian living in Connecticut, voluntarily contacted the Federal Bureau of Investigation after 9/11 to tell the agency that he had met four of the hijackers and given them a ride to Virginia in June 2001. He was arrested and held incommunicado in solitary confinement for over four months for his trouble. There was also the barakaat (a money transfer service used by Somali immigrants in the U.S.) in a Seattle strip mall that was raided as a putative financial arm of terrorist organizations and stripped of all its contents (including the coffee makers, food, and baked goods from its accompanying minimart). It took more than six months and the intervention of Senator Patty Murray (D-Washington) for the owner to recover the cash seized in the raid (which turned up no evidence of any wrongdoing); he was never compensated for the interruption of his business or the loss of his inventory and equipment.

The Patriot Act permits searches and seizures without immediate notification of the target (notice can be delayed for at least 90 days) and wiretapping (including the surveillance of e-mail) on the basis of a dec-

> *"The USA Patriot Act . . . represents a dangerous, unprecedented—and above all, unjustifiable—threat to civil liberties."*

laration that the information sought is "relevant to an ongoing criminal investigation" rather than the Fourth Amendment standard of probable cause. The act also authorizes the FBI to secretly obtain the books and records of any person or organization—most notoriously, bookstores' and libraries' information about their patrons' reading and Internet browsing habits—and to preclude any disclosure of the request. Each FBI office may issue these "National Security Letters," which do not require a court order of any kind, even one from the Foreign Intelligence Surveillance Act (FISA) court established to handle subpoenas and warrants in espionage and counterterrorism cases. The crux of these provisions is to remove the "neutral and detached magistrate" so dear to the hearts of the Founders from the process of searches, seizures, and surveillance. Even where the Patriot Act requires some judicial oversight, Bovard notes, citing a *Florida Law Review* article, it "require[s] that the order be granted if the application is properly filled out," effectively negating any judicial discretion.

An executive order that President George [W.] Bush originally issued in November 2001 permits the secretary of defense to order the indefinite detention of any alien—including U.S. residents—suspected of supporting international terrorist activities. As Bovard reports in heavily footnoted detail, more than 1,200 "special interest" suspects—temporary and resident aliens—were arrested in the months after 9/11, and more than 600 were eventually deported after secret trial, but all for various immigration or petty criminal offenses: "No evidence surfaced linking any of those people to the terrorist attacks." The government refused to release the names of the detainees or to disclose the precise numbers being held. Almost all were denied

> *"During wartime, constitutional safeguards have been repeatedly compromised on the basis of purportedly imminent threats."*

access to counsel either overtly or by subterfuge (lists of available lawyers' phone numbers contained only numbers that were out of service, or detainees were only allowed their one phone call a week after business hours, when no one would be there to answer their call).

U.S. Department of Defense secretary Donald Rumsfeld and Attorney General John Ashcroft have since asserted, in the prosecution of the so-called enemy combatant case (*Hamdi v. Rumsfeld*) against Yaser Hamdi, that the Bush order extends to U.S. citizens, even if arrested here and not on a foreign battlefield. Hamdi, a Louisiana-born American captured in Afghanistan, has been held incommunicado in a Navy brig in Norfolk, Virginia, for more than a year after his transfer from Guantanamo Bay in Cuba.[1] As Hentoff points out, Hamdi's detention is based on a two-page declaration by a special adviser to the Defense Department that Hamdi was "affiliated with a Taliban[2] unit and received weapons training." The federal district court judge presiding over a hear-

---

1. Hamdi was captured in Afghanistan in 2001 and has been held by the United States since then. As of this writing, his case was awaiting trial by the U.S. Supreme Court. 2. The Taliban is an Islamist movement that ruled most of Afghanistan from 1996 until 2001.

ing in the case (which Hamdi was not allowed to attend) concluded that the declaration "makes no effort to explain what 'affiliated' means nor under what criteria this 'affiliation' justifies Hamdi's classification as an enemy combatant. . . . Indeed, a close inspection of the declaration reveals that [it] never claims that Hamdi was fighting for the Taliban or was a member of the Taliban. . . ."

> *"The Patriot Act was drafted in the U.S. Senate in closed-door sessions attended only by legislators handpicked by the administration."*

The administration has since made good on extending the doctrine to Americans seized in America. Jose Padilla, a U.S. citizen arrested in Chicago for purportedly plotting to detonate a [radioactive] "dirty bomb," has also been held [since May 2002] without access to counsel, in the same brig as Hamdi, after being declared an enemy combatant by President Bush. Heymann's devastating conclusion: "Quite simply, a country cannot be free if the executive retains the power, on its own determination that certain conditions are met, to detain citizens for an indefinite period." At least one court has agreed with him. On December 18, 2003, a divided panel of the U.S. Court of Appeals for the Second Circuit ruled that the "president, acting alone, possesses no inherent constitutional authority to detain an American citizen seized in the U.S., away from the zone of combat, as an enemy combatant." The court ordered the government to release, charge, or hold Padilla as a material witness within 30 days; as of this writing, the Justice Department is seeking a stay of the order and has said it will appeal.[3]

The Declaration of a Permanent State of Emergency

During wartime, constitutional safeguards have been repeatedly compromised on the basis of purportedly imminent threats to the body politic, from [former U.S. president Abraham] Lincoln's suspension of the writ of habeas corpus during the Civil War to the internment of Japanese Americans during World War II. Conventional wars are bounded in time and space, with beginnings and endings, fronts and rears, and the curtailment of civil liberties purportedly justified by their exigencies is usually temporary as well. But the Bush administration has defined the "war on terrorism" as a global "crusade" to "rid the world of evildoers," per the president's speech on September 16, 2001; the battlefield is global, the time frame indefinite. "For so long as anybody's terrorizing established governments, there needs to be a war," the president repeated in an October 2001 interview.

If war is perpetual, so is the danger that justifies "emergency" powers. There's no due process on the battlefield. Bovard's conclusion: "Because of the actions of a handful of terrorists on September 11, federal agents could have

---

3. On February 20, 2004, the U.S. Supreme Court agreed to hear the appeal.

more power over all Americans in perpetuity. . . . The Bush administration carried off the biggest bait-and-switch in U.S. constitutional history. Rather than targeting terrorists, Bush and Congress awarded new powers [under the Patriot Act and the Homeland Security Act] to use against anyone suspected of committing any one of the 3,000 federal crimes on the books." Heymann's verdict is more measured, but just as damning: The administration has "carefully exploited the right to use selective enforcement of rarely used statutes and powers to act against a group or activity for purposes largely unconnected with the purposes of the Congress in passing the statute."

Short-Circuiting Democratic Decision Making

Governing is about making choices and assessing trade-offs. What are the benefits and the costs of the new post-9/11 security regime? Do the potential gains in public safety and peace of mind it promises outweigh the potential damage to democratic values and traditions it may cause? Heymann writes: "When there is a true conflict between greater security and preserving historic democratic freedoms . . . we must do our best to choose wisely—not an easy assignment in times of danger and fear." The Bush administration and Congress flunked the test.

As all three authors recount, the Patriot Act was drafted in the U.S. Senate in closed-door sessions attended only by legislators handpicked by the administration. It was bulldozed through Congress without substantive hearings in four weeks, under the lash of crisis rhetoric and the threat of members being attacked as unpatriotic for countenancing any deliberation. ("The American people do not have the luxury of unlimited time in erecting the necessary defenses to future terrorist attacks . . . ," Ashcroft lectured the House Judiciary Committee. "Each day that passes [before the Patriot Act is enacted] is a day that terrorists have a competitive advantage. Until Congress makes these changes, we are fighting an unnecessarily uphill battle.") The congressional leadership refused to consider an alternative bill unanimously reported out by the Judiciary Committee, forcing an up-or-down, no-amendment vote on the Senate version (which was not even printed and distributed to the representatives voting to approve it, most of whom never read it).

> *"The Patriot Act . . . [is] a loaded gun lying on the table, aimed at the heart of American democracy."*

Dismantling the Bill of Rights

The results? Hentoff: "A reckless dismantling of the Bill of Rights." Bovard: "The war on terrorism is the first political growth industry of the new millennium. . . . After 9/11, the Bush administration rushed to increase the power of federal agencies across the board . . . result[ing] in maximum intimidation and minimum deliberation by Congress." Heymann: "What isn't permissible is the view that Attorney General Ashcroft has repeatedly enunciated: that the job of the Justice Department is to go as far as legally possible in protecting even limited amounts of security without consideration of the long-term costs in democratic freedoms. . . . What [the Bush administration] has sought to do is to ignore the responsibility of the executive to consider the impact of precedent and practice on the character of the country and to deny Congress and the courts the opportunity to exercise oversight. Furthermore, it has sought to deny the American people full knowledge of what is being done.". . .

As [former U.S. Supreme Court] Justice Robert Jackson memorably wrote in his dissent in *Korematsu v. United States*, the World War II internment case: "A military order, however unconstitutional, is not apt to last longer than the military emergency. Even during that period a succeeding commander may revoke it all. But once a judicial opinion rationalizes such an order to show that it conforms to the Constitution, or rather rationalizes the Constitution to show that the Constitution sanctions such an order, the Court for all time has validated the principle of racial discrimination in criminal procedure and of transplanting American citizens. The principle then lies about like a loaded weapon ready for the hand of any authority that can bring forward a plausible claim of an urgent need. Every repetition imbeds that principle more deeply in our law and thinking and expands it to new purposes."

Hentoff, Heymann, and Bovard have made it clear that the Patriot Act and the Homeland Security Act are a loaded gun lying on the table, aimed at the heart of American democracy, ready for the hand of anyone—not just John Ashcroft or George Bush—who would fire it. The capability is there, whatever the intentions of our current leaders. The media and the federal courts have been all too complaisant in the face of the administration's response to the threat. Lawyers, too, are officers of the court, and the last line of defense for the rule of law. We have been warned.

Using Military Tribunals to Try Suspected Terrorists Violates Civil Liberties

by Elisa Massimino

About the author: *Elisa Massimino is director of the Washington, D.C., office of the Lawyers Committee for Human Rights, where she is responsible for advancing all aspects of the Lawyers Committee's human rights agenda in Washington, D.C.*

This is not the draft of an ACLU [American Civil Liberties Union] press release on the recent military order signed by President [George W.] Bush. It is an excerpt about Egypt from the *U.S. Department of State Country Reports on Human Rights Practices for 2000.* Similarly, when American Lori Berenson was convicted on terrorism charges in a military court in Peru, the United States vigorously objected, and included in its report the following analysis: "Proceedings in these military courts . . . do not meet internationally accepted standards of openness, fairness, and due process. Military courts hold . . . trials in secret."

After the president's order authorizing secret military trials, what will the United States be able to say?

The Bush administration has shown some initial signs that it will not forsake the U.S. criminal justice system—for example, deciding in early December [2002] to try French citizen Zacarias Moussaoui for conspiracy to commit terrorism and other related crimes in federal district court in Virginia.[1] However, the administration is defending its military order with great intensity and is not providing much advance information on how and when military commissions could be used.

---

1. The trial of Moussaoui, in connection with the September 11, 2001, terrorist attacks, was ongoing as of this writing.

Chapter 3

Forsaking a Strong System

Many societies have faced the violent scourge of terrorism and attacks on innocent civilians. But of these the United States has the strongest constitutionally based institutions of justice. In this time of crisis, we should view these institutions as a source of strength, not a liability. So why does the administration insist on having the authority to turn away from that system now, in favor of an extraconstitutional process that will surely be seen by many in the Muslim world as lacking in credibility?

Some argue that only Americans deserve American-style justice, with its presumption of innocence and other due process guarantees. Others insist that the extenuating circumstances of the war on terrorism make speedy convictions the overriding

"[In a military court] there is no right to appeal, no protection against coerced confession . . . and no presumption of innocence."

goal. [Former Supreme Court justice] Oliver Wendell Holmes said that hard cases make bad law; some have argued that the only way to inoculate our criminal justice system from the inevitable bad law is to forsake that system and set up a parallel scheme for trying terrorist suspects.

That is what President Bush has said he wants to do. In his capacity as Commander-in-Chief of the Armed Forces, and pursuant to his declaration of national emergency, the president issued a military order on November 13 [2001] regarding the "Detention, Treatment, and Trial of Certain Non-Citizens in the War against Terrorism." By this order, which has no expiration date, the president grants himself the power to turn any non-U.S. citizen whom he suspects is a terrorist, over to the secretary of defense to be tried by a "military commission" under whatever rules the secretary of defense creates.

No court would decide who goes before such a commission; the president need only state that he has reason to believe a certain person is a terrorist. This could be anyone, from an Al Qaeda [terrorist group] operative captured during battle, to one of the many thousands of immigrants in the United States now being rounded up for questioning by the FBI.

Potential Loss of Rights

The Moussaoui indictment makes it hard to imagine a case that could justify the use of military courts inside the United States. However, the order's definition of "terrorist" is so extraordinarily broad that, as written, it could include a person who harbored someone who aided someone in committing an act in preparation for an act of international terrorism that was designed to have an adverse effect on the U.S. economy. The military order's jurisdiction goes way beyond [terrorist leader] Osama bin Laden, and even Al Qaeda. Under the expansive terms of the order, the potential defendant described above could be sentenced to death in a trial held entirely in secret. There is no right to appeal, no protection against coerced confession, no provision for access to counsel, and no presumption of innocence. To the contrary, it's a presumption of guilt on which the military tribunal system is justified: "Somebody who comes into the United States illegally, who conducts a terrorist operation killing thousands of innocent Americans" does not deserve the safeguards of the American criminal justice system, Vice President [Dick] Cheney has argued. When asked about the type of procedures we can expect the secretary of defense to establish, Mr. Cheney said that the president's order "guarantees that we'll have the kind of treatment of these individuals that we believe they deserve."

In addition to the rights afforded criminal suspects under the U.S. Constitution, the United States has committed itself to upholding certain international human rights standards, including those set out in the International Covenant on Civil and Political Rights (Covenant), which the United States ratified in 1992. This international human rights framework for protecting civil and political rights is based on the premise that security and justice are mutually reinforcing goals. Neither can be fully realized in the absence of fundamental human rights guarantees. The treaty explicitly provides that some of its obligations may be set aside in times of national emergency; but

> *"The United States has committed itself to upholding certain international human rights standards [for criminal suspects]."*

even then, there are limits. The UN [United Nations] Human Rights Committee is the expert body charged with interpreting the treaty and providing guidance to countries with regard to compliance. Less than two weeks before the September 11 attacks, the UN Committee wrote in a General Comment on Article 4 of the treaty (which sets out the process and limits for derogation from the obligations of the treaty in situations that "threaten the life of the nation"): "It is inherent in the protection of rights explicitly recognized as non-derogable in Article 4, Paragraph 2, that they must be secured by procedural guarantees, including, often, judicial guarantees. . . . Thus, for example . . . any trial leading to the imposition of the death penalty during a state of emergency must conform to the provisions of the Covenant, including all the prerequisites of Articles 14 and 15."

Article 14 requires, among other things, that defendants benefit from a presumption of innocence and that they have the right to appeal a conviction to a higher tribunal. And there can be no derogation from Article 7, which prohibits torture and cruel, inhuman or degrading treatment or punishment, even in times of national emergency. None of these rights is protected in the president's military order.

Before the president signed the November 13 order, there were intense discussions within the administration about the so-called "justice options"—the methods under which suspected terrorists could be brought to book. Administration representatives have said that the military tribunal remains only one tool at the president's disposal; it does not rule out other options.

But what are the other options? The first, obviously, is to try terrorist suspects under standard procedures in regular U.S. courts, as the administration has decided to do in the Moussaoui case. This decision builds on a successful history of cases. Those indicted in the attack on the World Trade Center in 1993 and in the U.S. embassy bombings in Kenya in 1998 were tried and convicted through the ordinary process of the U.S. criminal justice system; some are now serving life sentences in U.S. jails.

Other Alternatives

For those apprehended outside the United States, a variety of other options have been suggested. The International Criminal Court (ICC) has been mentioned as a possible venue for terrorist trials. This body, intended to provide a standing forum in which those accused of the worst human rights crimes could be brought to justice, would seem like a natural choice to try such enemies of civilization as bin Laden and his associates. Although the court has not yet come into existence, and its jurisdiction is prospective only, the requisite sixty ratifications likely will be obtained in a few months. Many international legal experts, including the UN High Commissioner for Human Rights, have concluded that the September 11 attacks constitute "crimes against humanity," a central feature of the ICC's jurisdiction. Though it could not try the perpetrators of these attacks, the events of September 11 make clear the importance of getting the ICC up and running as soon as possible. The closest U.S. allies in the current military effort—including the United Kingdom, which ratified the ICC treaty in the midst of offering the U.S. its support in the war on terror—believe that the ICC represents the future of international justice in the new millennium. Yet, the United States continues to spurn it, even in the aftermath of our national tragedy, signaling support of a bill sponsored by Senator Jesse Helms (R-N.C.) that

> *"The military commissions authorized by the president's order have no place in a country committed to protecting liberty through rule of law and separation of powers."*

would prevent the ICC from ever coming into existence. Ultimately, however, the hard-headed multilateralism that the Bush administration now preaches must lead it to overcome its objections to the ICC and join with its allies in supporting this important new institution. When the gavel comes down at the start of the ICC's first trial of an international terrorist, U.S. opposition will likely start to come down too.

Of course, the international options for trying terrorist suspects are not limited to the ICC. Some experts have suggested expanding the jurisdiction of the

Yugoslav war crimes tribunal[2] to include terrorist offenses and war crimes committed in Afghanistan. Others suggest that the UN Security Council establish a new tribunal to try Al Qaeda members. Additional alternatives include some type of hybrid, Lockerbie-style court[3] or military trials conducted in jurisdictions outside the United States.

Although each of these options carries its own set of complications, none would require us to forsake our cherished institutions of justice. The military commissions authorized by the president's order have no place in a country committed to protecting liberty through the rule of law and separation of powers. The United States stands for these principles internationally, and will be judged by how well it cleaves to them in this time of crisis.

On November 13, President Bush announced he had signed the order permitting use of military commissions. As Bush was leaving for his Texas ranch for a meeting with Russian President [Vladimir] Putin, Deputy White House Counsel Timothy Flanigan announced "The order's signed and nobody's ashamed of it."

Someone should be.

---

2. UN tribunal created to prosecute war crimes committed in former Yugoslavia   3. trial in a neutral country

Racial Profiling in the War on Terrorism Has Violated Civil Liberties

by Nadine Strossen and Timothy Edgar

About the authors: *Nadine Strossen is president and Timothy Edgar is legislative counsel of the American Civil Liberties Union, an organization that works to safeguard civil liberties in the United States.*

On behalf of the American Civil Liberties Union [ACLU] and its over 400,000 members, dedicated to defending the principles enshrined in the Constitution and civil rights laws, with their promise of due process under law for all persons, we welcome this opportunity to appear at this hearing [before the United States Commission on Civil Rights on March 19, 2004,] on the impact of federal anti-terrorism efforts on civil liberties since [the terrorist attacks of] September 11, 2001.

We commend the Commission for coming together to examine how our nation's efforts to preserve freedom can be enhanced without sacrificing the very liberties we are trying to protect. This country needs exactly this public discussion, and the ACLU is privileged to urge the government to see its responsibility as preserving our rights and our system of checks and balances while it ensures our safety.

America faces a crucial test. That test is whether we—the political descendants of [former U.S. presidents Thomas] Jefferson and [James] Madison, and citizens of the world's oldest democracy—have the confidence, ingenuity and commitment to secure our safety without sacrificing our liberty.

For here we are at the beginning of the 21st century, in a battle with global terror. Terrorism is a new and different enemy. As a nation, we learned this on September 11, 2001, when a group of terrorists attacked us here at home, and within the space of minutes murdered nearly 3,000 of our fellow Americans and citizens of other nations, innocent civilians going about their everyday lives.

Nadine Strossen and Timothy Edgar, written statement before the U.S. Commission on Civil Rights, March 19, 2004.

ACLU lawyers and activists can never forget that day. Our national offices in New York and near the Capitol in Washington were evacuated. We pledged on that day to support President [George W.] Bush in the battle against terror, while standing strong against any efforts to use the attacks to abridge civil liberties or our system of checks and balances.

Freedom at Risk

We must be ready to defend liberty, for liberty cannot defend itself. We as a nation have no trouble understanding the necessity of a military defense. But there is another equally powerful defense that is required, and that is the defense of our Constitution—the defense of our most cherished freedoms.

Put aside our popular culture which changes by the day, and our material success which is now vulnerable to the vicissitudes of the global economy—strip away all that is truly superficial. What is left that distinguishes us if not our constitutional values? These values—freedom, liberty, equality and tolerance—are the very source of our strength as a nation and the bulwark of our democracy. They are what have permitted us to grow abundantly, and to absorb wave after wave of immigrants to our shores, reaping the benefits of their industrious energy.

Now, we are in danger of allowing ourselves to be governed by our fears, rather than our values. How else can we explain the actions of our government over the last two years to invade the privacy of our personal lives and to curtail immigrants' rights, all in the name of increasing our security?

One particularly troubling—and ineffective—government policy which has been advanced in the name of security is the practice of racial profiling. Racial profiling occurs when law enforcement relies on race, ethnicity, national origin, or religion in selecting which individuals to subject to law enforcement investigations. This practice not only violates our nation's basic constitutional commitment to equality before the law, but it also violates international principles aimed at eliminating racism.

Every year, thousands of minorities experience the humiliation of being stopped while driving, flying, or even walking simply because of their race, ethnicity or religion. These individuals are not stopped because they have committed a crime, but because of an erroneous assumption that they have committed a crime, simply because of their appearances. The practice fuels and confirms the belief in minority communities that the criminal justice systems and national security policies are unfair, which undermines the trust between the police and the communities they serve.

> *"We are in danger of allowing ourselves to be governed by our fears, rather than our values."*

Racial profiling is opposed by many law enforcement officials, who fear it will not only lead to the targeting of innocent people, but will also prompt security officers to overlook suspicious behavior by those who are not members of a targeted ethnic group. Despite the efforts of some state, local, and federal law enforcement agencies to address racial profiling within their departments, the practice persists and has become more pervasive over the last few years, particularly for the Arab American community.

In June 2003, the Department of Justice issued racial profiling guidelines to address racial profiling, but the guidelines are weak and are insufficient to eliminate racial profiling practices in this country. The guidelines do not apply on the state and local level, where the vast majority of profiling occurs. They require no data collection, which is essential to identifying and stopping profiling, and they lack an enforcement mechanism to end the practice. Unless the government makes racial profiling illegal, it will undoubtedly continue. Federal legislation is key to ending racial profiling in this country. Congress and the American people must step in—now—to preserve the freedoms that have been steadily eroding before and after September 11, 2001. . . .

> *"Congress and the American people must step in—now—to preserve the freedoms that have been steadily eroding before and after September 11, 2001."*

Increasing Inequality

"Equal Justice Under Law" is the motto inscribed above the Supreme Court building, but the legal system's treatment of the Arab and Muslim community in this country since September 11 has been separate, unequal and wrong.

Military detention of both citizen and non-citizen Arab and Muslim terrorism suspects stands in stark contrast to the treatment of homegrown terrorists like Timothy McVeigh [executed in 2001 for the Oklahoma City bombing that killed 168 people and injured hundreds]. Arab and Muslim non-citizens—who enjoy protection under the Constitution no less than citizens—are facing what amounts to an entirely new legal system, with basic due process suspended. Not only do they face potential trial before special military tribunals—with access to counsel and information limited severely, unlike ordinary military courts— but they also can be whisked away without a hearing to face injustice in the legal netherworld of Guantanamo Bay [detention facility in] Cuba, or to detention and interrogation by governments with some of the worst human rights records in the word. . . .

Many more Arab and Muslim non-citizens, who have not faced the harrowing ordeal of detention without due process, had to undergo a demeaning registration process that did more to tarnish America's image abroad, and inhibit international cooperation, than large sums spent on public diplomacy could wash away. Special registration severely exacerbated the problem of unwarranted, discriminatory detentions and selective deportation.

The special registration process did not apply equally to all immigrants and visitors, but rather requires registration, fingerprinting, photographing and questioning only of citizens and nationals of countries within the Arab and Muslim world, as well as North Korea. In December 2002, the INS [Immigration and Naturalization Service] used the first stage of this program to round-up hundreds of Arab and Muslim men on minor immigration infractions, many of which were caused by the INS' own bureaucratic incompetence. The agency detained a full one-quarter of all those who sought to comply with the new requirements at its Los Angeles office. . . .

The Record: Powers Misused, Powers Abused

Serious civil liberties abuses have occurred as a result of both the PATRIOT Act, and other post-9/11 anti-terrorism powers. . . .

Here are just a few examples of the impact of the practices documented by the DOJ's [Department of Justice] own inspector General on the 762 September 11, [2001,] immigration detainees. These examples are similar to the stories of detainees the ACLU interviewed and, in some cases, assisted with habeas corpus petitions:

• Mr. H., a Pakistani, has lived in the United States for the last eighteen years and is the sole provider for his wife and four-year-old son, who is a U.S. citizen. In November 2001, Mr. H was arrested after a co-worker at the hospital where Mr. H. worked as a registered nurse called the FBI to complain about Mr. H. "behaving suspiciously," because the co-worker was concerned with his wearing a surgical mask more than necessary. He was detained at Passaic [New Jersey] County Jail for six months, despite the fact that an immigrant visa that Mr. H had applied for was *granted* six weeks after his arrest in December 2001. In January 2002, Mr. H. was at last "cleared" and in May 2002 he was released on parole.

• Sidina Ould Moustapha, a citizen of Mauritania, arrived in the United States in April 2001 on a valid visitor's visa. On October 11, 2001, Mr. Moustapha was charged with overstaying his visa, and detained at Passaic County Jail. At his immigration hearing on October 30, 2001, the Immigration Judge granted his request to voluntarily leave the country. The INS did not

> *"Arab and Muslim non-citizens . . . are facing what amounts to an entirely new legal system, with basic due process suspended."*

appeal, but continued to detain him for five *months* after the Immigration Judge's order. Throughout this time, Mr. Moustapha could not contact his wife and two young children in Mauritania. Finally, Mr. Moustapha's attorney filed a petition for a writ of habeas corpus, and the INS allowed him to leave.

• After Altin Elezi was arrested by the FBI at his home in Kearney, New Jersey on October 3, 2001, he effectively disappeared. Mr. Elezi's brother, Albert

Elezi, learned about the arrest from neighbors, and desperately contacted government officials to find out where his brother was. After failing to hear from him for two weeks, Albert Elezi hired an attorney for his brother. The attorney contacted government officials who told him Albert Elezi's brother was being held in a detention facility in New York. When the attorney called the facility, however, he was told that Mr. Elezi was not there. The attorney called another detention facility and the Bureau of Prisons "Federal Prisoner Locator" service, but still could not find his new client. Finally, on October 22, 2001, the attorney filed a habeas corpus petition in federal court. Albert Elezi stated in an affidavit ac-

> *"The government has no business prying into the personal lives and the political and religious beliefs of citizens and others who are suspected of no criminal activity."*

companying the petition, "Our entire family has been terrified since the disappearance . . . I respectfully beg this Court [to] allow my brother to visit with his lawyer and his family."

• Asif-Ur-Rehman Saffi, a citizen of France, came to the United States on July 6, 2001. On September 30, 2001, Mr. Saffi was arrested by the INS and charged with working in the United States without authorization. He was held in the most restrictive conditions possible—the administrative maximum special housing unit at the Metropolitan Detention Center [MDC] in New York. In Mr. Saffi's case, as with other September 11 detainees, the Bureau of Prisons deferred to the FBI's "interest" classification for September 11 detainees, abdicating its own internal policies for classifying the security risks presented by detainees in its custody. As a result, garden-variety immigration violators like Mr. Saffi were held in "lockdown" 23 hours a day in cells that were continuously lighted, allowed only a very limited ability to contact attorneys and families; placed in handcuffs, leg irons, and a heavy chain linking the leg irons to the handcuffs for interviews and visitation; and subjected to body-cavity searches after all visits. Mr. Saffi was also subjected to severe physical and verbal abuse. Guards at MDC bent back his thumbs, stepped on his bare feet with their shoes, and pushed him into a wall so hard that he fainted. After Mr. Saffi fell to the floor, they kicked him in the face. The lieutenant in charge told Mr. Saffi that he would be treated harshly because of his supposed involvement in the September 11 attacks. . . .

What Can Be Done

Our government must say yes to responsible anti-terrorism powers by saying no to these excesses. . . .

We . . . strongly support efforts to draft legislation that would end secret detentions and deportations, provide for a meaningful custody hearing before an Immigration Judge and otherwise protect the civil liberties of immigrants.

Much more needs to be done, including restoring the rule of law to military tribunals and detentions, and reining in the use of terrorism powers for non-terrorism cases.

Finally, the ACLU strongly opposes any establishment of a new domestic intelligence gathering agency, separate from the FBI. Such a proposal would further sever government spying from the investigation of criminal wrongdoing, posing serious dangers for civil liberties. The government has no business prying into the personal lives and the political and religious beliefs of citizens and others who are suspected of no criminal activity. The Commission should firmly reject any such proposal.

Immigration Measures Used in the War on Terrorism Have Harmed Civil Liberties

by Muzaffar A. Chishti

About the author: *Muzaffar A. Chishti is the director of the Migration Policy Institute at the New York University School of Law.*

Editor's Note: This viewpoint was originally given as testimony before the U.S. Senate on November 18, 2003.

The devastating [terrorist] attacks of September 11 [2001] demanded a wide-ranging response. The United States has responded with military action, as in [the 2001 invasion of] Afghanistan; through intelligence operations to disrupt [the terrorist group] al Qaeda and arrest its members; and by re-organizing homeland security.

But our new security measures must be effective rather than merely dramatic, and must not destroy what we are trying to defend. The government's post–September 11 immigration measures have failed these tests.

These actions have not only done great harm to the nation; they have also been largely ineffective in their stated goal of improving our domestic security. Despite the government's heavy-handed immigration tactics, many of the September 11 terrorists would probably be admitted to the United States today [2003].

Al Qaeda's hijackers were carefully chosen to avoid detection: all but two were educated young men from middle-class families with no criminal records and no known connection to terrorism. To apprehend such individuals before they attack requires a laser-like focus on the gathering, sharing and analysis of intelligence, working hand-in-glove with well-targeted criminal and immigration law enforcement.

Muzaffar A. Chishti, testimony before the U.S. Senate on the Judiciary, Washington, DC, November 18, 2003.

Instead, the government conducted roundups of individuals based on their national origin and religion. These roundups failed to locate terrorists, and damaged one of our great potential assets in the war on terrorism: the communities of Arab- and Muslim-Americans.

We believe it is possible both to defend our nation and to protect core American values and principles, but doing so requires a different approach. It is too easy to say that if we abandon our civil liberties the terrorists win. It is just as easy to say that without security there will be little room for liberty. What is hard is to take both arguments with equal seriousness and to integrate them within a single framework. We set out to reach that important balance in our report.

[We are] convinced that more than security and civil liberties—that is, the rights of individuals—are at stake. There is a third element: the character of the nation. Our humblest coin, the penny, bears the words *e pluribus unum*, or "from many, one." The phrase goes to the heart of our identity as a nation and to the strength we derive from diversity. We strongly believe that fully embracing Muslim and Arab communities as part of the larger American society would not only serve this American value but help break the impasse between security and liberty, strengthening both. . . .

Government Immigration Actions
Threaten Fundamental Civil Liberties

The U.S. government has imposed some immigration measures more commonly associated with totalitarian regimes. . . . There have been too many instances of long-time U.S. residents deprived of their liberty without due process of law, detained by the government and held without charge, denied effective access to legal counsel, or subjected to closed hearings. These actions violate bedrock principles of U.S. law and society.

Take the experience of Tarek Mohamed Fayad, an Egyptian dentist arrested in southern California on Sept. 13, 2001, for violating his student visa. During Fayad's first 10 days of incarceration he was not allowed to make any telephone calls. Thereafter, he was allowed sporadic "legal" calls and only a single "social" call per month. The "legal" call was placed by a Bureau of Prisons counselor either to a designated law office or to one of the organizations on the INS's [Immigration and Naturalization Service's] list of organizations providing free legal services in the region. The privilege of making a call was deemed satisfied once the call was placed, regardless of whether the

> *"Our new security measures must be effective rather than merely dramatic, and must not destroy what we are trying to defend."*

call was answered. Of the agencies on the list provided to Fayad, only one number was a working contact for an agency providing legal counseling to detainees and none of the organizations agreed to provide representation. In the meantime, Fayad's friends had hired an attorney for him, but the attorney was unable to determine his location for more than a month. Even after the attorney found out that Fayad was being detained at a federal facility in New York, the Bureau of Prisons continued to deny having Fayad in custody.

Rather than relying on individualized suspicion or intelligence-driven criteria, the government has used national origin as a proxy for evidence of dangerousness. By targeting specific ethnic groups with its new measures, the government has violated another core principle of American justice: the Fifth Amendment guarantee of equal protection.

> *"Fully embracing Muslim and Arab communities as part of the larger American society would . . . help break the impasse between security and liberty, strengthening both."*

The government also conducted a determined effort to hide the identity, number and whereabouts of its detainees, violating the First Amendment's protection of the public's right to be informed about government actions. This right is at the heart of our democracy, and is crucial to maintaining government accountability to the public.

The government's post-September 11 actions follow a repeating pattern in American history of rounding up immigrant groups during national security crises, a history we review as part of our report. Like the internment of Japanese-Americans during World War II, the deportation of Eastern-European immigrants during the [Communist] Red Scare of 1919–20, and the harassment and internment of German-Americans during World War I, these actions will come to be seen as a stain on America's heritage as a nation of immigrants and a land where individual rights are valued and protected.

Government Secrecy

More than 1,200 people—the government has refused to say exactly how many, who they are, or what has happened to all of them—were detained after September 11. Despite the government's determined efforts to shroud these actions in secrecy, as part of our research we were able to obtain information about 406 of these detainees. . . .

• Unlike the hijackers, the majority of non-citizens detained since September 11 had significant ties to the United States and roots in their communities. Of the detainees for whom relevant information was available, over 46 percent had been in the United States at least six years. Almost half had spouses, children, or other family relationships in the United States.

• Even in an immigration system known for its systemic problems, the post–September 11 detainees suffered exceptionally harsh treatment. Many were detained for weeks or months without charge or after a judge ordered them released. Of the detainees for whom such information was available, nearly 52 percent were subject to an "FBI hold," keeping them detained after a judge released them or ordered them removed from the United States. More than 42 percent of detainees were denied the opportunity to post bond. Many of the detainees were subjected to solitary confinement, 24-hour lighting of cells and physical abuse.

• Although detainees in theory had the legal right to secure counsel at their own expense and to contact family members and consular representatives, the government frequently denied them these rights, especially in the first weeks after September 11.

• Many of the detainees were incarcerated because of profiling by ordinary citizens, who called government agencies about neighbors, coworkers and strangers based on their ethnicity, religion, name or appearance. In Louisville, Ky., the FBI and INS detained 27 Mauritanians after an outpouring of tips from the public; these included a tip from a suspicious neighbor who called the FBI when a delivery service dropped off a box with Arabic writing on it.

In New York, a man studying airplane design at the New York Institute of Technology went to a Kinko's store to make copies of airplane photos. An employee went into the wastebasket to get his information and then called the FBI; after nearly two months in detention, he accepted voluntary departure. Nearly 28 percent of the detainees were arrested because of a tip to the authorities by private citizens.

Most importantly, immigration arrests based upon tips, sweeps and profiling have not resulted in any terrorism-related convictions against these detainees. Of the four detainees in our sample who had terrorism-related charges brought against them, all four were arrested based on traditional investigative techniques, not as the result of immigration enforcement initiatives. One has since been convicted and two have been acquitted; charges were dropped against the fourth individual and he was deported.

Undermining National Unity

The government's actions against Arabs and Muslims have terrified and alienated hard-working communities across the nation.

President [George W.] Bush's visit to a Washington mosque shortly after September 11 had a temporary positive impact on Arab- and Muslim-American communities. But the subsequent failure of government leaders to speak out on a sustained basis against discrimination, coupled with the Justice Department's aggressive immigration initiatives, sent a message to individuals and companies that discrimination against Arabs and Muslims was acceptable, leaders of these communities said. These views emerged in a coast-to-coast series of interviews that the Migration Policy Institute con-

> *"The U.S. government has imposed some immigration measures more commonly associated with totalitarian regimes."*

ducted to gauge the impact of the crisis on Arab- and Muslim-Americans.

"September 11 has created an atmosphere which suggests that it is okay to be biased against Arab-Americans and Muslims," said a regional director of an Arab-American civil rights organization.

The Justice Department's decision to conduct closed immigration proceedings for many of the detainees only increased suspicion that Arab- and Muslim-Americans were being treated under a different standard of due process. "The automatic association with terrorism is present in all these proceedings," said a prominent Arab-American lawyer in Michigan.

"Even in an immigration system known for its systemic problems, the post–September 11 detainees suffered exceptionally harsh treatment."

There is a strong belief among Arab- and Muslim-Americans that these measures are ineffective in responding to threats of terrorism, but are being undertaken for political expediency or public relations at a huge price to their communities. "This is political smoke to make people feel good," said the spokesman of a national Arab-American organization.

In a striking consensus, however, many leaders of the community have developed a positive reaction to law enforcement agencies since September 11, especially to local police. "The local police are our friends," said the chief imam of a New York Islamic center, citing their constant presence to protect his mosque.

Discrimination in the workplace soared after September 11. So overwhelming was the number of complaints it received that the Equal Employment Opportunity Commission (EEOC) created a new category to track acts of discrimination against Middle Eastern, Muslim and South Asian workers after September 11. In the 15 months between Sept. 11, 2001, and Dec. 11, 2002, the EEOC received 705 such complaints. Many more went unreported. And to add insult to injury, some of those who were detained after September 11 have been fired by their employers as a result. . . .

International Consequences of U.S. Actions

Unfortunately, U.S. actions since September 11 have encouraged foreign governments to restrict their citizens' freedoms in the name of security. There is now growing evidence that governments in many parts of Europe, Central Asia, Africa, South Asia, and the Far East have either adopted new measures, or amplified existing legislations, to give police wide powers to investigate, search and detain suspects. Detention for long periods of time without trial is becoming more common, as is monitoring electronic communications and commercial transactions.

Similarly, torture of political prisoners and summary executions have intensified after September 11, according to a number of investigative reports. The new measures have frequently been used by governments to squelch political dissent. Our government's policies may have even influenced the terminology of new measures. For example, press reports suggest that in Liberia, the now-exiled President Charles Taylor declared three of his critics "illegal combatants", to be tried in a military court.

An Alternative Framework

America's challenge is to meet new security demands while defending and strengthening the civil liberties and national unity that contribute to our great strength as a nation. The terrorist threat demands a reaction that is strong but also smart. The necessary measures may please neither civil libertarians nor those who believe civil liberties are a luxury we can no longer afford.

To meet this challenge, Congress must reassert leadership. Congress has accorded extraordinary deference to the executive branch since September 11. This may have been understandable immediately after the attacks. But in our constitutional system, it is now vital for Congress to assert its policy and oversight role, and to closely monitor the executive branch's use of its expanded domestic security powers.

The primary domestic security responses to terrorism should be strengthened intelligence and analysis, compatible information systems and information-sharing, and vigorous law enforcement and investigations. Improved immigration controls and enforcement can support good antiterrorism enforcement, but they are not enough by themselves.

> *"The government's actions against Arabs and Muslims have terrified and alienated hard-working communities across the nation."*

The broad framework that should guide the nexus between immigration policy and counterterrorism should center on four broad policy imperatives:

• Mobilizing intelligence and information capabilities: More than anything else, September 11 demonstrated the need to dramatically improve the nation's intelligence capabilities. The immigration system captures voluminous amounts of data that can be important in "connecting the dots" about individuals under investigation. But for this to be effective, information from visa and immigration data systems must be fully linked to establish complete immigration histories of visitors and residents, and government agencies must greatly improve their information-sharing and their systems for maintaining watch-lists.

• Protecting the security of air, land and sea borders and beyond: Border enforcement must permit vast numbers of legitimate crossings while identifying and stopping a very small, but potentially lethal, number of wrongdoers. This calls for new systems, infrastructure, and policies rooted in risk management principles that identify reliable people and traffic, so that enforcement officials can concentrate on unknown and high-risk travelers that may constitute security threats.

• Supporting vigorous law enforcement and law enforcement cooperation: Strengthened enforcement of immigration laws can play an important role in combating terrorism. In specific cases, immigration violations and charges may be a method for identifying or developing criminal or terrorism-related charges, just as tax evasion has been used to thwart organized crime. But safeguards must also be established so that violations of immigration status requirements, for example, do not serve as a pretext for avoiding due process requirements.

Tools such as the use of classified information in terrorism prosecutions should be allowed only on a case-by-case basis and only with judicial authorization. Arrests and detentions for immigration violations should be subject to time limits that may be extended, but only in exceptional instances, case-by-case, and with a showing before and authorization from an immigration judge. And individuals detained for immigration violations, who do not now enjoy the right to government-appointed counsel because immigration proceedings are civil matters, should be granted that right when immigration charges result in detention.

• Engaging Arab- and Muslim-American communities: It is crucial for law enforcement to engage Arab- and Muslim-American communities as it works to identify terrorism-related conspiracies, recruitment, and financial networks. This requires cultivating new relationships and building trust. The government should also embrace these communities as bridges of understanding to societies and peoples around the world who are deeply alienated from the United States. . . .

A New System

Unfortunately, by targeting and alienating [Arab and Muslim] communities, the U.S. government's immigration actions since September 11 have deepened the perception abroad that America is anti-Muslim and that its principles are hypocritical. This strengthens the voices of radicals in their drive to recruit followers and expand influence, at the expense of moderates and others more sympathetic to Western philosophies and goals. Thus, in the name of buttressing security, current U.S. immigration policy may be making us more vulnerable to terrorism.

In the post-September 11 era, immigration policy must be part of a new security system in which the measures we take to protect ourselves also help us win the war for hearts and minds around the world. We urge Congress to take action now to help us win that war.

Civil Liberties Have Not Been Compromised by the Patriot Act

by John Ashcroft

About the author: *John Ashcroft served as the attorney general of the United States from 2000 to 2004.*

Editor's Note: The following viewpoint was originally given as a speech at the Federalist Society National Convention on November 15, 2003.

[Since the September 11, 2001, terrorist attacks, there has been] debate about how best to preserve and protect our liberty in the face of a very real terrorist threat.

America has an honored tradition of debate and dissent under the First Amendment. It is an essential piece of our constitutional and cultural fabric. As a former politician, I have heard a few dissents in my time, and even expressed a couple of my own.

The Founders believed debate should enlighten, not just enliven. It should reveal truth, not obscure it. The future of freedom demands that our discourse be based on a solid foundation of facts and a sincere desire for truth. As we consider the direction and destiny of our nation, the friends of freedom must practice for themselves . . . and demand from others . . . a debate informed by fact and directed toward truth.

Take away all the bells and whistles . . . the rhetorical flourishes and occasional vitriol . . . and the current debate about liberty is about the rule of law and the role of law.

"Ordered Liberty"

The notion that the law can enhance, not diminish, freedom is an old one. [Philosopher] John Locke said the end of law is, quote, ". . . not to abolish or

John Ashcroft, prepared remarks before the Federalist Society National Convention, November 15, 2003.

restrain but to preserve and enlarge freedom." George Washington called this, "ordered liberty."

There are some voices in this discussion of how best to preserve freedom that reject the idea that law can enhance freedom. They think that passage and enforcement of any law is necessarily an infringement of liberty.

Ordered liberty is the reason that we are the most open and the most secure society in the world. Ordered liberty is a guiding principle, not a stumbling block to security.

> *"The [Patriot] Act uses court-tested safeguards and time-honored ideas to aid the war against terrorism, while protecting the rights and lives of citizens."*

When the first societies passed and enforced the first laws against murder, theft and rape, the men and women of those societies unquestionably were made more free.

A test of a law, then, is this: does it honor or degrade liberty? Does it enhance or diminish freedom?

The Founders provided the mechanism to protect our liberties and preserve the safety and security of the Republic: the Constitution. It is a document that safeguards security, but not at the expense of freedom. It celebrates freedom, but not at the expense of security. It protects us *and* our way of life.

Since September 11, 2001, the Department of Justice has fought for, Congress has created, and the judiciary has upheld, legal tools that honor the Constitution . . . legal tools that are making America safer while enhancing American freedom.

It is a compliment to all who worked on the Patriot Act to say that it is not constitutionally innovative. The Act uses court-tested safeguards and time-honored ideas to aid the war against terrorism, while protecting the rights and lives of citizens.

[Former U.S. president James] Madison noted in 1792 that the greatest threat to our liberty was centralized power. Such focused power, he wrote, is liable to abuse. That is why he concluded a distribution of power into separate departments is a first principle of free governments.

The Patriot Act honors Madison's "first principles" . . . giving each branch of government a role in ensuring both the lives and liberties of our citizens are protected. The Patriot Act grants the executive branch critical tools in the war on terrorism. It provides the legislative branch extensive oversight. It honors the judicial branch with court supervision over the Act's important powers.

Tools for the Executive Branch

First, the executive branch.

At the Department of Justice, we are dedicated to detecting, disrupting, and dismantling the networks of terror before they can strike at our nation. In the past two years [since 2001] no major terrorist attack has been perpetrated on our soil.

Consider the bloodshed by terrorism elsewhere in that time:
• Women and children slaughtered in Jerusalem;
• Innocent, young lives snuffed out in Indonesia;
• Saudi citizens savaged in Riyadh;
• Churchgoers in Pakistan murdered by the hands of hate.

We are using the tough tools provided in the USA Patriot Act to defend American lives and liberty from those who have shed blood and decimated lives in other parts of the world.

The Patriot Act does three things:

First, it closes the gaping holes in law enforcement's ability to collect vital intelligence information on terrorist enterprises. It allows law enforcement to use proven tactics long used in the fight against organized crime and drug dealers.

Second, the Patriot Act updates our anti-terrorism laws to meet the challenges of new technology and new threats.

Third, with these critical new investigative tools provided by the Patriot Act, law enforcement can share information and cooperate better with each other. From prosecutors to intelligence agents, the Act allows law enforcement to "connect the dots" and uncover terrorist plots before they are launched.

Success Due to the Patriot Act

Here is an example of how we use the Act. Some of you are familiar with the Iyman Faris case. He is a naturalized American citizen who worked as a truck driver out of Columbus, Ohio. Using information sharing allowed under the Patriot Act, law enforcement pieced together Faris's activities:
• How Faris met senior Al Qaeda operatives in a training camp in Afghanistan.
• How he was asked to procure equipment that might cause train derailments and sever suspension systems of bridges.
• How he traveled to New York to scout a potential terrorist target.

Faris pleaded guilty on May 1, 2003, and on October 28, he was sentenced under the Patriot Act's tough sentences. He will serve 20 years in prison for providing material support

> *"The Patriot Act provides for close judicial supervision of the executive branch's use of Patriot Act authorities."*

to Al Qaeda and conspiracy for providing the terrorist organization with information about possible U.S. targets for attack.

The Faris case illustrates what the Patriot Act does. One thing the Patriot Act does not do is allow the investigation of individuals, quote, ". . . solely upon the basis of activities protected by the first amendment to the Constitution of the United States."

Even if the law did not prohibit it, the Justice Department has neither the time nor the inclination to delve into the reading habits or other First Amendment activities of our citizens.

Despite all the hoopla to the contrary, for example, the Patriot Act . . . which allows for court-approved requests for business records, including library records . . . has never been used to obtain records from a library. Not once.

> *"We are protecting the American people while honoring the Constitution and preserving the liberties we hold dear."*

Senator Dianne Feinstein recently said, quote, "I have never had a single abuse of the Patriot Act reported to me. My staff e-mailed the ACLU [American Civil Liberties Union] and asked them for instances of actual abuses. They e-mailed back and said they had none."

The Patriot Act has enabled us to make quiet, steady progress in the war on terror.

Since September 11, was have dismantled terrorist cells in Detroit, Seattle, Portland, Tampa, Northern Virginia, and Buffalo.

We have disrupted weapons procurement plots in Miami, San Diego, Newark, and Houston.

We have shut down terrorist-affiliated charities in Chicago, Dallas and Syracuse.

We have brought criminal charges against 286 individuals. We have secured convictions or guilty pleas from 155 people.

Terrorists who are incarcerated, deported or otherwise neutralized threaten fewer American lives. For two years, our citizens have been safe. There have been no major terrorist attacks on our soil. American freedom has been enhanced, not diminished. The Constitution has been honored, not degraded.

Legislative Oversight

Second, the role Congress plays.

In six weeks of debate in September and October of 2001, both the House of Representatives and the Senate examined studiously and debated vigorously the merits of the Patriot Act. In the end, both houses supported overwhelmingly its passage.

Congress built into the Patriot Act strict and structured oversight of the Executive Branch. Every six months, the Justice Department provides Congress with reports of its activities under the Patriot Act.

Since September 24, 2001, Justice Department officials, myself included, have testified on the Patriot Act and other homeland security issues more than 115 times. We have responded to hundreds of written and oral questions and provided reams of written responses.

To date, no congressional committee has found any evidence that law enforcement has abused the powers provided by the Patriot Act.

Legislative oversight of the executive branch is critical to "ordered liberty." It ensures that laws and those who administer them respect the rights and liberties of the citizens.

There has not been a major terrorist attack within our borders in the past two years. Time and again, Congress has found the Patriot Act to be effective against terrorist threats, and respectful and protective of citizens' liberties. The Constitution has been honored, not degraded.

Additional Protection Through Judicial Supervision

Finally, the judiciary.

The Patriot Act provides for close judicial supervision of the executive branch's use of Patriot Act authorities.

The Act allows the government to utilize many long-standing, well-accepted law enforcement tools in the fight against terror. These tools include delayed notification, judicially-supervised searches, and so-called roving wiretaps, which have long been used in combating organized crime and in the war on drugs.

In using these tactics to fight terrorism, the Patriot Act includes an *additional* layer of protection for individual liberty. A federal judge supervises the use of each of these tactics.

Were we to seek an order to request business records, that order would need the approval of a federal judge. Grand jury subpoenas issued for similar requests by police in standard criminal investigations are issued without judicial oversight.

Throughout the Patriot Act, tools provided to fight terrorism require that the same predication be established before a federal judge as with similar tools provided to fight other crime.

In addition, the Patriot Act includes yet another layer of judicial scrutiny by providing a civil remedy in the event of abuse. Section 223 of the Patriot Act allows citizens to seek monetary damages for willful violations of the Patriot Act. This civil remedy serves as a further deterrent against infringement upon individual liberties.

> *"Again and again, Congress has determined and the courts have determined that our citizens' rights have been respected."*

Given our overly litigious society, you are probably wondering how many such civil cases have been filed to date. It is a figure as astronomical as the library searches. Zero.

There is a simple reason for this . . . the Patriot has *not* been used to infringe upon individual liberty.

Many of you have heard the hue and cry from critics of the Patriot Act who allege that liberty has been eroded. But more telling is what you have not heard. You have not heard of one single case in which a judge has found an abuse of the Patriot Act because, again, *there have been no abuses.*

It is also important to consider what we have not *seen* . . . no major terrorist attacks on our soil over the past two years.

The Patriot Act's record demonstrates that we are protecting the American people while honoring the Constitution and preserving the liberties we hold dear.

While we are discussing the judiciary, allow me to add one more point. To be at its best, the judiciary requires a full bench. This is not like football or basketball, where the bench consists of reserves who might not see action. The judicial bench, to operate best for the people, must be at full strength.

Let me say this . . . President [George W.] Bush has performed his duties admirably in selecting and nominating highly qualified jurists to serve.

The language in a judge's commission reads, and I quote, "George W. Bush, President of the United States of America . . . to all who shall see this, presents greeting: Know ye that reposing special confidence and trust in the wisdom, uprightness and learning, I have nominated . . . ", you can fill in the blank, with the name Janice Rogers Brown, or Bill Pryor, or Priscilla Owen, or Carolyn Kuhl [Cool].

The commission's language may seem anachronistic. The ideals the men and women of the bench must uphold are not: Wisdom. Uprightness. Learning.

The president's nominees personify those noble ideals. They are proven defenders of the rule of law. They should be treated fairly. They deserve to be treated with the dignity that befits the position to which they seek to serve our country and its citizens.

The Power of Freedom

You may think that some of the best of the president's nominees are being treated unfairly. In that case, *you* may want to exercise your right to dissent. The future of freedom and the rule of law depend on citizens informed by fact and directed toward truth.

To be sure, the law depends on the integrity of those who make it, enforce it, and apply it. It depends on the moral courage of lawyers . . . and our citizens . . . to insist on being heard, whether in town hall meetings, county council meetings, or the Senate.

There is nothing more noble than fighting to preserve our God-given rights. Our proven tactics against the terrorist threat are helping to do just that.

For more than two years, we have protected the lives of our citizens here at home. Again and again, Congress has determined and the courts have determined that our citizens' rights have been respected.

Twenty-six months ago, terrorists attacked our nation thinking our liberties were our weakness.

They were wrong. The American people have fulfilled the destiny shaped by our forefathers and founders, and revealed the power of freedom.

Time and again, the spirit of our nation has been renewed and our greatness as a people has been strengthened by our dedication to the cause of liberty, the rule of law and the primacy and dignity of the individual.

I know we will keep alive these noble aspirations that lie in the hearts of all our fellow citizens, and for which our young men and women are at this moment fighting and making the ultimate sacrifice.

What we are defending is what generations before us fought for and defended: a nation that is a standard, a beacon, to all who desire a land that promises to uphold the best hopes of all mankind. A land of justice. A land of liberty.

Using Military Tribunals to Try Suspected Terrorists Is Not a Violation of Civil Liberties

by Pierre-Richard Prosper

About the author: *Pierre-Richard Prosper is the ambassador-at-large for war crimes issues in the U.S. Department of State.*

Editor's Note: This viewpoint was originally given as congressional testimony on December 4, 2001.

After the tragic events of September 11th, we as a nation were forced to re-examine our traditional notions of security, our conceptions of our attackers, and our approaches to bringing the perpetrators to justice. The conventional view of terrorism as isolated acts of egregious violence did not fit. The [September 11, 2001, terrorist attacks] committed by the al Qaida [terrorist] organization at the World Trade Center in New York, at the headquarters of our Department of Defense, and in Pennsylvania were of the kind that defied the imagination and shocked the conscience.

These atrocities are just as premeditated, just as systematic, just as evil as the violations of international humanitarian law that I have seen around the world. As the President's [November 13, 2001, order allowing the military trial of suspected terrorists] recognizes, we must call these attacks by their rightful name: war crimes.

President [George W.] Bush recognized that the threat we currently face is as grave as any we have confronted. While combating these war crimes committed against U.S. citizens, it is important that the President be able to act in the interest of this country to protect the security of our citizens and ensure that justice

Pierre-Richard Prosper, testimony before the U.S. Senate Committee on the Judiciary, Washington, DC, December 4, 2001.

is achieved. He has repeatedly promised to use all the military, diplomatic, economic and legal options available to ensure the safety of the American people and our democratic way of life. The President should have the full range of options available for addressing these wrongs. The Military Order adds additional arrows to the President's quiver.

Should we be in a position to prosecute [terrorist leader Osama] Bin Laden, his top henchmen, and other members of al Qaida, this option should be available to protect our civilian justice system against this organization of terror. We should all ask ourselves whether we want to bring into the domestic system dozens of persons who have proved they are willing to murder thousands of Americans at a time and die in the process.

> *"Because military commissions are empowered to try violations of the law of war, their jurisdiction is dependent upon the existence of an armed conflict, which we have."*

We all must think about the safety of the jurors, who may have to be sequestered from their families for up to a year or more while a complex trial unfolds. We all ought to remember the employees in the civilian courts, such as the bailiff, court clerk, and court reporter and ask ourselves whether this was the type of service they signed up for—to be potential victims of terror while justice was pursued. And we all must think also about the injured city of New York and the security implications that would be associated with a trial of the al Qaida organization.

With this security threat in mind, we should consider the option of military commissions from two perspectives. First, the President's Military Order is consistent with the precepts of international law. And second, military commissions are the customary legal option for bringing to justice the perpetrators of war crimes during times of war.

The Military Order's conclusion that we are in a state of armed conflict deserves comment. Because military commissions are empowered to try violations of the law of war, their jurisdiction is dependent upon the existence of an armed conflict, which we have.

War Crimes

It is clear that this series of attacks against the United States is more than isolated and sporadic acts of violence, or other acts of a similar nature. Rather, a foreign, private terrorist network, with the essential harboring and other support of the Taliban-led Afghanistan,[1] has issued a declaration of war against the United States. It has organized, campaigned, trained, and over the course of years repeatedly carried out cowardly, indiscriminate attacks, including the

---

1. The Taliban is an Islamist group that ruled most of Afghanistan from 1996 until 2001. In 2001 it was removed from power by the United States, who accused it of supporting al Qaida.

largest attack in history against the territory of the United States in terms of number of persons killed and property damage.

Tracing the criminal history of the organization further confirms the state of armed conflict. A decade's worth of hostile statements by Bin Laden over and over and over again state that he is at war against the United States. He has instructed his followers to kill each and every American civilian. We should also consider the intensity of the hostilities and the systematic nature of the assaults. Consider the fact that al Qaida is accused of bombing the World Trade Center in 1993 and attacking U.S. military service personnel serving in Somalia in the same year. Consider that Bin Laden and al Qaida are accused of attacking and bombing our embassies in Nairobi, Kenya and Dar es Salaam, Tanzania. Remember that al Qaida is accused of perpetrating last year's [2000] bombing of the U.S.S. Cole. And of course, added to this history are the horrifying and unprovoked air assaults on the twin towers in New York, the Pentagon, and the airplane tragedy in Pennsylvania.

It is clear that the conduct of al Qaida cannot be considered ordinary domestic crimes, and the perpetrators are not common criminals. Indeed, one needs to look no further than the international reaction to understand that September 11 was perceived as an armed attack on the United States. NATO [North Atlantic Treaty Organization]'s North Atlantic Council declared that the attack was directed from abroad and "regarded as an action covered by Article V of the Washington Treaty, which states that an armed attack

> *"It is clear that the conduct of al Qaida cannot be considered ordinary domestic crimes, and the perpetrators are not common criminals."*

against one or more of the Allies in Europe or North America shall be considered an attack against them all." The Organization of American States, Australia and New Zealand activated parallel provisions in their mutual defense treaties. UN [United Nations] Security Council Resolutions 1368 and 1373 recognized our inherent right to exercise self-defense. And UN Security Council Resolution 1377 added: "acts of international terrorism constitute one of the most serious threats to international peace and security in the twenty-first century."

Unlawful Combatants

We can also look at our domestic response, including the joint resolution passed by this Congress authorizing "the use of all necessary and appropriate force" in order to prevent any future acts of international terrorism. . . .

We are at war, an unconventional war conducted by unconventional means by an unprecedented aggressor. Under long established legal principles, the right to conduct armed conflict, lawful belligerency, is reserved only to states and recognized armed forces or groups under responsible command. Private persons lacking the basic indicia of organization and the ability or willingness to conduct operations in accordance with the laws of armed conflict have no legal right to wage warfare against a state. In waging war the participants become unlawful combatants.

Because the members of al Qaida do not meet the criteria to be lawful combatants under the law of war, they have no right to engage in armed conflict and are unlawful combatants. And because their intentional targeting and killing of civilians in time of international armed conflict amount to war crimes, military commissions are available for adjudicat-

> *"Because the members of al Qaida do not meet the criteria to be lawful combatants under the law of war, they have no right to engage in armed conflict."*

ing their specific violations of the laws of war. As the U.S. Supreme Court unanimously stated in *Ex Parte Quirin*: "by universal agreement and practice, the law of war draws a distinction between the armed forces and the peaceful populations of belligerent nations, and also between those who are lawful and unlawful combatants. Lawful combatants are subject to capture and detention as prisoners of war by opposing military forces. Unlawful combatants are likewise subject to capture and detention, but, in addition, they are subject to trial and punishment by military tribunals for acts which render their belligerency unlawful."

In this campaign against terrorism, it is important that the President have the full range of available forums for seeking criminal accountability against persons for their individual and command responsibility for violations of the law of war. The military commission provides a traditionally available mechanism to address these unconventional crimes.

A History of Military Commissions

Military commissions have been utilized and legally accepted throughout our history to prosecute persons who violate the laws of war. They were used by General Winfield Scott during his operations in Mexico, in the Civil War by President [Abraham] Lincoln, and in 1942 by President [Franklin D.] Roosevelt. They are an internationally accepted practice with deep historical roots. The international community has utilized military commissions and tribunals to achieve justice, most notably at Nuremberg and in the Far East. The tribunals which tried most of the leading perpetrators of Nazi and Japanese war crimes were military tribunals. These tribunals were followed by thousands of Allied prosecutions of the lower-level perpetrators under the Control Council Law No. 10.

By the end of 1958, the Western Allies had used military tribunals to sentence 5,025 Germans for war crimes. In the Far East, 4,200 Japanese were convicted before military tribunals convened by U.S., Australian, British, Chinese, Dutch, and French forces for their atrocities committed during the war.

Today [in 2001], the commissions as envisioned by the President in the Military

Order, while different from those found in our Article III courts, are in conformity with these historical precedents and the world's current efforts to prosecute war crimes through the United Nations in the International Criminal Tribunals for the Former Yugoslavia and Rwanda. To understand this it may be helpful for me to articulate the commonalities. Like its predecessors, in the Nuremberg and Far East International Military Tribunals, the Allied Control Council Law No. 10 proceedings, and the International Criminal Tribunals for the former Yugoslavia and Rwanda, the judges sit as both triers of law and of fact. In addition, decisions such as judicial orders, judgments, and sentences are reached by a majority vote and not unanimity. Evidence of a probative value is admitted. And in the United Nations International Criminal Tribunals for the former Yugoslavia and Rwanda, portions of the proceedings have been and are authorized to be closed, just as is contemplated by the President's military order. . . .

Since September 11th [2001] I have also been asked why we do not create an international tribunal? In our view, the international practice should be to support sovereign states seeking justice domestically when it is feasible and would be credible. . . . International tribunals are not and should not be the courts of first redress, but of last resort. When domestic justice is not possible for egregious war crimes due to a failed state or a dysfunctional judicial system, the international community may through the Security Council or by consent, step in on an ad hoc basis. . . . That is not the case in the United States.

Our goal should be and this administration's policy is to encourage states to pursue credible justice rather than abdicating the responsibility. Because justice and the administration of justice are a cornerstone of any democracy, pursuing accountability for war crimes while respecting the rule of law by a sovereign state must be encouraged at all times. The President understands our sovereign responsibility and has taken action to fulfill his duty to the American people. In creating an additional option, the nation is now prepared and will have an additional forum to address these wrongs when needed.

Racial Profiling Is Justified to Fight Terrorism

by Mark Steyn

About the author: *Mark Steyn is a columnist for London's* Daily Telegraph *and the* Spectator.

New Hampshire

When political correctness [PC] got going in the Eighties, the laconic wing of the conservative movement was inclined to be relaxed about it. To be sure, the tendency of previously pithy identity labels to become ever more polysyllabically ornate ('person of colour', 'Native American') was time-consuming, but otherwise PC was surely harmless. Some distinguished persons of non-colour, among them [writer] Sir Peregrine Worsthorne, even argued that conservatives should support political correctness as merely the contemporary version of old-fashioned courtliness and good manners.

Alas, after [the 11 September 2001 terrorist attacks] this position seems no longer tenable. Instead, we have to ask a more basic question: does political correctness kill?

Consider the extraordinary memo sent . . . by FBI agent Coleen Rowley to the agency's director Robert Mueller, and now [in 2002], despite his best efforts, all over *Time* magazine. Ms Rowley works out of the Minneapolis field office, whose agents, last 16 August [2001] took action to jail a French citizen of Middle Eastern origin. Zacarias Moussaoui had shown up at a Minnesota flight school and shelled out 8,000 bucks in cash in order to learn how to fly 747s, except for the landing and take-off bit, which he said he'd rather skip. On investigation, he proved to have overstayed his visa and so was held on an immigration violation. Otherwise, he would have been the 20th hijacker, and, so far as one can tell, on board United Flight 93, the fourth plane, the one which crashed in a Pennsylvania field en route, as we now know, to the White House. In Mr Moussaoui's more skilled hands—Flight 93 wound up with the runt of Osama's litter—it might well have reached its target.

Ms Rowley and her colleagues established that Moussaoui was on a French intelligence watch list, had ties to radical Islamist groups, was known to have recruited young Muslims to fight in Chechnya, and had been in Afghanistan and Pakistan immediately before arriving in the US. They wanted to search his computer, but to do that they needed the OK from HQ [headquarters]. Washington was not only uncooperative, but set about, in the words of Ms Rowley's memo, 'thwarting the Minneapolis FBI agents' efforts', responding to field-office requests with ever lamer brush-offs. How could she be sure it was the same guy? There could be any number of Frenchmen called 'Zacarias Moussaoui'. She checked the Paris phone book which listed only one. After 11 September, when the Minneapolis agents belatedly got access to Moussaoui's computer, they found among other things the phone number of Mohammed Atta's room-mate.[1]

> *"Alas, after [the 11 September 2001 terrorist attacks] . . . we have to ask a . . . basic question: does political correctness kill?"*

Fear of Ethnic Profiling

What was the problem at HQ? According to the *New York Time*'s William Safire, 'Intimidated by the brouhaha about supposed ethnic profiling of Wen Ho Lee, lawyers at [U.S. attorney general] John Ashcroft's Justice Department wanted no part of going after this Arab'. Wen Ho Lee was a Taiwan-born scientist at Los Alamos [National Laboratory] accused of leaking nuclear secrets to the Chinese and arrested in 1999. His lawyers mobilised the Asian-American lobby, his daughter embarked on a coast-to-coast speaking tour, and pretty soon the case had effectively collapsed, leaving the Feds with headlines like 'Investigator Denies Lee Was Victim of Racial Bias' (the *San Francisco Chronicle*).

This was during an election campaign in which [former U.S. vice president] Al Gore was promising that his first act as president would be to sign an executive order forbidding police from pulling over African-Americans for 'driving while black'. Dr Lee had been arrested, wrote the columnist Lars-Erik Nelson, for 'working in a nuclear weapons laboratory while Chinese'. In August 2001, invited to connect the dots on the Moussaoui file, Washington bureaucrats foresaw only scolding editorials about 'flying while Arab'.

Example number two: another memo from last summer [2001], this time the so-called 'Phoenix memo' sent by Kenneth Williams. This is Kenneth Williams the crack FBI Arizona agent, not Kenneth Williams of [the film] *Carry On Up the Khyber* fame, though in the end it might just as well have been. Agent Williams filed a report on an alarming trend he'd spotted and, just to make sure you didn't have to plough through a lot of stuff to get to the meat, the Executive

---

1. Mohammed Atta was one of the September 11 hijackers.

Summary at the top of the memo read, '[terrorist leader] Usama bin Laden and Al-Muhjiroun [British extremist Islamic group] supporters attending civil aviation universities/colleges in Arizona'.) . . .

FBI director Mueller was asked why the Bureau had declined to act on the memo. He said, 'There are more than 2,000 aviation academies in the United States. The latest figure I think I heard is something like 20,000 students attending them. And it was perceived that this would be a monumental undertaking without any specificity as to particular persons'.

A 'monumental undertaking'? OK, there are 20,000 students. Eliminate all the women, discount Irv Goldbloom of Queens and Gord MacDonald of Winnipeg and Stiffy Farquahar-ffarquahar of Little Blandford-on-the-Smack and just concentrate on fellows with names like . . . oh, I dunno, Mohammed, and Waleed, and Ahmed. How many would that be? 150? 200? Say it's 500. Is Mueller really saying that the FBI with all its resources cannot divert ten people to go through 2,000 names apiece and pull out the ones worth running through the computer?

Well, yes, officially, he is. But what he really means is not that the Bureau lacked 'any specificity as to particular persons', but that the specificity itself was the problem. In August 2001, no FBI honcho was prepared to fire off a memo saying 'Check out the Arabs'.

On 15 September [2001] Robert Mueller said, 'The fact that there were a number of individuals that happened to have received training at

> *"Washington bureaucrats foresaw only scolding editorials about 'flying while Arab'."*

flight schools here is news, quite obviously. If we had understood that to be the case, we would have—perhaps one could have averted this'. Indeed. There weren't a lot of dots to connect. Last summer [2001], within a few weeks of each other, the Phoenix flight-school memo and Moussaoui warrant request landed on the desk of Dave Frasca, head of the FBI's radical-fundamentalist unit. He buried the first, and refused the second.

Rehearsal for 9/11

Example three: On 1 August [2001] James Woods, the motion-picture actor, was flying from Boston to Los Angeles. With him in the first-class cabin were half-a-dozen guys, four of whom were young Middle Eastern men. Woods, like all really good actors, is a keen observer of people, and what he observed as they flew west persuaded him that they were hijackers. The FBI has asked him not to reveal all the details, but he says he asked the flight attendant if he could speak to the pilot. After landing at LAX [Los Angeles International Airport] the crew reported Woods's observations to the Federal Aviation Administration [FAA]. The FAA did . . . nothing. Two of the four were on board the 11 September planes. There are conflicting rumours about the other two. Woods turned out to be sitting in on a rehearsal for the big day.

After 9/11, the standard line was that Osama bin Laden had pulled off an ingenious plan. But he didn't have to be ingenious, just lucky. And he was luckiest of all in that the obviousness of what was happening paradoxically made investigating it all the more problematic. His men aren't that smart—not in the sense of IRA [Irish Republican Army] smart, or [terrorist] Carlos the Jackal smart. The details Woods is permitted to discuss are in themselves very revealing: the four men boarded with no hand luggage. Not a thing. That's what he noticed first. Everyone going on a long flight across a continent takes something: a briefcase, a laptop, a shopping bag with a couple of airport novels, a *Wall Street Journal* or a *Boston Globe.*

But these boys had zip. They didn't use their personal headsets, they declined all food and drink, they did nothing but stare ahead to the cockpit and engage in low murmurs in Arabic. They behaved like conspirators. And Woods was struck by the way they treated the stewardess: 'They literally ignored her like she didn't exist, which is sort of a kind of Taleban,[2] you know, idea of womanhood, as you know, not even a human being'.

So they weren't masters of disguise, adept at blending into any situation. They weren't like the Nazi spies in war movies, urbane and charming in their unaccented English. It apparently never occurred to them to act natural, read *Newsweek*, watch the movie, eat a salad, listen to Lite Rock Favourites of the Seventies, treat the infidel-whore stewardess the way a Westerner would. Everything they did stuck out. But it didn't matter. Because the more they stuck out, the more everyone who mattered was trained not to notice them. The sort of fellows willing to fly aeroplanes into buildings turn out, not surprisingly, to be fairly stupid. But they benefited from an even more profound institutional stupidity. In August 2001, no one at the FBI or FAA or anywhere else wanted to be seen to be noticing funny behaviour by Arabs. In mid-September [2001], I wrote that what happened was a total systemic failure. But, as the memos leak out, one reason for that failure looms ever larger. Thousands of Americans died because of ethnic squeamishness by federal agencies.

But that was before 11 September. Now we know better . . . don't we? The federal government surely wouldn't want to add to that grim body-count . . . would they?

Faintheartedness

Well, here's an easy experiment that any *Spectator* reader can perform while waiting to board at Newark or LaGuardia [airports]. Fifteen of the 19 hijackers were young Saudi males, Osama himself is (was) a youngish Saudi male, and some 80 per cent of all those folks captured in Afghanistan and carted off to Guantanamo [Bay detention facility] turn out to be young Saudi males (though,

2. Islamist group that ruled most of Afghanistan from 1996 until 2001

out of the usual deference to our Saudi friends, the administration is keeping studiously quiet on the last point). So you're at Newark standing in line behind a young Saudi male and an 87-year-old arthritic nun from Des Moines. Who'll be asked to remove his or her shoes? Six out of ten times, it'll be the nun. Three out of ten times, you. One out of ten, Abdumb al-Dumber. Even if this is just for show, what it's showing is profound official faintheartedness.

Norm Mineta, the transportation secretary, is resistent that fairness demands the burden of inconvenience be spread among all ethnic and age-groups. 'Any specificity as to particular persons' is strictly forbidden. Meanwhile, his colleagues have spent the last three weeks assuring us that another catastrophe is now inevitable. 'There will be another terrorist attack', Robert Mueller told the National Association of District Attorneys . . . : 'We will not be able to stop it'.

> *"No one at the FBI or FAA or anywhere else wanted to be seen to be noticing funny behaviour by Arabs."*

We must, I suppose, take him and [Vice President Richard] Cheney and Rummy [U.S. secretary of defense Donald Rumsfeld] and all the rest at their word. They wouldn't scare us if they hadn't done all they believe they can do. So, naturally, the mind turns to all the things they haven't done: as I write [in June 2002], young Saudi males are still arriving at US airports on routinely is-sued student visas. If it lessened the 'inevitability' of that second attack just ever so slightly, wouldn't it be worth declaring a temporary moratorium on Saudi visitors, or at least making their sojourns here extremely rare and highly discretionary? Oh, no. Can't be done.

Dying for Political Correctness

Ask why the Saudis are allowed to kill thousands of Americans and still get the kid-gloves treatment, and you're told the magic word: oil. Here's my an-swer: blow it out your Medicine Hat. The largest source of imported energy for the United States is the Province of Alberta. Indeed, whenever I'm asked how America can lessen its dependence on foreign oil, I say it's simple: annex Al-berta. The Albertans would be up for it, and, to be honest, they're the only as-similable Canadian province, at least from a Republican standpoint. In 1972, the world's total proven oil reserves added up to 550 billion barrels; today, a single deposit of Alberta's tar shales contains more than that. Yet no Albertan government minister or trade representative gets the access in Washington that the Saudis do. No premier of Alberta gets invited to Bush's Crawford ranch. No Albertan bigshot, if you'll forgive the oxymoron, gets [U.S. secretary of state] Colin Powell kissing up to him like 'Crown' 'Prince' Abdullah and 'Prince' Bandar do. In Washington, an Albertan can't get . . . well, I was going to say an Albertan can't get arrested, but funnily enough that's the one thing he can get. While Bush was governor of Texas, he even managed to execute an Albertan, which seems to be more than the administration is likely to do to any Saudis.

So it's not oil, but rather that even targeting so obvious an enemy as the Saudis is simply not politically possible. Cries of 'Islamophobia' and 'racism' would rend the air. The Saudis discriminate against Americans all the time: American Jews are not allowed to enter the 'Kingdom', nor are American Episcopalians who happen to have an Israeli stamp in their passports. But America cannot be seen to take any similar measures, though it has far more compelling reasons to.

James Woods puts it very well: 'Nineteen of 19 killers on 11 September were Arab Muslims—not a Swede among them'. But au contraire, in a world where the EU [European Union] officially chides the BBC [British Broadcasting Corporation] for describing Osama as an 'Islamic fundamentalist', we must pretend that al-Qa'eda contains potentially vast numbers of Swedish agents, many female and elderly. Even after 11 September, we can't revoke the central fiction of multiculturalism—that all cultures are equally nice and so we must be equally nice to them, even if they slaughter large numbers of us and announce repeatedly their intention to slaughter more. *National Review*'s John Derbyshire calls this 'the reductio ad absurdum of racial sensitivity: better dead than rude'.

Last October [2001], urging Congress to get tough on the obvious suspects, the leggy blonde commentatrix Ann Coulter declared, 'Americans aren't going to die for political correctness'.

They already have.

Chapter 4

Has the Battle Against Terrorism Been Successful?

CURRENT CONTROVERSIES

Chapter Preface

In October 2001 letters containing anthrax powder were mailed to three news organizations and two members of Congress. Five people died after inhaling the deadly anthrax spores, and seventeen became sick. Thousands of others who feared exposure, including many postal workers, took courses of antibiotics. Across the country, anxiety about bioterrorism was high, and some people hoarded antibiotics and purchased gas masks and hazardous-materials suits. While the 2001 mailings resulted in only five deaths, they showed how vulnerable America was to a bioterrorist attack. Since then, as part of its war on terrorism, the United States has taken a variety of actions to guard against the possibility of a future attack. However, there is widespread concern that America is still extremely vulnerable.

While it may be impossible to completely eliminate the possibility of such an attack, the U.S. government claims that America has become more prepared to respond quickly and effectively to bioterrorism. Federal spending for countering bioterrorism has increased dramatically since 2001. According to President George W. Bush, this increase will help make America safer. He argues, "It's money that will enable me to say we're doing everything we can to protect America." Parney Albright, assistant secretary for science and technology at the Department of Homeland Security, argues that the measures America has taken to fight bioterrorism have "certainly made the nation more safe than it was before." Albright states:

> We've mass trained our public health community in their ability to respond to [a bioterrorist attack]. Our colleagues in HHS [U.S. Department of Health and Human Services] have taken their role extraordinarily seriously. We have significant research development efforts to develop new vaccines and medical countermeasures to respond to such an epidemic. We have scenarios in place with which we plan so we can be assured that all the logistics of the structure that you need to have to respond to such a threat can occur. So absolutely, we are far, far better to respond to an epidemic than we were even a short time ago.

However, many people believe that efforts to protect against bioterrorism have not made America safer. Anthony S. Fauci, director of the National Institute of Allergy and Infectious Diseases, uses the anthrax attacks as an example of how easily terrorists could launch a lethal biological attack against America. "It certainly underscored the potential for a mass attack," said Fauci. "If the same amount and grade of anthrax that was in the [Senator Tom] Daschle letter had been put into the ventilation intake system of the Hart Senate Office Building or the Washington Metro or the New York Subway, you would have many, many more deaths. Hundreds, if not thousands of people could have gotten sick." Veronique de Rugy and Charles V. Peña believe that America is still vulnerable to a devastating bioterrorist attack. According to them, "The . . . anthrax cases point to the possibility of a future bioterrorist attack. . . . The nature of terrorism is such that it is impossible to accurately predict the probability of such an attack, but the potential consequences are catastrophic. Therefore, it is a serious threat that deserves serious attention."

The United States recognizes the seriousness of this threat and continues to take action to ensure America's safety. However, there is widespread debate over whether its actions against bioterrorism have actually made the United States safer. The level of threat from bioterrorism is just one part of the debate over America's success in the war on terrorism. The authors in the following chapter offer various perspectives on whether or not America's actions against terrorism have been successful.

The Battle Against Terrorism Has Made America Safer

by Jack Spencer and Ha Nguyen

About the authors: *Jack Spencer is a senior policy analyst for defense and national security, and Ha Nguyen is a research assistant at the Davis Institute for International Studies at the Heritage Foundation in Washington, D.C.*

On the second anniversary of the September 11 [2001, terrorist] attacks, many are asking the question: Are we safer today then we were two years ago? Unfortunately, a simple yes or no answer oversimplifies a complex situation. Therefore, a conditional "yes" is the more appropriate response.

While confronting and engaging terrorism around the world may increase the likelihood of the United States falling victim to another attack in the near-term, this is a necessary risk to ensure the long-term safety of the nation. It is also true, however, that no terrorists have successfully executed a major attack on American soil since 9-11. Of course, that does not mean an attack will not occur tomorrow, but it is indicative of the progress that the nation has made over the past two years.

The United States has essentially instituted a policy of defense at home and offense abroad. America's activities can roughly be placed in two categories: the war on terrorism and homeland security initiatives. In each category, the United States has taken concrete steps that will make the nation safer in the long run if the American government and public remain committed to the monumental task at hand.

The War on Terrorism

The United States, along with a broad coalition of allies, is successfully conducting a global war on terrorism. This war is not only being fought with armed forces, but also with economic, diplomatic, financial and political power. And it is being fueled with intelligence. Victories in the war on terrorism that will make the United State safer include:

Eliminating two of the world's leading state sponsors of terrorism. On September 11, 2001 the Taliban [Islamist group] ruled Afghanistan, and Saddam Hussein ruled Iraq. Today, neither is in power, and the United States is a safer place for that reason. A deadly synergy is created when states like Iraq and Afghanistan choose to work with terrorist groups. States have resources—including territory, finances, an international diplomatic presence, and trade—that non-state actors do not have. On the other hand, non-state actors are able to operate globally and can act largely undetected. The reality of the 21st century is that a state like Iraq could harness its resources to develop a weapon of mass destruction and collude with non-state actors to deliver that weapon. This symbiotic relationship can operate undercover, possibly without the knowledge of the American government. Thus, a state hostile to the United States may appear to be acting within the bounds of acceptable diplomatic behavior while at the same time covertly supporting aggressive endeavors of its non-state allies. This is exactly what both the Taliban and Saddam Hussein's Iraq were doing before they were removed from power.

> *"While it is true that Osama bin Laden's [terrorist organization] al Qaeda still exists, the organization has been disrupted and is on the run."*

Denying terrorist organizations the ability to freely operate. While it is true that Osama bin Laden's [terrorist organization] al Qaeda still exists, the organization has been disrupted and is on the run. Thousands of terrorists have been detained and/or killed over the past two years. These not only include low-level henchman like Richard C. Reid (the so-called shoe-bomber)[1] but also high-level strategists Khalied Shaik Mohammad, Riduan Isamuddin (also known as Hambali), and Uday and Qusay Hussein. Furthermore, the enablers of terrorist activity are also under assault. For example, financial flows that were the life-blood of organizations like al Qaeda are being disrupted; there are far fewer gaping security loopholes that terrorists can exploit. States like Saudi Arabia that have often enabled terrorists—if not outright supported them—can no longer ignore such activity.

America is developing a deterrence strategy appropriate for the threats of the 21st century. Both Osama bin Laden and the Taliban could have predicted that the United States would respond to their attacks, yet they were not deterred. Although terrorists attacked U.S. interests on many occasions prior to that day, and although numerous reports and studies warned of the growing threat of catastrophic terrorism, the United States, for the most part, ignored those warn-

---

1. In December 2001 Reid was arrested for attempting to destroy a passenger airliner by igniting explosives hidden in his shoes.

ings. The prevailing belief was that no state would attack the United States out of fear of the consequences; the activities of worldwide, organized terrorist networks were treated as criminal behavior. On September 11, 2001, however, that policy failed miserably. In response, President [George W.] Bush unveiled the Bush Doctrine, which is founded on the principle that the United States would actively engage, militarily if necessary, rogue nations that support terrorists and develop weapons of mass destruction. The president's description of these states as forming an "Axis of Evil" put the world on alert. While America's anti-terrorist activities in Afghanistan, Africa, the Philippines, and Indonesia have supported this principle, the president's willingness to wage full-scale war with Saddam Hussein's Iraq [in 2003] demonstrated to the world his commitment to uphold this new doctrine. The outcome of this policy is a deterrent that will help compel future states not to directly or indirectly support violence against the United States or its interests.

The United States better understands it own vulnerability. While many successes over the past two years may make America safer, nothing is as important as America's new willingness to understand its own vulnerability. Until September 11, 2001, most Americans and the American government believed that the United States faced no real security dangers. They largely ignored the proliferation of weapons of mass destruction, the spread of ballistic missile technology, the increasingly violent terrorist attacks that were occurring against U.S. interests abroad, and the increasingly belliger-

> *"The government and the public remain committed to developing strong policies both for security at home and for the war on terrorism abroad."*

ent and hostile rhetoric being propagated from the Osama bin Ladens and Saddam Husseins of the world. On September 11, however, the United States was forced to reevaluate its own vulnerability. The result was a series of policy changes that address the new dangers that America was facing. However, that was not the end. Indeed, America's policy makers have been continuously identifying weaknesses, oversights, and mistakes. And to the credit of the American people, they have for the most part been patient and understanding. It is also true that politics has snuck into the debate. Some have attempted to undermine the credibility of the president's policies in order to advance their own political agenda. The important point is, though, that the government and the public remain committed to developing strong policies both for security at home and for the war on terrorism abroad.

Homeland Security

Securing the homeland is a massive task by any measure. Making the task even more difficult was the fact that prior to September 11, the functions that are considered under the rubric of "homeland security" were spread throughout the federal government. To bring all of these related agencies—twenty-two in all—under one command, the Bush Administration established the Department of Homeland Security (DHS).

This was a major accomplishment in the effort to make America safer. While many of the functions of those agencies remained the same, the homeland security elements of their portfolios emerged as a top priority.

Although the DHS has been moving in the right direction, it will need several years to become truly effective. It needs to continue its efforts to become more organized, develop a national response plan as well as strategies for information technology, intelligence sharing and personnel needs. Congress needs to supply funding for emergency responders, intelligence reforms and critical infrastructure security. Similarly, state and local governments need to develop regional cooperation plans, share information and methods, and work with the DHS to develop a true national emergency response plan. In all aspects, the DHS should invest in human capital and training programs to institute an efficient homeland security process and to ensure that a safer America is on the horizon.

While there is much to be done, progress has been made over the past two years that has better prepared the United States for 21st century threats. These include:

Strides are being made to decrease the loopholes in immigration policy that terrorists have used to gain access to the United States. The United States cannot guarantee that no terrorists will gain entry onto its territory. However, policies are being implemented that make it more difficult for terrorists to enter and easier for authorities to identify potentially dangerous individuals. The terror attacks on 9/11 uncovered many loopholes in the U.S. immigration process. The Bureau of Immigration and Customs Enforcement (BICE) at the DHS was established to consolidate all the previously fragmented documentation and investigative functions of immigration. While documenting people entering, exiting, and residing in the United States is important, ensuring immigration flows is essential to the American way of life and promotes economic growth. The BICE has begun numerous initiatives such as the Student Exchange Visitor and Information System (SEVIS) to secure and facilitate legitimate immigration.

Vital intelligence is being shared among government agencies. Intelligence sharing has been a crucial focus within the DHS as well as in interagency relations, especially with the Central Intelligence Agency, the Federal Bureau of Investigation, the De-

> **"Since 9/11, authorities have broken up four alleged terrorist cells located within the United States."**

partment of Defense, the State Department and with state and local officials. Initiatives such as the creation of an intelligence fusion center, the Terrorism Threat Integration Center (TTIC), begin to establish a strategic plan for intelligence sharing. However, overcoming cultural barriers between different intelligence agencies and logistically modifying intelligence systems to render them more compatible will take time to research, develop, test, and deploy. Even if much remains to be done, the intelligence reforms that have taken place have allowed the United States to apprehend potential terrorists, break apart terrorist cells, and thwart likely attacks. Since 9/11, authorities have broken up four alleged terrorist cells located within the United States.

> *"Americans may never be completely safe again, but we can reasonably expect that terrorists won't run our lives or attack us with impunity."*

America's emergency response capabilities are better prepared to mitigate the consequences of a major terrorist attack. State and local first response agencies, such as emergency medical technicians, are at the forefront of the nation's ability to respond to terrorist acts. In fact, these local agencies will nearly always be first to respond to an incident and will be the determining factor in mitigating the consequences of an attack. The Federal government attempted to streamline and consolidate the grant funding process for emergency responders under the Office of State and Local Government Coordination (OSLGC). Furthermore, the Secretary of Homeland Security, Tom Ridge, is working to establish regional offices to better coordinate efforts between federal, state, and local officials.

America has decreased the likelihood that a terrorist will smuggle dangerous contraband into the nation. Over the past two years [since September 11, 2001] America has not necessarily begun inspecting more of what comes into the nation. However, it has implemented smarter inspection procedures. That is to say that inspectors are more able and better equipped to profile what is entering the nation and distinguish between what should be inspected and what should not. The DHS has dedicated a lot of effort to secure America's borders by developing numerous initiatives such as the Container Security Initiative [CSI]—through which the U.S. Customs will negotiate and enter into bilateral arrangements with foreign governments to screen U.S.-bound containers at key foreign ports. Up to date, the United States has signed bilateral CSI arrangements with nineteen of the world's top twenty ports. The DHS's Bureau of Customs and Border Protection (BCBP) has also engaged private industry through partnerships to enhance the security of international supply chains. Furthermore, the Transportation Security Administration (TSA) is currently researching a system to inspect air cargo, still a gaping hole in the system. These programs will not only help secure our borders, but also [will be] very beneficial to the industries because tighter security measures will ultimately facilitate and expedite the movement of cargo and containers.

More Work Remains

The events of 9/11 brought Americans to the realization that we need [to] secure our homeland against terror threats. Many immediate steps were taken in reaction to 9/11 in order to prevent another attack. But, given the patience and determination of our enemies—and the fact that two armed conflicts have yet to dampen their enthusiasm for attacking America—it's safe to say we have much more work ahead of us than behind us.

America's enemies have demonstrated their staying power—they spent seven years planning the attacks on New York and Washington—and we must demonstrate ours. We'll have to spend billions of dollars and suffer more casualties before we prevail.

Americans may never be completely safe again, but we can reasonably expect that terrorists won't run our lives or attack us with impunity. We will continue to thrive even as we hound our enemies until they join the Soviets in the back pages of history books.

The Bush Administration's Policies Are Protecting America

by Condoleezza Rice

About the author: *Condoleezza Rice was appointed as the U.S. national security advisor in 2001.*

Editor's Note: The following viewpoint was originally given as opening remarks to the National Commission on Terrorist Attacks upon the United States on April 8, 2004.

The terrorist threat to our Nation did not emerge on September 11th, 2001.[1] Long before that day, radical, freedom-hating terrorists declared war on America and on the civilized world. The attack on the Marine barracks in Lebanon in 1983, the hijacking of the [passenger ship] *Achille Lauro* in 1985, the rise of [terrorist group] al-Qaida and the bombing of the World Trade Center in 1993, the attacks on American installations in Saudi Arabia in 1995 and 1996, the East Africa embassy bombings of 1998, the attack on the USS *Cole* in 2000, these and other atrocities were part of a sustained, systematic campaign to spread devastation and chaos and to murder innocent Americans.

The terrorists were at war with us, but we were not yet at war with them. For more than 20 years, the terrorist threat gathered, and America's response across several administrations of both parties was insufficient. Historically, democratic societies have been slow to react to gathering threats, tending instead to wait to confront threats until they are too dangerous to ignore or until it is too late. Despite the sinking of the [passenger ship] *Lusitania* [by a German submarine] in 1915 and continued German harassment of American shipping, the United States did not enter the First World War until two years later. Despite Nazi Ger-

---

1. the date of the worst terrorist attack to occur in the United States

Condoleezza Rice, address to the National Commission on Terrorist Attacks upon the United States, Washington, DC, April 8, 2004.

many's repeated violations of the Versailles Treaty [which restricted the German armed forces] and its string of provocations throughout the mid-1930s, the Western democracies did not take action until 1939. The U.S. Government did not act against the growing threat from Imperial Japan until the threat became all too evident at Pearl Harbor [when the Japanese attacked the United States]. And, tragically, for all the language of war spoken before September 11th, this country simply was not on a war footing.

Since then, America has been at war. And under President [George W.] Bush's leadership, we will remain at war until the terrorist threat to our Nation is ended. The world has changed so much that it is hard to remember what our lives were like before that day. But I do want to describe the actions this Administration was taking to fight terrorism before September 11th, 2001.

Taking Over the Work of the Clinton Administration

After President Bush was elected, we were briefed by the [Bill] Clinton Administration on many national security issues during the transition. The President-elect and I were briefed by [director of Central Intelligence] George Tenet on terrorism and on the al-Qaida network. Members of [former national security advisor] Sandy Berger's NSC [National Security Council] staff briefed me, along with other members of the new national security team, on counterterrorism and al-Qaida. This briefing lasted about one hour, and it reviewed the Clinton Administration's counterterrorism approach and the various counterterrorism activities then underway. Sandy and I personally discussed a variety of other topics, including North Korea, Iraq, the Middle East, and the Balkans.

Because of these briefings and because we had watched the rise of al-Qaida over the years, we understood that the network posed a serious threat to the United States. We wanted to ensure there was no respite in the fight against al-Qaida. On an operational level, we decided immediately to continue pursuing the Clinton Administration's covert action authorities and other efforts to fight the network. President Bush retained George Tenet as Director of Central Intelligence [DCI] and Louis Freeh remained the Director of the FBI. I took the unusual step of retaining Dick Clarke and the entire Clinton Administration's counterterrorism team on the NSC staff. I knew Dick to be an expert in his field, as well as an experienced crisis manager. Our goal was to ensure continuity of operations while we developed new and more aggressive policies.

> *"Under President [George W.] Bush's leadership, we will remain at war until the terrorist threat to our Nation is ended."*

At the beginning of the Administration, President Bush revived the practice of meeting with the Director of Central Intelligence almost every day in the Oval Office—meetings which I attended, along with the Vice President and the Chief of Staff. At these meetings, the President received up-to-date intelligence and asked questions of his most senior intelligence officials. From January 20 [2001] through September 10 [2001] the President received at these daily meetings more than 40 briefing items on al-Qaida, and 13 of these were in response to questions he or his top advisers had posed. In addition to seeing DCI Tenet almost every morning, I generally spoke by telephone every morning at 7:15 with Secretaries [Colin] Powell and [Donald] Rumsfeld. I also met and spoke regularly with the DCI about al-Qaida and terrorism.

> *"President Bush understood the threat, and he understood its importance. He made clear to us that he did not want to respond to al-Qaida one attack at a time."*

Of course, we also had other responsibilities. President Bush had set a broad foreign policy agenda. We were determined to confront the proliferation of weapons of mass destruction [WMD]. We were improving America's relations with the world's great powers. We had to change an Iraq policy that was making no progress against a hostile regime which regularly shot at U.S. planes enforcing U.N. Security Council Resolutions. And we had to deal with the occasional crisis, for instance, when the crew of a Navy plane was detained in China for 11 days.

We also moved to develop a new and comprehensive strategy to eliminate the al-Qaida terrorist network. President Bush understood the threat, and he understood its importance. He made clear to us that he did not want to respond to al-Qaida one attack at a time. He told me he was "tired of swatting flies."

Al-Qaida Is a Top Priority

This new strategy was developed over the Spring and Summer of 2001, and was approved by the President's senior national security officials on September 4. It was the very first major national security policy directive of the Bush Administration—not Russia, not missile defense, not Iraq, but the elimination of al-Qaida.

Although this National Security Presidential Directive was originally a highly classified document, we arranged for portions to be declassified to help the Commission in its work, and I will describe some of those today. The strategy set as its goal the elimination of the al-Qaida network. It ordered the leadership of relevant U.S. departments and agencies to make the elimination of al-Qaida a high priority and to use all aspects of our national power—intelligence, financial, diplomatic, and military—to meet this goal. And it gave Cabinet Secretaries and department heads specific responsibilities. For instance:

• It directed the Secretary of State to work with other countries to end all sanctuaries given to al-Qaida.

• It directed the Secretaries of the Treasury and State to work with foreign governments to seize or freeze assets and holdings of al-Qaida and its benefactors.

• It directed the Director of Central Intelligence to prepare an aggressive program of covert activities to disrupt al-Qaida and provide assistance to anti-Taliban[2] groups operating against al-Qaida in Afghanistan.

• It tasked the Director of OMB [Office of Management and Budget] with ensuring that sufficient funds were available in the budgets over the next five years to meet the goals laid out in the strategy.

• And it directed the Secretary of Defense to—and I quote—"ensure that the contingency planning process includes plans: against al-Qaida and associated terrorist facilities in Afghanistan, including leadership, command-control-communications, training, and logistics facilities; against Taliban targets in Afghanistan, including leadership, command-control, air and air defense, ground forces, and logistics; to eliminate weapons of mass destruction which al-Qaida and associated terrorist groups may acquire or manufacture, including those stored in underground bunkers." This was a change from the prior strategy—Presidential Decision Directive 62, signed in 1998—which ordered the Secretary of Defense to provide transportation to bring individual terrorists to the U.S. for trial, to protect DOD [Department of Defense] forces overseas, and to be prepared to respond to terrorist and weapons of mass destruction incidents.

More importantly, we recognized that no counterterrorism strategy could succeed in isolation. As you know from the Pakistan and Afghanistan strategy documents that we made available to the Commission, our counterterrorism strategy was part of a broader package of strategies that addressed the complexities of the region.

Integrating our counterterrorism and regional strategies was the most difficult and the most important aspect of the new strategy to get right. Al-Qaida was both client of and patron to the Taliban, which in turn was supported by Pakistan. Those relationships provided al-Qaida with a powerful umbrella of protection, and we had to sever them. This was not easy.

"When threat reporting increased during the Spring and Summer of 2001, we moved the U.S. Government at all levels to a high state of alert and activity."

Not that we hadn't tried. Within a month of taking office, President Bush sent a strong, private message to [Pakistani] President [Pervez] Musharraf urging him to use his influence with the Taliban to bring Bin Laden to justice and to close down al-Qaida training camps. Secretary Powell actively urged the Pakistanis, including Musharraf himself, to abandon support for the Taliban. I met with Pakistan's Foreign Minister in my office in June of 2001. I delivered a very tough message, which was met with a rote, expressionless response.

America's al-Qaida policy wasn't working because our Afghanistan policy

2. The Taliban was an Islamist group that ruled most of Afghanistan from 1996 to 2001, and was believed to be supporting al-Qaida during that time.

wasn't working. And our Afghanistan policy wasn't working because our Pakistan policy wasn't working. We recognized that America's counterterrorism policy had to be connected to our regional strategies and to our overall foreign policy. . . .

While we were developing this new strategy to deal with al-Qaida, we also made decisions on a number of specific anti-al-Qaida initiatives that had been proposed by Dick Clarke. Many of these ideas had been deferred by the last Administration, and some had been on the table since 1998. We increased counterterror assistance to Uzbekistan; we bolstered the Treasury Department's activities to track and seize terrorist assets; we increased funding for counterterrorism activities across several agencies; and we moved quickly to arm Predator unmanned surveillance vehicles for action against al-Qaida.

> *"There was no silver bullet that could have prevented the 9/11 attacks."*

When threat reporting increased during the Spring and Summer of 2001, we moved the U.S. Government at all levels to a high state of alert and activity. Let me clear up any confusion about the relationship between the development of our new strategy and the many actions we took to respond to threats that summer. Policy development and crisis management require different approaches. Throughout this period, we did both simultaneously. . . .

Working Hard Against Nonspecific Threats

The threat reporting that we received in the Spring and Summer of 2001 was not specific as to time, nor place, nor manner of attack. Almost all of the reports focused on al-Qaida activities outside the United States, especially in the Middle East and North Africa. In fact, the information that was specific enough to be actionable referred to terrorist operations overseas. More often, it was frustratingly vague. Let me read you some of the actual chatter that we picked up that Spring and Summer:

• "Unbelievable news in coming weeks" "Big event . . . there will be a very, very, very, very big uproar" "There will be attacks in the near future"

Troubling, yes. But they don't tell us when; they don't tell us where; they don't tell us who; and they don't tell us how. . . .

Throughout this period of heightened threat information, we worked hard on multiple fronts to detect, protect against, and disrupt any terrorist plans or operations that might lead to an attack. For instance:

• The Department of Defense issued at least five urgent warnings to U.S. military forces that al-Qaida might be planning a near-term attack, and placed our military forces in certain regions on heightened alert.

• The State Department issued at least four urgent security advisories and public worldwide cautions on terrorist threats, enhanced security measures at certain embassies, and warned the Taliban that they would be held responsible for any al-Qaida attack on U.S. interests.

• The FBI issued at least three nationwide warnings to Federal, State, and local law enforcement agencies, and specifically stated that, although the vast majority of the information indicated overseas targets, attacks against the homeland could not be ruled out. The FBI also tasked all 56 of its U.S. Field Offices to increase surveillance of known or suspected terrorists and reach out to known informants who might have information on terrorist activities.

• The FAA [Federal Aviation Administration] issued at least five Civil Aviation Security Information Circulars to all U.S. airlines and airport security personnel, including specific warnings about the possibility of hijackings.

• The CIA worked round the clock to disrupt threats worldwide. Agency officials launched a wide-ranging disruption effort against al-Qaida in more than 20 countries.

• During this period, the Vice President, DCI Tenet, and the NSC's Counterterrorism staff called senior foreign officials requesting that they increase their intelligence assistance and report to us any relevant threat information.

This is a brief sample of our intense activity over the Summer of 2001.

"No Silver Bullet"

Yet there was no silver bullet that could have prevented the 9/11 attacks. In hindsight, if anything might have helped stop 9/11, it would have been better information about threats inside the United States, something made difficult by structural and legal impediments that prevented the collection and sharing of information by our law enforcement and intelligence agencies.

So the attacks came. A band of vicious terrorists tried to decapitate our government, destroy our financial system, and break the spirit of America. As an officer of government on duty that day, I will never forget the sorrow and the anger I felt. Nor will I forget the courage and resilience shown by the American people and the leadership of the President that day.

Now, we have an opportunity and an obligation to move forward together. Bold and comprehensive changes are sometimes only possible in the wake of catastrophic events—events which create a new consensus that allows us to transcend old ways of thinking and acting. Just as World War II led to a fundamental reorganization of our national defense structure and to the creation of the National Security Council, so has September 11th made possible sweeping changes in the ways we protect our homeland.

> *"President Bush is leading the country during this time of crisis and change. He has unified and streamlined our efforts to secure the American Homeland."*

President Bush is leading the country during this time of crisis and change. He has unified and streamlined our efforts to secure the American Homeland by creating the Department of Homeland Security, established a new center to integrate and analyze terrorist threat information, directed the transformation of the FBI into an agency dedicated to fighting terror, broken down the bureaucratic walls and legal barriers that prevented the sharing of vital threat information between our domestic law enforcement and our foreign intelligence agencies, and, working with the Congress, given officials new tools, such as the USA PATRIOT Act, to find and stop terrorists. And he has done all of this in a way that is consistent with protecting America's cherished civil liberties and with preserving our character as a free and open society.

More Work Needed

But the President also recognizes that our work is far from complete. More structural reform will likely be necessary. Our intelligence gathering and analysis have improved dramatically [since September 11, 2001], but they must be stronger still. The President and all of us in his Administration welcome new ideas and fresh thinking. We are eager to do whatever is necessary to protect the American people. . . .

We are at war and our security as a nation depends on winning that war. We must and we will do everything we can to harden terrorist targets within the United States. Dedicated law enforcement and security profes-

> *"Under [President George W. Bush's] leadership, the United States and our allies are disrupting terrorist operations, cutting off their funding, and hunting down terrorists."*

sionals continue to risk their lives every day to make us all safer, and we owe them a debt of gratitude. And, let's remember, those charged with protecting us from attack have to succeed 100 percent of the time. To inflict devastation on a massive scale, the terrorists only have to succeed once, and we know they are trying every day.

That is why we must address the source of the problem. We must stay on offense, to find and defeat the terrorists wherever they live, hide, and plot around the world. If we learned anything on September 11th, 2001, it is that we cannot wait while dangers gather.

After the September 11th attacks, our Nation faced hard choices. We could fight a narrow war against al-Qaida and the Taliban or we could fight a broad war against a global menace. We could seek a narrow victory or we could work for a lasting peace and a better world. President Bush chose the bolder course.

He recognizes that the War on Terror is a broad war. Under his leadership, the United States and our allies are disrupting terrorist operations, cutting off their funding, and hunting down terrorists one-by-one. Their world is getting smaller. The terrorists have lost a home-base and training camps in Afghanistan. The Governments of Pakistan and Saudi Arabia now pursue them with energy and force.

We are confronting the nexus between terror and weapons of mass destruction. We are working to stop the spread of deadly weapons and prevent them from getting into the hands of terrorists, seizing dangerous materials in transit, where necessary. Because we acted in Iraq, [former Iraqi president] Saddam Hussein will never again use weapons of mass destruction against his people or his neighbors. And we have convinced Libya to give up all its WMD-related programs and materials.

And as we attack the threat at its sources, we are also addressing its roots. Thanks to the bravery and skill of our men and women in uniform, we removed from power two of the world's most brutal regimes—sources of violence, and fear, and instability in the region. Today, along with many allies, we are helping the people of Iraq and Afghanistan to build free societies. And we are working with the people of the Middle East to spread the blessings of liberty and democracy as the alternatives to instability, hatred, and terror. This work is hard and dangerous, yet it is worthy of our effort and our sacrifice. The defeat of terror and the success of freedom in those nations will serve the interests of our Nation and inspire hope and encourage reform throughout the greater Middle East.

In the aftermath of September 11th, those were the right choices for America to make—the only choices that can ensure the safety of our Nation in the decades to come.

The United States Is Successfully Working with the United Nations to Fight Terrorism

by George W. Bush

About the author: *George W. Bush, former governor of Texas, is the forty-third president of the United States.*

Editor's Note: The following speech was given to the United Nations General Assembly on September 23, 2003.

Twenty-four months ago [on September 11, 2001]—and yesterday in the memory of America—the center of New York City became a battlefield, and a graveyard, and the symbol of an unfinished war.[1] Since that day, terrorists have struck in Bali, Mombasa, in Casablanca, in Riyadh, in Jakarta, in Jerusalem—measuring the advance of their cause in the chaos and innocent suffering they leave behind.

Last month [in August 2003], terrorists brought their war to the United Nations [U.N.] itself. The U.N. headquarters in Baghdad stood for order and compassion—and for that reason, the terrorists decided it must be destroyed. Among the 22 people who were murdered was Sergio Vieira de Mello. Over the decades, this good and brave man from Brazil gave help to the afflicted in Bangladesh, Cyprus, Mozambique, Lebanon, Cambodia, Central Africa, Kosovo, and East Timor, and was aiding the people of Iraq in their time of need. America joins you, his colleagues, in honoring the memory of Señor

---

1. On September 11, 2001, almost three thousand people died in a series of terrorist attacks against the Pentagon and the World Trade Center.

George W. Bush, address to the United Nations General Assembly, New York, September 23, 2003.

Vieira de Mello, and the memory of all who died with him in the service to the United Nations.

By the victims they choose, and by the means they use, the terrorists have clarified the struggle we are in. Those who target relief workers for death have set themselves against all humanity. Those who incite murder and celebrate suicide reveal their contempt for life itself. They have no place in any religious faith; they have no claim on the world's sympathy; and they should have no friend in this [U.N.] chamber.

A Clear Divide

Events during the past two years have set before us the clearest of divides: between those who seek order, and those who spreads chaos; between those who work for peaceful change, and those who adopt the methods of gangsters; between those who honor the rights of man, and those who deliberately take the lives of men and women and children without mercy or shame.

Between those alternatives there is no neutral ground. All governments that support terror are complicit in a war against civilization. No government should ignore the threat of terror, because to look the other way gives terrorists the chance to regroup and recruit and prepare. And all nations that fight terror, as if the lives of their own people depend on it, will earn the favorable judgment of history.

The former regimes of Afghanistan and Iraq knew these alternatives, and made their choices. The Taliban[2] was a sponsor and servant of terrorism. When confronted, that regime chose defiance, and that regime is no more. Afghanistan's President . . . now represents a free people who are building a decent and just society; they're building a nation fully joined in the war against terror.

The regime of Saddam Hussein cultivated ties to terror while it built weapons of mass destruction. It used those weapons in acts of mass murder, and refused to account for them when confronted by the world. The [U.N.] Security Council was right to be alarmed. The Security Council was right to demand that Iraq destroy its illegal weapons and prove that it had done so. The Security Council was right to vow serious consequences if Iraq refused to comply. And because there were consequences, because a coalition of nations acted to defend the peace, and the credibility of the United Nations, Iraq is free, and today we are joined by representatives of a liberated country.

> *"No government should ignore the threat of terror, because to look the other way gives terrorists the chance to regroup and recruit and prepare."*

Saddam Hussein's monuments have been removed and not only his statutes. The true monuments of his rule and his character—the torture chambers, and

2. Islamist group that ruled most of Afghanistan from 1996 until it was removed in 2001 by a U.S.-led coalition

the rape rooms, and the prison cells for innocent children—are closed. And as we discover the killing fields and mass graves of Iraq, the true scale of Saddam's cruelty is being revealed.

The Iraqi people are meeting hardships and challenges, like every nation that has set out on the path of democracy. Yet their future promises lives of dignity and freedom, and that is a world away from the squalid, vicious tyranny they have known. Across Iraq, life is being improved by liberty. Across the Middle East, people are safer because an unstable aggressor has been removed from power. Across the world, nations are more secure because an ally of terror has fallen.

Common Goals

Our actions in Afghanistan and Iraq were supported by many governments, and America is grateful to each one. I also recognize that some of the sovereign nations of this assembly disagreed with our actions. Yet there was, and there remains, unity among us on the fundamental principles and objectives of the United Nations. We are dedicated to the defense of our collective security, and to the advance of human rights. These permanent commitments call us to great work in the world, work we must do together. So let us move forward.

First, we must stand with the people of Afghanistan and Iraq as they build free and stable countries. The terrorists and their allies fear and fight this progress above all, because free people embrace hope over resentment, and choose peace over violence.

> *"In the nation of Iraq, the United Nations is carrying out vital and effective work every day."*

The United Nations has been a friend of the Afghan people, distributing food and medicine, helping refugees return home, advising on a new constitution, and helping to prepare the way for nationwide elections. NATO [North Atlantic Treaty Organization] has taken over the U.N.-mandated security force in Kabul. American and coalition forces continue to track and defeat al Qaeda terrorists and remnants of the Taliban. Our efforts to rebuild that country go on. I have recently proposed to spend an additional $1.2 billion for the Afghan reconstruction effort, and I urge other nations to continue contributing to this important cause.

In the nation of Iraq, the United Nations is carrying out vital and effective work every day. By the end of 2004, more than 90 percent of Iraqi children under age five will have been immunized against preventable diseases such as polio, tuberculosis and measles, thanks to the hard work and high ideals of UNICEF [United Nations International Children's Emergency Fund]. Iraq's food distribution system is operational, delivering nearly a half-million tons of food per month, thanks to the skill and expertise of the World Food Program.

Our international coalition in Iraq is meeting it[s] responsibilities. We are conducting precision raids against terrorists and holdouts of the former regime.

These killers are at war with the Iraqi people. They have made Iraq the central front in the war on terror, and they will be defeated. Our coalition has made sure that Iraq's former dictator will never again use weapons of mass destruction. We are interviewing Iraqi citizens and analyzing records of the old regime to reveal the full extent of its weapons programs and its long campaign of deception. We're training Iraqi police and border guards and a new army, so the Iraqi people can assume full responsibility for their own security.

> *"America is working with friends and allies on a new Security Council resolution, which will expand the U.N.'s role in Iraq."*

And at the same time, our coalition is helping to improve the daily lives of the Iraqi people. The old regime built palaces while letting schools decay, so we are rebuilding more than a thousand schools. The old regime starved hospitals of resources, so we have helped to supply and reopen hospitals across Iraq. The old regime built up armies and weapons, while allowing the nation's infrastructure to crumble, so we are rehabilitating power plants, water and sanitation facilities, bridges and airports. I proposed to Congress that the United States provide additional funding for our work in Iraq, the greatest financial commitment of its kind since the Marshall Plan.[3] Having helped to liberate Iraq, we will honor our pledges to Iraq, and by helping the Iraqi people build a stable and peaceful country, we will make our own countries more secure.

Democracy in Iraq

The primary goal of our coalition in Iraq is self-government for the people of Iraq, reached by orderly and democratic process. This process must unfold according to the needs of Iraqis, neither hurried, nor delayed by the wishes of other parties. And the United Nations can contribute greatly to the cause of Iraq's self-government. America is working with friends and allies on a new Security Council resolution, which will expand the U.N.'s role in Iraq. As in the aftermath of other conflicts, the United Nations should assist in developing a constitution, in training civil servants, and conducting free and fair elections.

Iraq now has a Governing Council, the first truly representative institution in that country. Iraq's new leaders are showing the openness and tolerance that democracy requires, and they're also showing courage. Yet every young democracy needs the help of friends. Now the nation of Iraq needs and deserves our aid, and all nations of goodwill should step forward and provide that support.

The success of a free Iraq will be watched and noted throughout the region. Millions will see that freedom, equality, and material progress are possible at the heart of the Middle East. Leaders in the region will face the clearest evi-

3. Between 1948 and 1951, the United States contributed more than $13 billion to assist the reconstruction of Europe after World War II.

dence that free institutions and open societies are the only path to long-term national success and dignity. And a transformed Middle East would benefit the entire world, by undermining the ideologies that export violence to other lands.

Iraq as a dictatorship had great power to destabilize the Middle East; Iraq as a democracy will have great power to inspire the Middle East. The advance of democratic institutions in Iraq is setting an example that others, including the Palestinian people, would be wise to follow. The Palestinian cause is betrayed by leaders who cling to power by feeding old hatreds and destroying the good work of others. The Palestinian people deserve their own state, and they will gain that state by embracing new leaders committed to reform, to fighting terror, and to building peace. All parties in the Middle East must meet their responsibilities and carry out the commitments they made at Aqaba. Israel must work to create the conditions that will allow a peaceful Palestinian state to emerge. And Arab nations must cut off funding and other support for terrorist organizations. America will work with every nation in the region that acts boldly for the sake of peace.

Weapons of Mass Destruction

A second challenge we must confront together is the proliferation of weapons of mass destruction. Outlaw regimes that possess nuclear, chemical and biological weapons—and the means to deliver them—would be able to use blackmail and create chaos in entire regions. These weapons could be used by terrorists to bring sudden disaster and suffering on a scale we can scarcely imagine. The deadly combination of outlaw regimes and terror networks and weapons of mass murder is a peril that cannot be ignored or wished away. If such a danger is allowed to fully materialize, all words, all protests, will come too late. Nations of the world must have the wisdom and the will to stop grave threats before they arrive.

"The United States of America is committed to the United Nations. And we show that commitment by working to fulfill the U.N.'s stated purposes."

One crucial step is to secure the most dangerous materials at their source. For more than a decade, the United States has worked with Russia and other states of the former Soviet Union to dismantle, destroy, or secure weapons and dangerous materials left over from another era. Last year [2002] in Canada, the G8[4] nations agreed to provide up to $20 billion—half of it from the United States—to fight this proliferation risk over the next 10 years. Since then, six additional countries have joined the effort. More are needed, and I urge other nations to help us meet this danger.

---

4. coalition of industrialized nations that includes Great Britain, France, Germany, Italy, Japan, Russia, the United States, and Canada

We're also improving our capability to interdict lethal materials in transit. Through our Proliferation Security Initiative, 11 nations are preparing to search planes and ships, trains and trucks carrying suspect cargo, and to seize weapons or missile shipments that raise proliferation concerns. These nations have agreed on a set of interdiction principles, consistent with legal—current legal—authorities. And we're working to expand the Proliferation Security Initiative to other countries. We're determined to keep the world's most destructive weapons away from all our shores, and out of the hands of our common enemies.

Because proliferators will use any route or channel that is open to them, we need the broadest possible cooperation to stop them. Today, I ask the U.N. Security Council to adopt a new anti-proliferation resolution. This resolution should call on all members of the U.N. to criminalize the proliferation of weapons—weapons of mass destruction, to enact strict export controls consistent with international standards, and to secure any and all sensitive materials within their own borders. The United States stands ready to help any nation draft these new laws, and to assist in their enforcement. . . .

America Is Committed to the United Nations

All the challenges I have spoken of this morning require urgent attention and moral clarity. Helping Afghanistan and Iraq to succeed as free nations in a transformed region [and] cutting off the avenues of proliferation . . . —these are the kinds of great tasks for which the United Nations was founded. In each case, careful discussion is needed, and also decisive action. Our good intentions will be credited only if we achieve good outcomes.

As an original signer of the U.N. Charter, the United States of America is committed to the United Nations. And we show that commitment by working to fulfill the U.N.'s stated purposes, and give meaning to its ideals. The founding documents of the United Nations and the founding documents of America stand in the same tradition. Both assert that human beings should never be reduced to objects of power or commerce, because their dignity is inherent. Both require—both recognize—a moral law that stands above men and nations, which must be defended and enforced by men and nations. And both point the way to peace, the peace that comes when all are free. We secure that peace with our courage, and we must show that courage together.

America Is Still at Risk for a Terrorist Attack

by George J. Tenet

About the author: *George J. Tenet is the U.S. director of Central Intelligence.*

Editor's Note: This viewpoint was originally given as testimony before the U.S. Senate on March 9, 2004.

I'll begin today on terrorism, with a stark bottom-line:

• The al-Qa'ida [terrorist group] leadership structure we charted after [the September 11, 2001, terrorist attacks] is seriously damaged—but the group remains as committed as ever to attacking the US homeland.

• But as we continue the battle against al-Qa'ida, we must overcome a movement—a global movement infected by al-Qa'ida's radical agenda.

• In this battle we are moving forward in our knowledge of the enemy—his plans, capabilities, and intentions.

• And what we've learned continues to validate my deepest concern: that this enemy remains intent on obtaining, and using, catastrophic weapons.

Now let me tell you about the war we've waged against the al-Qa'ida organization and its leadership.

• Military and intelligence operations by the United States and its allies overseas have degraded the group. Local al-Qa'ida cells are forced to make their own decisions because of the central leadership's disarray.

Al-Qa'ida depends on leaders who not only direct terrorist attacks but who carry out the day-to-day tasks that support operations. Over the past 18 months, we have killed or captured key al-Qa'ida leaders in every significant operational area—logistics, planning, finance, training—and have eroded the key pillars of the organization, such as the leadership in Pakistani urban areas and operational cells in the al-Qa'ida heartland of Saudi Arabia and Yemen. . . .

We are creating large and growing gaps in the al-Qa'ida hierarchy.

And, unquestionably, bringing these key operators to ground disrupted plots

George J. Tenet, testimony before the U.S. Senate Armed Services Committee, Washington, DC, March 9, 2004.

that would otherwise have killed Americans.

Meanwhile, al-Qa'ida central continues to lose operational safehavens, and [al-Qa'ida leader Usama] Bin Ladin has gone deep underground. We are hunting him in some of the most unfriendly regions on earth. We follow every lead.

Al-Qa'ida's finances are also being squeezed. This is due in part to takedowns of key moneymen in the past year, particularly the [Persian] Gulf, Southwest Asia, and even Iraq.

And we are receiving a broad array of help from our coalition partners who have been central to our effort against al-Qa'ida.

> *"[Al-Qa'ida] remains intent on obtaining, and using, catastrophic weapons."*

• Since the 12 May bombings, the Saudi government has shown an important commitment to fighting al-Qa'ida in the Kingdom, and Saudi officers have paid with their lives.

• Elsewhere in the Arab world, we're receiving valuable cooperation from Jordan, Morocco, Egypt, Algeria, the UAE, Oman, and many others.

• President Musharraf of Pakistan remains a courageous and indispensable ally who has become the target of assassins for the help he's given us.

• Partners in Southeast Asia have been instrumental in the roundup of key regional associates of al-Qa'ida.

• Our European partners worked closely together to unravel and disrupt a continent-wide network of terrorists planning chemical, biological and conventional attacks in Europe.

The United States Is Still at War

So we have made notable strides. But do not misunderstand me. I am not suggesting al-Qa'ida is defeated. It is not. We are still at war. This is a learning organization that remains committed to attacking the United States, its friends and allies.

Successive blows to al-Qa'ida's central leadership have transformed the organization into a loose collection of regional networks that operate more autonomously. These regional components have demonstrated their operational prowess in the past year.

• The sites of their attacks span the group's broad reach—Morocco, Kenya, Turkey, Jordan, Saudi Arabia, Kuwait, Afghanistan, Pakistan, Indonesia.

• And al-Qa'ida seeks to influence the regional networks with operational training, consultations, and money. Khalid Shaykh Muhammad [al-Qa'ida operations chief] sent Hambali [senior operational planner for al-Qa'ida] $50,000 for operations in Southeast Asia.

You should not take the fact that these attacks occurred abroad to mean the threat to the US homeland has waned. As al-Qa'ida and associated groups undertook these attacks overseas, detainees consistently talk about the importance the group still attaches to striking the main enemy: the United States. Across the operational spectrum—air, maritime, special weapons—we have time and again uncovered plots that are chilling.

• On aircraft plots alone, we have uncovered new plans to recruit pilots and to evade new security measures in Southeast Asia, the Middle East, and Europe.

• Even catastrophic attacks on the scale of 11 September remain within al-Qa'ida's reach. Make no mistake: these plots are hatched abroad, but they target US soil or that of our allies.

So far, I have been talking only about al-Qa'ida. But al-Qa'ida is not the limit of the terrorist threat worldwide. Al-Qa'ida has infected others with its ideology, which depicts the United States as Islam's greatest foe. . . . What I want to say to you now may be the most important thing I tell you today.

Spread of Anti-Americanism

The steady spread of Usama bin Ladin's anti-US sentiment—through the wider Sunni extremist movement and through the broad dissemination of al-Qa'ida's destructive expertise—ensures that a serious threat will remain for the foreseeable future . . . with or without al-Qa'ida in the picture.

A decade ago, bin Ladin had a vision of rousing Islamic terrorists worldwide to attack the United States. He created al-Qa'ida to indoctrinate a worldwide movement in global jihad, with America as the enemy—an enemy to be attacked with every means at hand.

> *"We are still at war. [Al-Qa'ida] is a learning organization that remains committed to attacking the United States, its friends and allies."*

• In the minds of Bin Ladin and his cohorts, September 11 was the shining moment, their "shot heard 'round the world," and they want to capitalize on it.

And so, even as al-Qa'ida has been weakened, other extremist groups within the movement it influenced have become the next wave of the terrorist threat. Dozens of such groups exist. Let me offer a few thoughts on how to understand this challenge.

• One of the most immediate threats is from smaller international Sunni [denomination of Islam] extremist groups who have benefited from al-Qa'ida links. They include groups as diverse as the al-Zarqawi network, the Ansar al-Islam in Iraq, the Libyan Islamic Fighting Group, and the Islamic Movement of Uzbekistan.

• A second level of threat comes from small local groups, with limited domestic agendas, that work with international terrorist groups in their own countries. These include the Salifiya Jihadia, a Moroccan network that carried out the May 2003 Casablanca [suicide] bombings, and similar groups throughout Africa and Asia.

These far-flung groups increasingly set the agenda, and are redefining the threat we face. They are not all creatures of Bin Ladin, and so their fate is not tied to his. They have autonomous leadership, they pick their own targets, they plan their own attacks.

Beyond these groups are the so-called "foreign jihadists"—individuals ready to fight anywhere they believe Muslim lands are under attack by what they see as "infidel invaders." They draw on broad support networks, have wide appeal, and enjoy a growing sense of support from Muslims who are not necessarily supporters of terrorism. The foreign jihadists see Iraq as a golden opportunity.

Let me repeat: for the growing number of jihadists interested in attacking the United States, a spectacular attack on the US Homeland is the "brass ring" that many strive for—with or without encouragement by al-Qa'ida's central leadership.

To detect and ultimately defeat these forces, we will continually need to watch hotspots, present or potential battlegrounds, places where these terrorist networks converge. Iraq is of course one major locus of concern. Southeast Asia is another. Even Western Europe is an area where terrorists recruit, train, and target.

• To get the global job done, foreign governments will need to improve bilateral and multilateral, and even inter-service cooperation, and strengthen domestic counterterrorist legislation and security practices.

I have consistently warned of al-Qa'ida's interest in chemical, biological, radiological and nuclear [CBRN] weapons. Acquiring these remains a "religious obligation" in Bin Ladin's eyes, and al-Qa'ida and more than two dozen other terrorist groups are pursuing CBRN materials.

• We particularly see a heightened risk of poison attacks. Contemplated delivery methods to date have been simple but this may change as non–al-Qa'ida groups share information on more sophisticated methods and tactics.

Over the last year we've also seen an increase in the threat of more sophisticated CBRN. For this reason we take very seriously the threat of a CBRN attack.

• Extremists have widely disseminated assembly instructions for an improvised chemical weapon using common materials that could cause a large numbers of casualties in a crowded, enclosed area.

"Even as al-Qa'ida has been weakened, other extremist groups within the movement it influenced have become the next wave of the terrorist threat."

• Although gaps in our understanding remain, we see al-Qa'ida's program to produce anthrax as one of the most immediate terrorist CBRN threats we are likely to face.

• Al-Qa'ida continues to pursue its strategic goal of obtaining a nuclear capability. It remains interested in dirty bombs. Terrorist documents contain accurate views of how such weapons would be used.

I've focused, and rightly so, on al-Qa'ida and related groups. But other terrorist organizations also threaten US interests. Palestinian terrorist groups in Israel, the West Bank, and Gaza remain a formidable threat and continue to use terrorism to undermine prospects for peace.

• Last year Palestinian terrorist groups conducted more than 600 attacks, killing about 200 Israelis and foreigners, including Americans.

Lebanese [terrorist group] Hizballah cooperates with these groups and appears to be increasing its support. It is also working with Iran and surrogate groups in Iraq and would likely react to an attack against it, Syria, or Iran with attacks against US and Israeli targets worldwide.

> *"Places that combine desperate social and economic circumstances with a failure of government . . . can often provide nurturing environments for terrorist groups."*

Iran and Syria continue to support terrorist groups, and their links into Iraq have become problematic to our efforts there.

Although Islamic extremists comprise the most pressing threat to US interests, we cannot ignore nominally leftist groups in Latin America and Europe. The Revolutionary Armed Forces of Colombia, or FARC, and the National Liberation Army (ELN), Colombia's second largest leftist insurgent group have shown a willingness to attack US targets. So has the Revolutionary People's Liberation Party/Front—a Turkish group that has killed two US citizens and targeted US interests in Turkey.

Finally, cyber vulnerabilities are another of our concerns, with not only terrorists but foreign governments, hackers, crime groups, and industrial spies attempting to obtain information from our computer networks. . . .

Transnational Issues

Let me conclude my comments . . . by briefly considering some important transnational concerns that touch on the war against terrorism.

We're used to thinking of that fight as a sustained worldwide effort to get the perpetrators and would-be perpetrator off the street. This is an important preoccupation, and we will never lose sight of it.

But places that combine desperate social and economic circumstances with a failure of government to police its own territory can often provide nurturing environments for terrorist groups, and for insurgents and criminals. The failure of governments to control their own territory creates potential power vacuums that open opportunities for those who hate.

• We count approximately 50 countries that have such "stateless zones." In half of these, terrorist groups are thriving. Al-Qa'ida and extremists like the Taliban, operating in the Afghanistan-Pakistan border area, are well known examples.

As the war on terrorism progresses, terrorists will be driven from their safe havens to seek new hideouts where they can undertake training, planning, and staging without interference from government authorities. The prime candidates for new "no man's lands" are remote, rugged regions where central governments have no consistent reach and where socioeconomic problems are rife.

Many factors play into the struggle to eradicate stateless zones and dry up the wellsprings of disaffection.

• Population trends. More than half of the Middle East's population is under the age of 22. "Youth bulges," or excessive numbers of unemployed young people, are historical markers for increased risk of political violence and recruitment into radical causes. The disproportionate rise of young age cohorts will be particularly pronounced in Iraq, followed by Syria, Kuwait, Iran and Saudi Arabia.

• Infectious disease. The HIV/AIDS [human immunodeficiency virus/acquired immune deficiency syndrome] pandemic remains a global humanitarian crisis that also endangers social and political stability. Although Africa currently [in 2004] has the greatest number of HIV/AIDS cases—more than 29 million infected—the disease is spreading rapidly. Last year [in 2003] I warned about rising infection rates in Russia, China, India, and the Caribbean. But the virus is also gaining a foothold in the Middle East and North Africa, where governments may be lulled into overconfidence by the protective effects of social and cultural conservatism.

• Humanitarian need. Need will again outpace international pledges for assistance. Sub-Saharan Africa and such conflict-ravaged places like Chechnya, Tajikistan, and the Palestinian Occupied Territories will compete for aid against assistance to Iraq and Afghanistan. Only 40 percent of UN [United Nations] funding requirements for 2003 had been met for the five most needy countries in Africa.

• Food insecurity. More than 840 million people are undernourished worldwide, a number that had fallen in the first half of the 1990s but is now on the increase. USDA [U.S. Department of Agriculture] estimates the food aid needed to meet annual recommended minimum nutrition levels at almost 18 million metric tons, far above the recent average of 11 million tons donated per annum.

The Bush Administration's Policies Have Increased the Terrorist Threat Against America

by Edward S. Herman

About the author: *Edward S. Herman is an economist, author, and media analyst, and is professor emeritus of finance at the Wharton School, University of Pennsylvania.*

One of the remarkable phenomena in this crazy political environment has been the Republican administration's success in getting President George [W.] Bush portrayed as the person who the citizenry can rely on to protect their security interests. This is amazing, given the Bush record and plans. I will argue that he has been a calamitous failure on security issues up to now [2003] and that he is busily engaged in sowing the seeds for security disasters in the future. In saying this I am using security in the narrow sense, concerned only with threats of terrorist and military attack. If we extend the concept to encompass the security of the U.S. citizenry from threats of unemployment, pension loss, lack of medical insurance, street crime, security state abuses of civil liberties, breakdowns in electrical, water, or transportation service, or damage to health resulting from environmental degradation, the Bush threat to security is overwhelming.

Bush has gotten away with this image of security-savior by stoking fears, stirring up patriotic ardor, manufacturing wars—or rather invasions of small and virtually defenseless countries—and strutting about looking very grave, pronouncing momentous words attempting to evoke Churchillian[1] grandeur ("I will

---

1. Former British prime minister Winston Churchill is known for his inspiring speeches given during World War II.

not yield; I will not rest; I will not relent in waging this struggle for freedom and security for the American people"), and acting his part in frequent photo-ops that portray the erstwhile draft-dodger as an active warrior chieftain (his jet-landing in Air Force garb on the USS *Abraham Lincoln*).

But he couldn't have done this without an ultra-compliant media that followed his agenda, featured virtually without comment his photo-ops, serial misrepresentations of fact, promoted scares, and refused to challenge their leader, serving him much in the manner of the media of a totalitarian state. Professor Lance Bennett refers to this media performance as a "near-perfect journalistic participation in government propaganda operations." The large right-wing segment of the media have functioned as literal press agents and cheerleaders for the Bush administration, setting the tone and helping cow the "liberal" sector of the corporate media into similar, if less vocal, subservience to the government (although most of them didn't need to be cowed). At a deeper level, this reflects the fact that the corporate community is very pleased with the Bush administration, which has been brazenly aggressive in providing business tax breaks, resource giveaways, reductions in environmental controls, cutbacks in the welfare state, and impediments to labor organization. Such service to the needs of the powerful feeds into the performance of the corporate and advertiser-funded media, which treats a Bush much differently than a [former president Bill] Clinton, [former vice president Al] Gore, or any other politician who may try hard to placate business, but is not prepared for 100 percent corporate service.

The 9/11 Security Failure

The Bush administration was directly responsible for the [security failure that led to the September 11, 2001, attacks], one of the greatest and most inexcusable in U.S. history. The Administration had been warned by the outgoing Clinton team of the [terrorist group] al Qaeda threat and essentially ignored that warning in its eight months in office before 9/11. The Administration failed to take any action based on a host of subsequent warning signals, including information on the flight training of suspicious individuals and explicit advisories of a threatened "spectacular" terrorist action provided by the intelligence agencies of half-a-dozen allied countries. Bush's August 6, 2001 intelligence briefing included an item, "Bin Laden Determined to Strike in US," which noted the "FBI judgment about pattern of activity consistent with preparation for hijackings and other types of attack." The Bush administration did nothing in response to these warnings in the way of checking out threatening "patterns of activity" like flight training or trying to strengthen airport security. On September 10, 2001,

> *"[George W. Bush] has been a calamitous failure on security issues up to now [2003] and . . . he is busily engaged in sowing the seeds for security disasters in the future."*

Attorney-General John Ashcroft submitted a Justice Department budget that reduced by $58 million FBI requests that would have provided for 149 counterterrorism field agents, 200 intelligence analysts, and 54 translators; and he proposed a $65 million cut for state and local governments for counterterrorism supplies, including radios and decontamination equipment. Ashcroft's priorities did not include terrorism; they featured "securing the rights of victims of crimes," immigration control, dealing with drug trafficking, and the threat of prostitutes in Louisiana.

The failure to deal with the al Qaeda terror threat may well have been connected to the relationships between the Bush family, friends, and oil interests and the Saudis, including members of the bin Laden family, some of whom were allowed to leave the country in the immediate wake of 9/11 with White House approval—while large numbers of Arabs with no known connections to bin Laden or al Qaeda were quickly rounded up for questioning, frequent mistreatment, and open-ended incarceration. The Bush administration went to great pains to impede and delay an investigation of the 9/11 security failure, refusing access to (national security advisor) Condoleeza Rice, many CIA and other personnel, as well as executive documents and, in the end, insisting on keeping from public scrutiny the 28 pages of the long-delayed report on the reasons for the security failure that dealt with the Saudi connection.

> *"The Bush administration was directly responsible for the [security failure that led to the September 11, 2001, terrorist attacks]."*

It is an amazing testimony to the power of the right wing that the Bush administration was able to get away with delaying and then successfully censoring the joint congressional committee's 9/11 report and without ever suffering any serious condemnation. Clearly 9/11 has been considered an event of overwhelming importance, with almost 3,000 U.S. dead, generating vast publicity and expressions of grief and anger, and providing the basis for an open-ended "war on terror." Recall also that some of the 19 plane hijackers had even trained in aircraft management in the United States, had coordinated this operation on U.S. soil without any interference from a security apparatus costing the taxpayers an estimated $30 billion a year. Then there is the record of warnings and evidence of Bush administration disinterest, possibly influenced by the Saudi-oil connection. Then there is the failure of the U.S. alert system to respond to the hijacking, and the evidence that leader George Bush became conspicuous by his absence following his hearing of the Twin Tower hits.

Many of the 9/11 victims' families have been appalled at the security failure cover-up and some have even pursued the issue with a great deal of energy. . . . But the media have been exceedingly quiet and from 9/11 to the present they have exerted little pressure on the Administration to explain their failure and they have not suggested that this dereliction of duty constitutes criminal and im-

peachable negligence. At the height of the disclosures of Bush's intelligence failures, in May 2002, the *New York Times* editorial stress was on the inability to assemble data and to act as a "chronic" problem and the need to focus on "what
really matters, which is preventing another assault" by bin Laden, rather than
blame assessment. In fact, the media have hardly admitted 9/11 to be a Bush
failure at all—the *Philadelphia In-
quirer* made 9/11 something that
might taint Clinton's legacy, without
even mentioning any possible Bush
responsibility.

> *"The failure to deal with the al
> Qaeda terror threat may well
> have been connected to the
> relationships between the Bush
> family . . . and the Saudis."*

I would submit that if Clinton had
been in office and displayed the same
record of non- and mal-performance
the media would have been unrelenting, their investigative efforts would have
been frenzied, and the security failure would have been pinned on Clinton along
with his immediate subordinates. (Dick Cheney, for example, was presented as
Bush's "point man on domestic terrorism" in May 2001, but he hadn't lifted a fin-
ger in dealing with this responsibility by 9/11.) If Clinton was impeached for lies
associated with the Lewinsky scandal,[2] can there be any doubt that he would have
been impeached—and convicted and removed from office—for this much more
serious crime? But he was not protected by the right wing and "liberal media," as
is George Bush, the more aggressive servant of the corporate community.

Security Failure to Fear-Mongering

Having egregiously failed to protect U.S. national security on 9/11, the Bush
team then rushed to the opposite extreme of inflating and manufacturing terrorist threats, stoking fear, and presenting themselves as the security-protectors
that the U.S. citizenry could rely upon. This took the heat off their catastrophic
failure—and the ongoing corporate and Bush administration's conflict-of-
interest scandals—and allowed them to use this new focus and diversion to
carry out external and internal policies that they had wanted to pursue but found
difficult to implement without a cover.

This new effort to work the security-protector gambit began with an immediate rush of naval vessels to New York harbor and elsewhere, and continuous Air
Force flights over New York and other major cities that continued for many
months. This was extremely silly, as it should have been obvious even to the editors of the *New York Times* that bin Laden, and even Saddam Hussein, had no
navy or air force that might attack New York City, that 9/11 was a long-planned
once-off project, and that further terrorist attacks, if they took place, were going
to be by low-tech methods. But the media didn't laugh or criticize. They didn't

---

2. In 1998, Bill Clinton was impeached after investigations revealed that he had had a sexual relationship with White House intern Monica Lewinsky, then lied about it to the American public.

point out the contrast between the failure to deal with the real threat and the idiotic (and wasteful) new rush to convey the image of alert security-protectors. No, they fell in line with that high gullibility quotient they so frequently display when dealing with alleged "security" or foreign policy issues (as they have done in dealing with the Bush pre-invasion claims of Saddam Hussein's threatening weapons of mass destruction).

Thereafter the Bush team made frequent announcements of terror threats and arrests of terror suspects, based on information far less compelling than that which they had completely ignored before 9/11 and often laughable. Ashcroft's claim that the FBI had disrupted a plan to launch a "dirty bomb" [radioactive bomb] attack on Washington by its May 8, 2002 arrest of a former member of a Chicago street gang, soon collapsed when it was revealed that there was no bomb, no access to nuclear material, not even a plan—only an alleged "intention." But the media played this up heavily and they regularly feature general claims of ominous threats, even when timed to coincide with embarrassing political moments for the Bush terror fighters. The new Homeland Security Administration concocted a system of color alerts for terror threats of different levels of seriousness and they were on frequently, dependably at politically convenient moments. These alerts were invariably false alarms. Despite all the fear propaganda, and barring the attacks via the anthrax mailings,[3] there was not a single real terrorist act on U.S. soil for the two years following 9/11. Theoretically this could have been the result of the arrests, alerts and heightened surveillance that had been put in place. The other possibility, which I believe to be the main reality is that al Qaeda was poorly represented in the United States and had temporarily exhausted its capabilities here.

> *"The media have . . . exerted little pressure on the Administration to explain their failure [to prevent the September 11, 2001, terrorist attacks]."*

Failure to Protect Against Terror

The Bush administration took advantage of the new fear environment and stoked patriotism to push its National Missile Defense (NMD) and other military projects that had absolutely nothing to do with combating al Qaeda and terrorism, but which neither the media nor Democrats contested. A very large fraction of the new money allocated to "security" after 9/11 went to these non-terrorism-related projects and military attacks abroad that served the semi-hidden Bush agenda of projecting U.S. imperial power on a global basis, and which are reliable producers of more anti-U.S. terrorism.

---

3. In late 2001 a number of letters were mailed containing anthrax powder, causing seventeen infections and five fatalities.

But while big money was being spent by Bush on NMD and other provocative and wasteful weapons systems, and wars, the Bush team was shortchanging programs that would actually help fend off and protect the public against terrorist acts. It wasted money and effort in putting up a huge Homeland Security bureaucracy, when even a relatively small bureaucracy like that of the FBI had not been able to coordinate information within its own ranks. It has put a great deal of money into increased surveillance, but shortchanged the security needs of airports, ports, and other vulnerable infrastructure such as electric and nuclear facilities, and water pumping stations.

> *"A very large fraction of the new money allocated to 'security' after 9/11 went to . . . non-terrorism-related projects . . . abroad that served the . . . Bush agenda."*

Although the front lines of defense against terrorist attacks are the local police, firefighters, and emergency workers, and although many new homeland security duties were placed upon them, U.S. cities have received only "a relative pittance" to fund these activities and because of Congress's combining new homeland security funds with existing federal monies for crime prevention, public safety, and emergency preparedness, "America's cities and towns actually experienced a net loss in federal support.". . .

The Department of Homeland Security alerts call for action by local emergency providers, although ordinary citizens are free to ignore them. These alerts therefore regularly require overtime payments for local police and others, and the U.S. Conference of Mayors estimates that cities have been spending an additional $70 million per week on personnel costs alone to keep up with Orange Alert demands. [Author] David Morris points out that "Bush's strategy of distinguishing between local and national security has led to a truly bizarre situation. Whenever the likelihood of a terrorist attack goes up, the capacity of our communities to cope goes down.". . . Add to this the fiscal crisis now besetting states and local governments, with virtually no aid from the Bush administration—which is busy pumping federal resources into military and occupation expenditures and tax cuts for Bush cronies and business supporters, and the local capacity to respond to terrorism is weakened further.

Manufacturing Terrorists

During the Vietnam War the U.S. military displayed its mastery of the art of creating enemies by its racist contempt for the little "yellow dwarves" ([former U.S. president] Lyndon Johnson) and the lavish use of firepower on "suspected Vietcong villages." This country also used chemicals on a large scale to destroy peasant rice crops (Operation Ranch Hand). The U.S. military succeeded in producing two enemy soldiers for every one they killed, but never quite grasped where these new replacement soldiers were coming from. But not everybody in the military was confused—as U.S. Army Master Sergeant Donald Duncan testified in 1966: "One day I asked one of our Vietnamese helicopter pilots what he thought of the last bomb raid. [He answered] 'I think maybe today we make many Vietcong'."

George Bush and his cabal have built on this tradition. The United States is using chemical and biological agents against drug-related crops, with spillover to other crops, in Colombia. This is a superb hate- and terrorist-producing operation.

The Bush administration has entered into a close alliance with "man of peace" [Israeli prime minister] Ariel Sharon and has given virtually unconditional support to Israel's ethnic cleansing, and it is completely unconcerned with Israel's nuclear (and chemical-biological) arsenal and threats while aggressively threatening any Israeli neighbor daring to pursue similar arms. Bush declared an openended "war on terror," first announced as a "crusade," with a very obvious anti-Islam bias, but is open to support of any government willing to align with the Bush team in its global projection of power. Many authoritarian governments have been happy to join the war as it has provided them with aid and protection in their own campaigns to attack and crush dissident movements.

The serial wars, first, Afghanistan, then Iraq, with others openly threatened, have been extremely well designed to produce terrorists. In both cases (as in Vietnam), by the lavish use of firepower that killed and injured large numbers of civilians, and by the ground behavior of U.S. troops (beating, handcuffing and blindfolding men, women and children, and shooting to kill at the slightest provocation)—taking numerous prisoners in blind sweeps, treating them badly, and holding them for long periods without charge or ability to communicate with their families. In Afghanistan, large numbers of Taliban[4] prisoners were murdered in prison and in transit to other locations, mainly by U.S. allies but with obvious U.S. acquiescence. There are thousands of prisoners in Iraq whose status and treatment are unclear but whose treatment is in clear violation of international law.

> *"The serial wars, first Afghanistan, then Iraq, with others openly threatened, have been extremely well designed to produce terrorists."*

Bush justified the attack on Iraq on the basis of Iraq's alleged providing "training and safe haven to terrorists . . . who would willingly use weapons of mass destruction against America and other peace-loving countries." But as [journalist] Jonathan Freedland has pointed out, "With astonishing speed, the United States and Britain are making their nightmares come true. Iraq is fast becoming the land that they warned about . . ." So while the Bush claim was a lie, "events have taken care of that little lacuna in the US argument."

But it would be a mistake to think that the Bush cabal regrets this wee mis-

---

4. Islamist movement that ruled most of Afghanistan from 1996 until 2001

take. They wanted an excuse to invade and occupy and used many lies as justification. Furthermore, I don't believe they are all that upset over the fact that their policies have produced more terrorism, although the difficulty and costs of pacifying Iraq is definitely a setback. But just as 9/11 was a Bush windfall, so further terrorist acts will give him and the cabal the further fear and "security" cover for the continued projection of power abroad and service to the corporate community and military-industrial complex at home. This works because the mainstream media get on each terrorist gambit bandwagon and refuse to point out the self-fulfilling character of the Bush policies in which wholesale terror elicits retail terror. The hope is that the costs of these cruel and dangerous policies, feeding back on ordinary citizens and making them steadily poorer and more insecure, will produce a public enlightenment and outcry that will affect the media and have political consequences.

U.S. Actions in the War on Terror Have Damaged the United Nations' Peacekeeping Power

by Matthew Rothschild

About the author: *Matthew Rothschild is editor of the* Progressive, *a monthly magazine that promotes peace and social justice around the world.*

Editor's Note: The following article was published immediately after the U.S.-led invasion of Iraq, which was launched on March 19, 2003.

On June 26, 1945, in San Francisco, the United Nations was born, and former Secretary of State Cordell Hull won the Nobel Prize for his efforts in creating the institution. He called the U.N. charter "one of the great milestones in man's upward climb toward a truly civilized existence." Almost six decades later, George W. Bush has done more to reverse this upward climb than anyone in the postwar period. The audacity of Bush's Iraq war maneuvers and his crude bullying threatens not only the United Nations but the dream of world governance and world peace. This dream animated [former U.S. presidents] Woodrow Wilson and Franklin D. Roosevelt and hundreds of millions of people across the globe who saw the world torn asunder by the hideous wars of the twentieth century. Roosevelt called the United Nations a "world organization for permanent peace." Now in the early hours of the twenty-first century, Bush returns international relations to the raw power politics of the nineteenth century and abandons international law for the law of the jungle.

The sign was clear back on September 12, 2002, when Bush first addressed the United Nations on the subject of Iraq. So relieved were member nations that the President deigned to appear before the international body that they seemed deaf to the insulting words he was hurling at them. "Will the United Nations serve the purpose of its founding, or will it be irrelevant?" Bush asked.

At the time, even the French were praising Bush. He has resisted "the temptation of unilateral action," said France's foreign minister, Dominique de Villepin. Amr Moussa, Secretary General of the Arab League, said "the turn President Bush has taken in asking the United Nations to take up its responsibility is a good one." They apparently did not realize that Bush was engaging in a mere charade and that he was fully prepared to render the United Nations irrelevant himself.

Making the Security Council Irrelevant

Bush tarred the Security Council with the brush of irrelevance for not enforcing previous resolutions Iraq had flouted. He repeated the charge at his March 6 [2003] press conference: "The fundamental question facing the Security Council is, will its words mean anything? When the Security Council speaks, will the words have merit and weight?"

But Bush's insistence that the Security Council back up its resolutions is selective in the extreme. Iraq is not the only country to violate Security Council resolutions. In fact, it is not the country that violates the most resolutions. That distinction belongs to Israel, which has violated thirty-two Security Council resolutions. Turkey has violated twenty-four, and Morocco sixteen, according to Stephen Zunes, associate professor of politics at the University of San Francisco and chair of its peace and justice studies program. By comparison, Iraq has violated seventeen resolutions.

Since Israel, Turkey, and Morocco are U.S. allies, Bush has not been browbeating the Security Council to make good on its word by threatening force against these countries. And you don't hear Bush talking about gathering a "coalition of the willing" to impose regime change in Jerusalem, Ankara, and Rabat. To see how outrageous Bush's action is, consider how Washington would have felt if Russia had told the U.N. Security Council that it was going to gather a "coalition of the willing" to impose regime change on those three countries. Bush, Congress, and the pundits would be condemning Russia as a reckless and renegade country. Today, the United States is that reckless and renegade country.

Bush's essential message is, the United Nations is irrelevant if it doesn't do exactly what Washington demands. And Bush has chided the United Nations not to become another failure like the League of Na-

> *"The audacity of Bush's Iraq war maneuvers and his crude bullying threatens not only the United Nations but the dream of world governance and world peace."*

tions, though the League of Nations collapsed [in 1946, replaced by the United Nations], in part, because the U.S. Senate never ratified U.S. entry into the organization.

"Bush has made it abundantly clear that he feels the United Nations is just a nuisance," says John Anderson, head of the World Federalist Association, who ran for President as an independent in 1980. "It's a very specious and hypocritical attitude to sigh and wonder whether the U.N. is going the way of the League of Nations when Bush himself has done everything in his power to see that this happens."

A mere glance back at the U.N. Charter reveals how far from its letter and spirit Bush has now traveled. Article 2, Section 3, states that "all members shall settle their international disputes by peaceful means." And Article 2, Section 4, says, "All members shall refrain in their international relations from the threat or use of force against the territorial integrity or political independence of any state." Bush's entire discussion of "regime change," his mobilizing of more than 200,000 troops [as of April 2003], and his constant threats of force since September [2002] are in clear violation of this article.

And if he goes on and wages aggressive war, which is "the ultimate crime" in international law, according to Michael Ratner of the Center for Constitutional Rights, he could be tried in an international court.[1] (In any event, Bush has been shirking his constitutional duty to enforce the laws, since treaties signed and ratified by the United States are supposed to be inviolable.)

"If the U.N. Security Council had been behaving in the way it ought to, it should have been saying all along that the United States was carrying out illegal acts by threatening force," says Stephen Shalom, professor of political science at William Paterson University in New Jersey. "The U.S. was in violation of the charter, and the council should have said so.". . .

> *"Bush's insistence that the [United Nations] Security Council back up its resolutions is selective in the extreme."*

The End of an International System

"We're seeing the end of the international system as we've known it since the Second World War," says Ratner.

"This is the most dangerous and depressing moment in my life," says Richard Falk, a professor of international law and practice at Princeton. "The United States is undeterred and undeterrable in the current situation. It repudiates any willingness to allow the United Nations to act independently, and it refuses to accept a set of restraints derived from international law. This is a free-fall situation."

In late February and early March [2003], Bush put the United Nations in an impossible bind. "He clearly has confronted the U.N. with an untenable dilemma of either being a rubber stamp for U.S. geopolitics or finding itself bypassed on a major threat to peace and security by the most important member of the institution," says Falk.

---

1. On March 19, 2003, a U.S.-led coalition invaded Iraq.

Using Corleone-style [Mafia-style] tactics, Bush pulled out all the stops to gain support of the council. "What's unique is the scale and the audacity of the bribing," says Phyllis Bennis, a fellow at the Institute for Policy Studies and co-author of the group's report "Coalition of the Willing or Coalition of the Coerced?" Almost every country faced "coercion, bullying, bribery, or the implied threat of U.S. action that would directly damage the interests of the country," the report says. Many

> *"A mere glance back at the U.N. Charter reveals how far from its letter and spirit [George W.] Bush has now traveled."*

nations may remember what the United States did to Yemen prior to the Gulf War in 1991. "When Yemen, the sole Arab country on the council, voted against the resolution authorizing war, a U.S. diplomat told the Yemeni ambassador, 'That will be the most expensive no vote you ever cast.' Three days later, the U.S. cut its entire aid budget to Yemen," the report notes.

Still, the resistance many countries put up was remarkable. From Turkey to Chile to Mexico, governments that Washington could usually rely on bucked the pressure at least for a while. That was because of the astonishing, unprecedented global peace movement that demanded, in country after country, that leaders not give in to Washington.

"The 'coalition of the coerced' stands in direct conflict with democracy," the report adds. "In most nations, including those most closely allied to the United States, over 70 percent of the public opposes U.S. military action against Iraq."

Washington further sullied its image by spying on Security Council members, according to a story the *London Observer* broke. That paper obtained a copy of a National Security Agency memo outlining its snooping to obtain "the whole gamut of information that could give U.S. policymakers an edge in obtaining results favorable to U.S. goals to head off surprises.". . .

Bush was positively cocksure when asked at his March 6 [2003] press conference whether the United States had the right to attack Iraq without Security Council approval. "If we need to act, we will act, and we really don't need United Nations approval to do so," he said. "We really don't need anybody's permission." As a matter of fact, the U.N. Charter says the only time a country can act alone is "if an armed attack occurs against" it.

"Assuming Bush is going to war anyway, it's better to have the U.N. not give Bush the endorsement," says Shalom. "That will help galvanize opposition, and it will make it impossible for Bush to claim he's acting in conformity with international law or the will of the international community."

Changes in Global Power

The Security Council was set up to reflect the global power arrangements at the end of World War II, and those arrangements no longer exist. Roosevelt "viewed the Security Council as a direct extension of the Big Three [United

States, United Kingdom, and Soviet Union] wartime alliance," Townsend Hoopes and Douglas Brinkley write in *FDR and the Creation of the U.N.* (Yale, 1997). "In his view, Big Power cooperation was imperative for settling or suppressing conflicts between and among the lesser nations. . . . At the same time, he understood that there was no mechanistic remedy for unresolved conflict between Big Powers."

But now the other "Big Powers" are not so big anymore. The Soviet Union has vanished. Britain and France are nowhere near as strong as they were at the time of the founding. China is not yet a full rival to the United States. And so Washington thinks it can have its way.

The old system was not perfect, by any means. The very establishment of these five permanent voting members on the Security Council was undemocratic. If the world body really wanted to be fair, it would have no permanent members and simply would rotate members through the council. But the establishment of the Security Council with the so-called Big Five each having veto power was a realistic bow to the powerful.

"The main lesson he [Roosevelt] drew from the League failure was that responsibility for world peace depended exclusively on the few nations that possessed real power and that they must 'run the world' for an indefinite transitional period," Hoopes and Brinkley write.

As the permanent members of the Security Council divided into Cold War blocs, they didn't run the world very well. Only by luck and icy nerves during the Cuban Missile Crisis did the two superpowers spare the world from nuclear annihilation. And many regional conflicts raged, most notably in the Middle East, Southern Africa, Central America, Southeast Asia, and the Indian subcontinent.

Precedents for U.S. Unilateralism

Nor is Bush by any means the first President to flout the United Nations. The United States was able to gain U.N. approval for the Korean War only by a fluke: The Soviet representative was boycotting the Security Council at the time. And [former U.S. president Harry] Truman acknowledged that he was ready to bypass the United Nations if need be. "No doubt about it," he said years later when asked if he would have gone to war against Korea without U.N. approval, according to Hoopes and Brinkley.

> *"'We're seeing the end of the international system as we've known it since the Second World War.'"*

The United States waged war against Vietnam, Cambodia and Laos without formal approval of the Security Council. It also attacked, among others, Panama, Grenada, the Dominican Republic, and Libya, and it destabilized many more countries without such approval.

"Bush's unilateralism has plenty of precedents," says [author] Noam Chomsky. But it has taken "a long step beyond" where previous Administrations have gone. "Its forthright declaration that it intends to rule the world by force" amounts to a kind of "fanaticism," Chomsky says.

Even Presidents who were flouting the United Nations tried to bow to international norms, Falk says. No one up to George W. Bush has been so reckless in disregarding the institution. "What worries me most is the absence of limits on Washington," Falk says. "We live in a unipolar world, you have the United States intent on pursuing a global dominance project, and there is no countervailing power.

> *"No one up to George W. Bush has been so reckless in disregarding the [United Nations]."*

The Cold War, at least, had the international benefit of a countervailing force. You were not as dependent on the law. There is a greater dependence on international law in a unipolar world." But Bush acts as though he is not bound by that law.

Franklin Roosevelt warned: "We shall have to take the responsibility for world collaboration, or we shall have to bear the responsibility for another world conflict." But Bush has disdained, and dispensed with, "world collaboration," and so world conflict is on the horizon.

Consequences of Unilateralism

What are the consequences of Bush's trashing the United Nations? "The unilateral path is horribly destructive, and almost certain to be self-destructive," says Falk. "As a precedent, it's horrible: An endless number of countries could invoke this kind of preemptive logic. China could use it against Taiwan, and it could lead to a nuclear war between India and Pakistan."

William Hartung of the World Policy Institute shares this fear. "Every regional tyrant will feel free to do to its enemies—internal and external what Bush and his clique are doing to Iraq," he says.

It also gives other nations a clear indication that their own self-interest lies not in taking issues to the United Nations but in establishing facts on the ground. North Korea's game of nuclear chicken[2] may not be the aberrant notion of a crazy ruler but a rational response to Washington's aggressiveness. Such actions may increasingly be the norm in a lawless future.

Even for U.S. security, the approach is counterproductive. "It will cause international backlash, generate more suicide bombings, lead to more religious and political extremism, and possibly cause a fundamentalist takeover in Pakistan or Egypt," says Falk. "It could be a geopolitical disaster."

Such a disaster is what impelled the career foreign service officer John Brady Kiesling, who was serving in the U.S. embassy in Greece, to resign from the

---

2. attempts to obtain an increasing number of nuclear weapons, in violation of international agreements

State Department on January 27 [2003]. "The policies we are now asked to advance are incompatible not only with American values but also with American interests," he wrote in his resignation letter to Secretary of State Colin Powell. "Our fervent pursuit of war with Iraq is driving us to squander the international legitimacy that has been America's most potent weapon of both offense and defense since the days of Woodrow Wilson. We have begun to dismantle the largest and most effective web of international relationships the world has ever known. Our current course will bring instability and danger, not security."

The flexing of sheer brute force that so typifies the Bush policy gives terrorists and other nonstate actors the message that the superpower cannot be restrained by traditional, legal channels but only by "asymmetrical" and extralegal means. Ratner at the Center for Constitutional Rights says the Bush approach, "in terms of our security and safety, is fatal." He worries the United States will alienate its allies in the war on terrorism, and that "by not using international law and peaceful methods, it will bring about a huge radicalization in parts of the world that are going to terrorize us further."

Ratner says the United Nations may never be the same again. "Like [author] F. Scott Fitzgerald after his nervous breakdown, who said he was like a plate that was glued back together and was no good for serving dinner on but useful only for snacks, the U.N. will be used for noncontroversial issues, but when it comes to the use of force, it will be a cracked plate," Ratner says.

The final cost of this policy is internal. "It could destroy democracy at home," Falk argues. "The rising tide of opposition here and abroad will play into fearmongering and an expansion of government control over citizen rights. There is a kind of proto-fascist dimension to the current set of circumstances." Falk says he usually is loath to throw the term "fascism" around. "But you have this crackdown, coupled with a consolidation of military power and a messianic view that the United States is the bearer of a benevolent future that justifies exterminating those who stand in the way," he explains. "You have the convergence of religious evangelicals in the White House with geopolitical fundamentalists like [political adviser] Richard Perle and [U.S. deputy secretary of defense] Paul Wolfowitz. We have never had this mixture of religious and secular extremists so close to the core of governmental power."

> *"The United Nations may never be the same again."*

Importance of the United Nations

Given the U.S. manipulation of the United Nations, there may be some progressive people who wonder why we should even bother with it. But not bothering would be a mistake.

"We should support the U.N. and international law for the same reasons we support democracy and other values," says Chomsky. "The fact that they are trampled to dust and treated with contempt by power centers does not mean that these values and institutions should be tossed into the ashcan of history."

Chomsky and other observers take note of the one hopeful sign in [early 2003]: the rise of the massive international peace movement. "We should never rest hopes in institutions," says Chomsky. "I have to admit that the basic truth of the matter appeared in the lead paragraphs of a front-page story in my favorite newspaper, *The New York Times*, a couple of days after the demos: *The Times* reported that there are now two superpowers on the planet, the U.S. and world opinion. Our hopes should rest in the second superpower."

Bennis of the Institute for Policy Studies says this second superpower can find a home at the United Nations. "People throughout the world are looking at the U.N. as part of this global anti-war movement." More hopeful than most, she believes Bush already may ironically be pushing the United Nations to assume a new, more powerful role. "He's trying to do enormous damage," she says. "But the ferocity of his attack has had exactly the opposite result. Right now, the United Nations is not only more relevant but is gaining more backbone because of Bush's blatant actions. The United Nations has a somewhat new identity as the centerpiece of the global movement against the U.S. empire. It's exactly where the U.N. belongs: organizing the defiance of the world against the superpower."

There will come a day when the United States is no longer king of the hill, when other powers arise to challenge Washington for dominance. The Roman Empire lasted 500 years. The British Empire lasted almost 400 years. The Soviet Empire vanished within seventy-five years. The 1,000 Year Reich lasted barely more than a single decade. The American Empire will fade, as well. At such a time, it would be in the interest of the United States to have still standing an institution that can act as a buffer against war.

But Bush and [Vice President Richard] Cheney and [Secretary of Defense Donald] Rumsfeld can't imagine that day, and so they can't imagine that need. They foresee, explicitly in their new strategic doctrine, indefinite U.S. military preeminence, and they are eager to go to war "preemptively" whenever another nation attempts to vie for power against the United States.

The founders of the United Nations, in the words of the charter, created an institution to save succeeding generations from "the scourge of war." But Bush does not consider war a "scourge." He uses it as a favorite tool to ensure the predominance of the United States, and thus he denies the basic purpose of the United Nations.

The War on Iraq Has United Muslims Against the United States

by Ed Blanche

About the author: *Ed Blanche is a contributing writer for the* Middle East, *a monthly magazine that offers analysis of events in the Middle East region.*

The conquest and occupation of Iraq [in 2003] has radicalised the Muslim world to an unprecedented degree, many believe to the point where Sunni and Shi'ite hardliners are now putting aside their historic differences and preparing to join forces against a common enemy—the West.

For years, the idea of an Islamic alliance between Sunni and Shi'ite has been a nightmare scenario for western intelligence agencies, their allies in the Muslim world and Israel. Ever since the 1980s, there have been indications that hardliners from both denominations have been setting aside the theological differences that have kept them apart for 14 centuries and are possibly already cooperating on particular operations in which the interests of all concerned are advanced. . . .

But no formalised hard-and-fast alliance between Shi'ite and Sunni hardliners, dedicated to attacking the West and its Arab friends, ever seemed to emerge. By some accounts, that may be changing, largely as a consequence of the 11 September 2001, and the United States' response to the unprecedented terrorist attack on its soil.

The issue is clouded by intrigue and political agendas, propaganda from all sides, Iran, Israel, the US and elsewhere. But there seems little doubt that George W. Bush's war against terrorism is increasingly perceived in the Muslim world as a new Judeo-Christian crusade against Islam and its people. The conquest and occupation of Iraq has radicalised the Muslim world to an unprecedented degree.

These days, Iran and its Shi'ite Lebanese ally, [political party] Hizbullah, are

Ed Blanche, "Brothers in Arms? An Old Arab Proverb Notes: My Brother and Me Against My Cousin, My Cousin and Me Against the Stranger," *The Middle East*, December 2003. Reproduced by permission.

actively aiding the Palestinian Sunni fundamentalists of [paramilitary and political organization] Hamas and [terrorist group] Islamic Jihad, and latterly secular Sunni-dominated forces loyal to [leader of the Palestinian Authority] Yasser Arafat as well.

That is a relationship that goes back to 1992, when Israel tried to deport 415 Sunni activists of Hamas to Lebanon. Beirut refused to let them in, leaving the activists stranded in no-man's land on the border for seven months, during which time the Shi'ite militants taught their Sunni cousins how to conduct suicide bombings. The Hamas men were eventually taken back into Israel and the first Palestinian suicide bombing followed in April 1994.

Cooperation with Al Qaeda?

As for [terrorist group] Al Qaeda, the Americans have . . . alleged that militant forces in Iran, such as the IRGC [Islamic Revolutionary Guard Corps] and its Qods (Jerusalem) Force, which is responsible for all clandestine activities outside Iran, are working hand-in-glove with Osama bin Laden's network, which is Sunni, and bringing them together with Hizbullah, a long-time enemy of the US.

It is difficult to verify these claims, but it is clear that Sunni and Shi'ite militants are increasingly finding common cause against the US and its principal Middle Eastern ally, Israel. While there are differences between the two Muslim denominations, which have flared into violence, as in Pakistan today [2003,] the perceived threat to Islam from the US since 9/11 has eroded those differences.

Still, it is difficult for some to accept that Iran's Shi'ite leadership has joined forces with Al Qaeda, an overwhelmingly Sunni network virulently opposed to Shi'aism. Al Qaeda was, and remains, a close ally of the Taliban,[1] whose hostility towards Tehran almost led to war on a couple of occasions before the Americans defeated the Afghan fundamentalists in late 2001.

One of Osama bin Laden's operatives, a former Egyptian soldier named Ali Mohammed, testified in a US court four years ago admitting that he arranged a face-to-face meeting between Bin Laden and one of Hizbullah's top masterminds, Imad Mughniyeh, in Sudan in 1993, and that Hizbullah provided explosives training for Al Qaeda fighters.

There have been reports of subsequent cooperation between the two groups, although Hizbullah has denied any dealings with Al Qaeda. Israel claims Sudan's Hasan Al Turabi, until a couple of years ago the power

> *"The conquest and occupation of Iraq has radicalised the Muslim world to an unprecedented degree."*

behind the Khartoum [Sudan] regime, and Abdallah Nuri, leader of Tajikistan's Islamic movement and a Bin Laden ally, sought to bring Hizbullah and Al Qaeda together on other occasions.

---

1. Islamist group that ruled most of Afghanistan from 1996 until 2001

"Recent history has demonstrated that there are few religious-ideological barriers in the world of international terrorism," according to a recent paper by Israel's Institute for Contemporary Affairs. "It would be a mistake to assume that Islamist international terror groups are driven primarily by the religious associations with radical Sunni or radical Shi'ite Islam. These groups have their own geopolitical interests in bridging this great Islamic divide—particularly their antipathy for the United States and its allies."

The *Washington Post* recently [in 2003] quoted US intelligence sources as saying that Osama bin Laden's 24-year-old son, Saad, and other high-ranking Al Qaeda figures were being given sanctuary in Iran, from where they are masterminding terrorist operations against the West. This all sounds remarkably like the Bush administration's efforts to link Al Qaeda with Saddam Hussein as a justification for invading Iraq.

That premise proved to be totally false—although, if the Americans are to be believed, Al Qaeda activists are now joining the Iraqi resistance to US occupation. "This looks like a US attempt to focus the war on terrorism on Iran, possibly to intensify the pressure over its nuclear programme," one European intelligence source told *The Middle East.*

Still, although the government of reformist President Mohammed Khatami may be seeking to improve Iran's relations with the West and curb Islamic militancy, his administration has no control over the IRGC and other hard-line organisations that oppose dialogue. Like other key centres of power in Iran, the IRGC remains in the hands of the hard-liners led by the nation's supreme leader, Ayatollah Ali Khamenei, with access to the huge wealth of foundations known as bonyads outside of government control. The bonyads, which control the vast holdings seized from the monarchy when it fell, are largely run by conservative organisations who in the past have been involved in clandestine operations, some intended to discredit political moderates.

> *"There seems little doubt that George W. Bush's war against terrorism is increasingly perceived . . . as a new Judeo-Christian crusade against Islam and its people."*

The Shi'ite hard-liners may well have made an alliance of convenience with the Sunnis of Al Qaeda to combat US forces now installed, far too close for comfort, in neighbouring Iraq and Afghanistan. But that arrangement could be subsumed by political expediency, for instance if Tehran surrenders to the Americans Al Qaeda operatives it says it holds in return for the Bush administration easing pressure on the Islamic republic.

Pushing Sunni and Shi'ite Together

It is ironic that the US invasion of Iraq may be the instrument that pushes Sunni and Shi'ite together. An emerging alliance of Shi'ites and Sunnis in postwar Iraq may be the path to stability and the answer to the Americans' inept efforts to end the chaos they engendered when they deposed Saddam's brutal regime. Despite the escalating guerrilla war against the Americans, so far, at least, there has been no manifestation of the blood bath between the long-repressed Shi'ites, who comprise some 60% of Iraq's 24 million population, and the minority Sunnis who dominated Saddam's regime, that many had feared would happen once the war ended.

> *"While there are differences between the two Muslim denominations [of Sunni and Shi'ite]... the perceived threat to Islam from the US ... has eroded those differences."*

Indeed, two key leaders of the rival denominations, the firebrand Shi'ite preacher Muqtada Al Sadr and the charismatic Ahmed Kubeisi of the Sunnis, have come together to oppose the US occupation and both command considerable grassroots support from their co-religionists. Both have preached unity among Sunnis and Shi'ites and both have fallen foul of the Americans, who view the alliance between the two clerics with concern and dismay and have blocked both from sitting on the US-appointed 25-member Governing Council of Iraq.

Given Saddam's brutal crackdown over the years on the Shi'ites, who dominate southern Iraq and pockets west of Baghdad, it came as little surprise that the US occupation found the most support among Iraq's largest religious group. But radicals like Sadr, the son of a revered Shi'ite cleric, Mohammed Sadiq Sadr, who was murdered in 1999 by Saddam's regime, have been taking an increasingly hostile position against the occupation that could extend the violence, so far [in December 2003] largely confined to the so-called Sunni Triangle north and west of Baghdad, to the volatile south as well.

Indications of an Alliance

An indication of the alliance between Sadr and Kubeisi have been the slogans that have recently appeared in mosques which read: No Sunni. No Shi'ite. Only Islam.

The opposite seems to be happening in Pakistan, the main arena of Sunni-Shi'ite bloodshed and there are many in the Muslim world who subscribe to the theory that the West has, over the years, sought to perpetuate and whenever possible exacerbate the Sunni-Shi'ite schism, with the intention of weakening political Islam.

Many Muslims believe that certain pro-western Arab regimes may have helped maintain the religious schism for political purposes, largely by financing militant Sunni factions in Pakistan, Afghanistan and elsewhere over the years.

"It is this unholy alliance of secular Arab nationalism of Saddam's Iraq, Islamic fundamentalism and western imperialism with its massive media resources that has created the present perception of a vast Shi'ite-Sunni divide," according to Islamic analyst Sultan Shahin.

"The fact that the widely predicted Shi'ite backlash against the decades long Sunni domination of Iraq has not materialised may mean that the imperialist project of divide and rule has not succeed[ed] in that country, at least so far," he wrote recently. "Now it is for the Shi'ites and Sunnis in other parts of [the] world to build on the Iraqi example and seek to bridge the gulf separating the two denominations to promote harmony and peace undeterred by the bigotry of extremism and the machinations of imperialist powers."

Chronology

1989

Osama bin Laden founds an international terrorist group known as al Qaeda (the Base).

1991

April: Saudi Arabia expels Bin Laden, and he takes up residence in Sudan.

1993

February 26: A bomb in a van explodes in the underground parking garage of New York's World Trade Center, killing six people and wounding more than a thousand.

1994

April: Saudi Arabia strips Bin Laden of his citizenship.

1995

April 19: A truck bomb at the federal building in Oklahoma City, Oklahoma, kills 168 people.

1996

Sudan offers to turn Bin Laden over to the United States or Saudi Arabia, but both countries refuse the offer. The United States lacks the evidence to indict him.

May 18: Sudan expels Bin Laden, and he moves to Afghanistan.

September 27: The fundamentalist Islamic Taliban takes power in Afghanistan.

1998

January 8: Ramzi Yousef, an associate of Bin Laden, is sentenced to life without parole for orchestrating the 1993 World Trade Center bombing.

February 22: Bin Laden issues an edict calling for attacks on American citizens.

August: Terrorist bombs destroy U.S. embassies in Kenya and Tanzania, killing hundreds and wounding thousands. Osama bin Laden is later indicted for this attack by a U.S. grand jury; the United States attacks targets in Afghanistan and Sudan in retaliation for the bombings.

2000

October 12: The navy destroyer USS *Cole* in the Yemeni port of Aden is attacked by terrorists linked to Bin Laden. Seventeen crew members are killed and approximately forty are injured.

2001

September 11: Arab terrorists hijack four U.S. airliners, crashing two into the World Trade Center, one into the Pentagon, and one into a field in western Pennsylvania. The attacks result in the deaths of approximately three thousand people.

September 13: Osama bin Laden is named as the prime suspect in the September 11 attacks.

October 7: The United States, with support from the United Kingdom and Afghanistan's Northern Alliance, launches Operation Enduring Freedom, an invasion of Afghanistan to oust the Taliban regime believed to be harboring al Qaeda.

October 26: The Uniting and Strengthening America by Providing Appropriate Tools Required to Intercept and Obstruct Terrorism Act (USA PATRIOT Act) is passed. This law expands the power of the federal government to gather information by wiretapping and other techniques.

October–November: Letters containing anthrax are sent to offices in several U.S. cities, killing five and sickening seventeen.

November: President George W. Bush signs an executive order allowing military tribunals against any foreigners suspected of having connections to terrorist acts or planned acts on the United States.

November 19: Bush signs the Aviation and Transportation Security Act, creating the Transportation Security Administration (TSA).

November 25: American John Walker Lindh is captured while fighting for the Taliban in Afghanistan. He is subsequently convicted of engaging in terrorist acts and sentenced to twenty years in federal prison.

December 6: The last major Taliban stronghold in Afghanistan falls to U.S.-led forces.

December 13: The U.S. Department of Defense releases a videotape of Osama bin Laden discussing the September 11 terrorist attacks. The tape shows Bin Laden saying that the devastation caused by the attacks far exceeded his expectations.

2002

January 12: The first group of al Qaeda prisoners from Afghanistan is taken to a U.S. camp at Guantánamo Bay, Cuba. There is international criticism over the treatment of the prisoners and the fact that they are being held indefinitely.

January 29: Bush delivers his annual State of the Union address. In it he describes Iraq, Iran, and North Korea as an "axis of evil" because they promote terrorism.

February: The Total Information Awarness (TIA) project is announced. The project is designed to collect, index, and consolidate all available information on everyone in America in a central repository for perusal by the U.S. government. Due to widespread protest, the program is suspended in late 2003.

May 8: American José Padilla is arrested under suspicion of participating in the construction of a radioactive "dirty bomb." He is held without access to a lawyer, and without legal proceedings. In December 2003 the U.S. Supreme Court orders the government to release him; however, the government appeals this decision and Padilla continues to be detained.

September: The Justice Department launches a special registration procedure for certain male noncitizens in the United States, requiring them to register in person at immigration service offices; Ramzi Binalshibh, believed to be one of the planners of the September 11 attacks, is captured in Pakistan.

October 4: Six suspected members of the al Qaeda terrorist network operating in new Buffalo, New York, are indicted.

October 12: Two bombs explode in a discotheque in Bali, killing more than two hundred people and injuring more than three hundred. Islamic terrorists are suspected.

November: Bush signs the Homeland Security Act of 2002, establishing the Department of Homeland Security, which consolidates twenty-two government agencies; the United Nations Security Council unanimously adopts Resolution 1441, which outlines an inspection regime for Iraq's disarmament. Iraq accepts the resolution and UN inspections are conducted there.

December: Iraq provides weapons inspectors with twelve thousand pages of information about the regime's chemical, biological, and nuclear weapons programs and declares that there are no weapons of mass destruction (WMDs) in Iraq.

2003

February: The United States, Great Britain, and Spain state that Iraq has failed to comply with Resolution 1441 and ask the UN Security Council to approve the use of force against the country. France, Germany, and Russia oppose the use of force and request that inspections be intensified.

March 1: Khalid Sheikh Mohammed, the alleged architect of the September 11 attacks, is captured in Pakistan.

March 17: The Homeland Security Department commences Operation Liberty Shield, an increase in protective measures to defend the homeland; without UN support, Bush issues an ultimatum that either Saddam Hussein and his sons leave Iraq within forty-eight hours or the United States will pursue military action against Iraq.

March 19: A U.S.-led campaign against Iraq begins as American missiles hit targets in Baghdad. U.S. and British ground troops enter Iraq from the south.

May 1: Bush declares an end to major combat operations in Iraq. The UN Security Council approves a resolution backing the U.S.-led administration of Iraq. The United States abolishes the Ba'ath Party and institutions of the former regime; the Terrorist Threat Integration Center, created to integrate intelligence on terrorism collected at home and abroad, begins operations.

July: Hussein's sons Uday and Qusay Hussein are killed by U.S. troops. U.S. forces in Iraq face guerrilla-style warfare from Iraqis opposed to the occupation.

August: U.S. and British casualties in Iraq reach 298.

August 12: Hemant Lakhani, a London arms dealer, is arrested for trying to smuggle surface-to-air missiles.

August 19: Iraqi vice president Taha Yasin Ramadan Al-Jizrawi, number twenty on the U.S. most-wanted list of terrorists, is captured.

October: According to an interim report by David Kay, the lead investigator searching for weapons of mass destruction in Iraq, none have been found.

November: Mohammed Hamdi al Ahdal, a top al Qaeda leader in Yemen, is captured; the number of U.S. and British deaths in Iraq reaches 510; the Bush administration agrees to transfer power to an interim Iraqi government early in 2004.

December 13: Saddam Hussein is captured by U.S. forces in Iraq.

2004

March 1: The Department of Homeland Security celebrates its one-year anniversary.

March 11: Terrorist bombings on commuter trains in Madrid, Spain, take hundreds of lives in the deadliest terrorist attack on a European target since World War II.

June: The United States turns over the administration of Iraq to the Iraqis.

Organizations to Contact

The editors have compiled the following list of organizations concerned with the issues debated in this book. The descriptions are derived from materials provided by the organizations. All have publications or information available for interested readers. The list was compiled on the date of publication of the present volume; names, addresses, phone and fax numbers, and e-mail addresses may change. Be aware that many organizations take several weeks or longer to respond to inquiries, so allow as much time as possible.

American Civil Liberties Union (ACLU)
125 Broad St., 18th Fl., New York, NY 10004
(212) 549-2500
e-mail: aclu@aclu.org • Web site: www.aclu.org

The American Civil Liberties Union is a national organization that works to defend Americans' civil rights guaranteed by the U.S. Constitution, arguing that measures to protect national security should not compromise fundamental civil liberties. It publishes and distributes policy statements, pamphlets, and press releases, including *Civil Liberties After 9-11: The ACLU Defends Freedom* and *Bigger Monster, Weaker Chains: The Growth of an American Surveillance Society.*

American Enterprise Institute (AEI)
1150 Seventeenth St. NW, Washington, DC 20036
(202) 862-5800 • fax: (202) 862-7177
e-mail: info@aei.org • Web site: www.aei.org

The American Enterprise Institute for Public Policy Research is a scholarly research institute that is dedicated to preserving a strong foreign policy and national defense. Its publications include articles in its magazine, *American Enterprise*, and books including *Study of Revenge: The First World Trade Center Attack and Saddam Hussein's War Against America* and *An End to Evil: How to Win the War on Terror*. Articles, speeches, and seminar transcripts on terrorism are available on its Web site.

Arab American Institute (AAI)
1600 K St. NW, Suite 601, Washington, DC 20006
(202) 429-9210
Web site: www.aaiusa.org

AAI is a nonprofit organization committed to the civic and political empowerment of Americans of Arab descent. The institute opposes ethnic profiling and the restriction of immigrants' civil liberties in the name of homeland security. It provides policy, research, and public affairs services to support a broad range of community activities. It publishes a quarterly newsletter called *Issues*, a weekly bulletin called *Countdown*, and the report *Healing the Nation: The Arab American Experience After September 11.*

Brookings Institution
1775 Massachusetts Ave. NW, Washington, DC 20036
(202) 797-6000 • fax: (202) 797-6004
e-mail: brookinfo@brook.edu • Web site: www.brookings.org

The Brookings Institution is a think tank that conducts research and education in foreign policy, economics, government, and the social sciences. Its Saban Center for Middle East Policy develops programs to promote a better understanding of policy choices in the Middle East. Articles on the war against terrorism can be found on the organization's Web site and in its publications, including the quarterly *Brookings Review.*

Cato Institute
1000 Massachusetts Ave. NW, Washington, DC 20001-5403
(202) 842-0200 • fax: (202) 842-3490
e-mail: cato@cato.org • Web site: www.cato.org

The Cato Institute is a libertarian public policy research foundation dedicated to limiting the role of government and promoting free markets and peace. It disapproves of an interventionist foreign policy and believes that the use of U.S. forces in other countries should be limited. The institute publishes the quarterly magazine *Regulation*, the bimonthly *Cato Policy Report*, and numerous papers dealing with foreign policy and terrorism, including "The Empire Strikes Out: 'The New Imperialism' and Its Fatal Flaws," and "Did U.S. Intervention Overseas Breed Terrorism?"

Center for Constitutional Rights (CCR)
666 Broadway, 7th Fl., New York 10012
(212) 614-6464 • fax: (212) 614-6499
Web site: www.ccr-ny.org

CCR is a nonprofit legal and educational organization dedicated to protecting and advancing the rights guaranteed by the U.S. Constitution and the Universal Declaration of Human Rights. The organization uses litigation to empower minority and poor communities and to strengthen the broader movement for constitutional and human rights. It opposes the government's curtailment of civil liberties since the September 11, 2001, terrorist attacks. CCR publishes books, pamphlets, fact sheets, and reports, such as *The State of Civil Liberties: One Year Later.*

Center for Strategic and International Studies (CSIS)
1800 K St. NW, Suite 400, Washington, DC 20006
(202) 887-0200 • fax: (202) 775-3199
Web site: www.csis.org

The center works to provide world leaders with strategic insights and policy options on current and emerging global issues. It publishes books, including *The "Instant" Lessons of the Iraq War*; the *Washington Quarterly*, a journal on political, economic, and security issues; and other publications, including reports that can be downloaded from its Web site.

Council on Foreign Relations
58 E. Sixty-eighth St., New York, NY 10021
(212) 434-9400 • fax: (212) 986-2984
e-mail: communications@cfr.org • Web site: www.cfr.org

The council specializes in foreign affairs and studies the international aspects of American political and economic policies and problems. Its journal *Foreign Affairs*, published five times a year, includes analyses of America's relations with countries around the world.

Department of Homeland Security (DHS)
Washington, DC 20528
Web site: www.dhs.gov

The DHS, created in March 2003, merges twenty-two previously disparate domestic agencies into one department to protect the nation against threats to the homeland. DHS's priority is to protect the United States against terrorist attacks. Component agencies analyze threats and intelligence, guard America's borders and airports, protect critical infrastructure, and coordinate the U.S. response to future emergencies. The DHS Web site offers a wide variety of information on homeland security, including press releases, speeches and testimony, and reports on topics such as airport security, weapons of mass destruction, planning for and responding to emergencies, and border control.

Foreign Policy Association (FPA)
470 Park Ave. South, 2nd Fl., New York, NY 10016
(212) 481-8100 • fax: (212) 481-9275
e-mail: info@fpa.org • Web site: www.fpa.org

FPA is a nonprofit organization that believes a concerned and informed public is the foundation for an effective foreign policy. Publications such as the annual *Great Decisions* briefing book and the quarterly *Headline Series* review U.S. foreign policy issues in China, the Persian Gulf and the Middle East, and Africa.

Global Exchange
2017 Mission St., #303, San Francisco, CA 94110
(415) 255-7296 • fax: (415) 255-7498
e-mail: info@globalexchange.org • Web site: www.globalexchange.org

Global Exchange is a human rights organization that exposes economic and political injustice around the world. In response to such injustices, the organization supports education, activism, and a noninterventionist U.S. foreign policy. It publishes *Global Exchanges* quarterly.

The Heritage Foundation
214 Massachusetts Ave. NE, Washington, DC 20002
(202) 546-4400 • fax: (202) 546-8328
e-mail: info@heritage.org • Web site: www.heritage.org

The Heritage Foundation is a conservative public-policy research institute. Its position papers and reports on America's foreign policy and the war on terrorism include "Turning Back the Terrorist Threat: America's Unbreakable Commitment," "Forging a Durable Post-War Political Settlement in Iraq," and "The Future of Transatlantic Relations."

Hoover Institution
Stanford University, Stanford, CA 94305-6010
(650) 723-1754 • fax: (650) 723-1687
e-mail: horaney@hoover.stanford.edu • Web site: www.hoover.stanford.edu

The Hoover Institution is a public policy research center devoted to advanced study of politics, economics, and international affairs. It publishes the quarterly *Hoover Digest* and *Policy Review*—which often include articles on terrorism—as well as a newsletter and special reports, including "Foreign Policy for America in the Twenty-First Century."

Institute for Policy Studies (IPS)
733 Fifteenth St. NW., Suite 1020, Washington, DC 20005
(202) 234-9382 • fax: (202) 387-7915
Web site: www.ips-dc.org

The Institute for Policy Studies is a progressive think tank that works to develop societies built around the values of justice and nonviolence. It publishes reports, including *Global Perspectives: A Media Guide to Foreign Policy Experts.* Numerous articles and interviews on the terrorist attacks of September 11, 2001, are available on its Web site.

Iraq Action Coalition
7309 Haymarket Ln., Raleigh, NC 27615
fax: (919) 846-7422 • e-mail: iac@leb.net
Web site: www.iraqaction.org

The Iraq Action Coalition is an online media and activists' resource center for groups and activists who opposed both international economic sanctions and U.S. military action against Iraq. It publishes books and reports on Iraq, including *Iraq Under Siege: The Deadly Impact of Sanctions and War.* Its Web site includes numerous links to other organizations opposed to the war against Iraq.

Middle East Forum
1500 Walnut St., Suite 1050, Philadelphia, PA 19102
(215) 546-5406 • fax: (215) 546-5409
e-mail: info@meforum.org • Web site: www.meforum.org

The Middle East Forum is a think tank that works to define and promote American interests in the Middle East. It supports strong American ties with Israel, Turkey, and other democracies as they emerge. It publishes the *Middle East Quarterly*, a policy-oriented journal. Its Web site includes articles, summaries of activities, and a discussion forum.

Middle East Institute
1761 N St. NW, Washington, DC 20036-2882
(202) 785-1141 • fax: (202) 331-8861
e-mail: mideasti@mideasti.org • Web site: www.themiddleeastinstitute.org

The institute's charter mission is to promote better understanding of Middle Eastern cultures, languages, religions, and politics. It publishes numerous books, papers, audiotapes, and videos as well as the quarterly *Middle East Journal.* It also maintains an Educational Outreach Department to give teachers and students of all grade levels advice on resources.

Middle East Media Research Institute (MEMRI)
PO Box 27837, Washington, DC 20038-7837
(202) 955-9070 • fax: (202) 955-9077
e-mail: memri@memri.org • Web site: www.memri.org

MEMRI translates and disseminates articles and commentaries from Middle East media sources and attempts to increase understanding between the West and the Middle East.

Middle East Policy Council
1730 M St. NW, Suite 512, Washington, DC 20036-4505
(202) 296-6767 • fax: (202) 296-5791
e-mail: info@mepc.org. • Web site: www.mepc.org

The Middle East Policy Council was founded in 1981 to expand public discussion and understanding of issues affecting U.S. policy in the Middle East. The council is a nonprofit educational organization that operates nationwide. It publishes the quarterly *Middle East Policy Journal.*

Middle East Research and Information Project (MERIP)
1500 Massachusetts Ave. NW, Washington, DC 20005
(202) 223-3677 • fax: (202) 223-3604
e-mail: ctoensing@merip.org • Web site: www.merip.org

MERIP is a nonprofit, nongovernmental organization with no links to any religious, educational, or political organizations in the United States or elsewhere. Its mission is to educate the public about the contemporary Middle East with particular emphasis on U.S. foreign policy, human rights, and social justice issues. It publishes the bimonthly *Middle East Report.*

National Security Agency
9800 Savage Rd., Ft. Meade, MD 20755
(301) 688-6524
Web site: www.nsa.gov

The National Security Agency coordinates, directs, and performs activities such as designing cipher systems, which protect American information systems and produce foreign intelligence information. It is the largest employer of mathematicians in the United States and also hires the nation's best code makers and code breakers. Speeches, briefings, and reports are available on its Web site.

Trilateral Commission
345 E. Forty-sixth St., New York, NY 10017
(212) 661-1180 • fax: (212) 949-7268
e-mail: trilat@panix.com • Web site: www.trilateral.org

The commission encourages shared leadership responsibilities among the countries in North America, Western Europe, and Japan. It publishes the annual magazine *Trialogue* and the report "Addressing the New International Terrorism: Prevention, Intervention, and Multilateral Cooperation."

United Nations (UN)
UN Headquarters, First Avenue at Forty-sixth Street, New York, NY 10017
Web site: www.un.org

The UN is an international organization dedicated to maintaining international peace and security, developing friendly relations among nations, and promoting international cooperation. Articles and speeches about terrorism are available on its Web site.

Washington Institute for Near East Policy
1828 L St. NW, Suite 1050, Washington, DC 20036
(202) 452-0650 • fax: (202) 223-5364
e-mail: info@washingtoninstitute.org • Web site: www.washingtoninstitute.org

The institute is an independent, nonprofit research organization that provides information and analysis on the Middle East and U.S. policy in the region. It publishes numerous books, periodic monographs, and reports on regional politics, security, and economics, including *Peace Watch*, which focuses on the Arab-Israeli peace process, and the reports "Democracy and Arab Political Culture" and "Radical Middle East States and U.S. Policy."

Bibliography

Books

Peter Andreas and Thomas J. Biersteker, eds.
The Rebordering of North America: Integration and Exclusion in a New Security Context. New York: Routledge, 2003.

Lee C. Bollinger and Geoffrey R. Stone, eds.
Eternally Vigilant: Free Speech in the Modern Era. Chicago: University of Chicago Press, 2002.

Kurt M. Campbell and Michelle A. Flourney
To Prevail: An American Strategy for the Campaign Against Terrorism. Washington, DC: Center for Strategic and International Studies, 2001.

Nancy Chang et al.
Silencing Political Dissent: How Post-September 11 Anti-Terrorism Measures Threaten Our Civil Liberties. New York: Seven Stories Press, 2002.

Eric Cody et al.
Chemical and Biological Warfare: A Comprehensive Guide for the Concerned Citizen. New York: Copernicus Books, 2002.

David Cole and James X. Dempsey
Terrorism and the Constitution: Sacrificing Civil Liberties in the Name of National Security. New York: New Press, 2002.

Anthony H. Cordesman
Terrorism, Asymmetric Warfare, and Weapons of Mass Destruction: Defending the U.S. Homeland. Westport, CT: Praeger, 2002.

Lynn E. Davis
Organizing for Homeland Security. Santa Monica, CA: Rand, 2002.

Alan M. Dershowitz
Shouting Fire: Civil Liberties in a Turbulent Age. Boston: Little, Brown, 2002.

Steven Emerson
American Jihad: The Terrorists Living Among Us. New York: Free Press, 2002.

William H. Frist
When Every Moment Counts: What You Need to Know About Bioterrorism from the Senate's Only Doctor. Lanham, MD: Rowman & Littlefield, 2002.

Simson Garfinkel
Database Nation: The Death of Privacy in the 21st Century. Cambridge, MA: O'Reilly, 2001.

Kathlyn Gay	*Silent Death: The Threat of Chemical and Biological Terrorism.* Brookfield, CT: Twenty-First Century Books, 2001.
Ted Gottfried	*Homeland Security vs. Constitutional Rights.* Brookfield, CT: Twenty-First Century Books, 2003.
Stanley Hauerwas and Frank Lentricchia, eds.	*Dissent from the Homeland: Essays After September 11.* Durham, NC: Duke University Press, 2002.
Katrina vanden Heuvel, ed.	*A Just Response: The Nation on Terrorism, Democracy, and September 11.* New York: Thunder's Mouth, 2002.
Jessica Kornbluth and Jessica Papin, eds.	*Because We Are Americans: What We Discovered on September 11, 2001.* New York: Warner Books, 2001.
Walter Laquer	*No End to War: Terrorism in the Twenty-First Century.* New York: Continuum, 2003.
Michael A. Ledeen	*The War Against the Terror Masters.* New York: St. Martin's, 2002.
Michael E. O'Hanlon et al.	*Protecting the American Homeland: A Preliminary Analysis.* Washington, DC: Brookings Institution, 2002.
John V. Parachini, Lynn E. Davis, and Timothy Liston	*Homeland Security: A Compendium of Public and Private Organizations' Policy Recommendations.* Santa Monica, CA: Rand, 2003.
Daniel Pipes	*Militant Islam Reaches America.* New York: W.W. Norton, 2002.
Marcus J. Ranum	*The Myth of Homeland Security.* Indianapolis, IN: John Wiley & Sons, 2003.
Phil Scranton, ed.	*Beyond September 11: An Anthology of Dissent.* London: Pluto, 2002.
Paul Wilkinson	*Terrorism Versus Democracy: The Liberal State Response.* London: Frank Cass, 2001.
Bob Woodward	*Bush at War.* New York: Simon & Schuster, 2002.

Periodicals

Ferry Biedermann	"Winning the Battle Against Terror, Losing the War of Ideas," www.salon.com, January 10, 2004.
David Corn	"Now They Tell Us: Postwar Truths and Consequences," *Nation*, May 19, 2003.
Helle Dale	"The State of Homeland Security and the War on Terrorism," www.heritage.org, January 21, 2004.
Shelly Delos	"A Dim View: The World Looks at Bush," *Political Affairs*, December 2003.
Bob Drogin	"The Vanishing—What Happened to the WMD?" *New Republic*, July 21, 2003.
Michael Duffy	"Could It Happen Again?" *Time*, August 4, 2003.

Bibliography

Economist	"Manifest Destiny Warmed Up?—America and Empire," August 16, 2003.
Economist	"Show Me the Way to Go Home: America and Empire," August 16, 2003.
Economist	"Still Out There: Al-Qaeda," January 10, 2004.
Timothy H. Edgar	"Watch Out America, the White House Is Seeking to Expand the Patriot Act," *Crisis*, November/December 2003.
Dan Eggen	"Center to Assess Terrorist Threat," *Washington Post*, May 1, 2003.
Ivan Eland	"Report Card on the Bush Administration's 'War on Terrorism,'" www.independent.org, August 28, 2003.
Hassan Fattah	"Baghdad Dispatch: Random Death," *New Republic*, August 11, 2003.
Stephen E. Flynn	"America the Vulnerable," *Foreign Affairs*, January 1, 2002.
Nick Gillespie	"Freedom for Safety," *Reason*, October 2002.
Richard Halloran	"Anti-Americanism on the Rise," *Washington Times*, December 20, 2002.
Victor Davis Hanson	"Iraq's Future—and Ours," *Commentary*, January 2004.
Gene Healy	"Libertarian Intervention: Will It Liberate?" *Liberty*, November 2003.
Jesse Helms	"Emerging Threats to United States National Security," *Imprimis*, January 2002.
Jacob G. Hornberger	"Keep the Borders Open," *World & I*, January 2002.
Derrick Z. Jackson	"Owning Up to Deceptions on the Iraq War," *Liberal Opinion Week*, October 13, 2003.
Penn Jillette	"Make the Terrorists Do the Profiling," *Regulation*, Spring 2002.
Daryl G. Kimball	"Iraq's WMD: Myth and Reality," *Arms Control Today*, September 2003.
Paul D. Lawrence	"Shredding the Bill of Rights," *People's Weekly World*, January/February 2004.
Herbert London	"Profiling as Needed," *Albany Law Review*, Winter 2002.
Timothy Lynch	"Breaking the Vicious Cycle," Preserving Our Liberties While Fighting Terrorism," *Policy Analysis*, June 26, 2002.
Dmitry Marin	"Why Do They Hate Us?" *Political Affairs*, December 2003.
Kate Martin	"Intelligence, Terrorism, and Civil Liberties," *Human Rights*, Winter 2002.
Bill McIntyre	"Crush the Terrorists . . . Not the Bill of Rights," *Shield*, Spring 2002.

Caryle Murphy	"The War on Terrorism: Why It Really Will Be a Long One," *America*, April 28, 2003.
John Podesta	"USA Patriot Act: The Good, the Bad, and the Sunset," *Human Rights*, Winter 2002.
Jack Snyder	"Imperial Temptations," *National Interest*, Spring 2003.
Jack Spencer and Ha Nguyen	"Are We Safer Today than Before 9/11?" www.heritage.org, September 10, 2003.
Scott L. Wheeler	"The Link Between Iraq and al-Qaeda; Saddam May Not Have Known the Details of 9/11, but a Senior Government Official Says the United States Has Uncovered Key Evidence That Iraq Was Funding al-Qaeda," *Insight on the News*, October 14, 2003.
Patricia J. Williams	"Loose Lips and Other Slips," *Nation*, March 17, 2003.

Index